Life Insurance Theory

Actuarial Perspectives

by

F. Etienne De Vylder

KLUWER ACADEMIC PUBLISHERS

BOSTON / DORDRECHT / LONDON

A C.I.P. Catalogue record for this book is available from the Library of Congress

ISBN 0-7923-9995-1

Published by Kluwer Academic Publishers,
P.O. Box 17, 3300 AA Dordrecht, The Netherlands.

Sold and distributed in the U.S.A. and Canada
by Kluwer Academic Publishers,
101 Philip Drive, Norwell, MA 02061, U.S.A.

In all other countries, sold and distributed
by Kluwer Academic Publishers,
P.O. Box 322, 3300 AH Dordrecht, The Netherlands.

Printed on acid-free paper

Printed in the Netherlands

TABLE OF CONTENTS

FIGURES AND TABLES

Figures

Tables

PREFACE

This book is different from all other books on Life Insurance by at least one of the following characteristics 1–4.

1. The treatment of life insurances at three different levels: time-capital, present value and price level.

We call **time-capital** any distribution of a capital over time:

$$(C_1,T_1) + (C_2,T_2) + \ldots + (C_N,T_N) \qquad (*)$$

is the time-capital with amounts $C_1, C_2, \ldots, C_N$ at moments $T_1, T_2, \ldots, T_N$ resp. For instance, let (x) be a life at instant 0 with future lifetime X. Then the whole life insurance $\bar{A}_x{}^{\circ\circ}$ is the time-capital (1,X). The whole life annuity $\ddot{a}_x{}^{\circ\circ}$ is the time-capital $(1,0) + (1,1) + (1,2) + \ldots + (1,'X)$, where 'X is the integer part of X.

The **present value** at 0 of time-capital (*) is the random variable

$$C_1 v^{T_1} + C_2 v^{T_2} + \ldots + C_N v^{T_N}. \qquad (**)$$

In particular, the present value of $\bar{A}_x{}^{\circ\circ}$ and $\ddot{a}_x{}^{\circ\circ}$ is

$$\bar{A}_x{}^{\circ} = v^X \text{ and } \ddot{a}_x{}^{\circ} = 1 + v + v^2 + \ldots + v^{'X} \text{ resp.}$$

The **price** (or premium) of a time-capital is the expectation of its present value. In particular, the price of $\bar{A}_x{}^{\circ\circ}$ and $\ddot{a}_x{}^{\circ\circ}$ is

$$\bar{A}_x = E(v^X) \text{ and } \ddot{a}_x = E(1 + v + v^2 + \ldots + v^{'X}) \text{ resp.}$$

It is important to know at what level relations are valid. For instance, the classical relation $\bar{A}_x = 1-\delta\,\bar{a}_x$ is in fact valid at present value level: $\bar{A}_x{}^{\circ} = 1-\delta\,\bar{a}_x{}^{\circ}$. The latter relation implies that $Var(\bar{A}_x{}^{\circ}) = \delta^2\,Var(\bar{a}_x{}^{\circ})$.

2. The introduction of general capital-functions c_τ ($\tau\geq 0$).

For instance, the variable whole life insurance with capital-function c_τ is the time-capital $\bar{A}_x(c_\tau)^{\circ\circ} = (c_X,X)$ with present value $\bar{A}_x(c_\tau)^{\circ} = c_X v^X$ and price $\bar{A}_x(c_\tau) = E(c_X v^X)$. Similarly, general variable annuities with capital-function c_τ are defined. Then all classical relations (between life insurances and life annuities, between yearly annuities and partitioned annuities, ...) can be resumed in simple general relations with general capital-functions.

3. The introduction of extinction graphs of a group of lives.

For instance, the evolution of the group of two lives (x) and (y) can be visualized by a graph with 4 states xy (x and y alive), x|y (x dead and y alive), y|x (y dead and x alive) and x|y| (x and y both dead). Annuities can be defined on the states and insurances can be connected with a transition from one state to another state. Very general relations at present value level can be proved on graphs. Models with decrements due to other causes than death (sickness, disablement,...) can be treated by graphs.

4. The consideration and evaluation of long term ruin probabilities of a life insurance company, under assumptions on true mortality, true interest rate and evolution of the volume of the company.

Acknowledgments

I am grateful to Kluwer Academic Publishers, in particular to Mr. Allard Winterink, Acquisitions Editor, to have accepted the publication of this book. Mr. Winterink remained in permanent pleasant contact during the complete submission and publication process.

Professor Hélène Cossette (Laval, Québec) and Professor Etienne Marceau (Laval, Québec) have developed computer programs for the numerical evaluation of ruin probabilities, based on Chapter 10, in a portfolio of a large Canadian life insurance company. Thanks, Hélène and Etienne, for this agreeable collaboration.

The first version of the book has been used in a life insurance course at a Belgian university. Thanks to Mr. Frederic Kint, one of my students, numerous misprints in the initial text have been detected and eliminated.

Finally, I want to thank Mrs. Anne Cocriamont for reading my manuscript, checking for language and spelling mistakes.

Ghent, June 1997, F. Etienne De Vylder

A GUIDE TO TERMINOLOGY AND NOTATION

The notations :=, =: , :⇔ , ⇔: are used for definitions. The defined symbol, or property, is on the side of the double point. The symbol ≡ connects identical quantities expressed in different notations, or it indicates that a function has a constant value on some domain

$$\mathbf{R} :=]-\infty, +\infty[\equiv (-\infty, +\infty), \quad \mathbf{R}_+ := [0, \infty[\equiv [0, \infty).$$

We call ≤ the **inequality symbol** and < the **strict inequality symbol** and we use a corresponding consistent terminology. Examples

$$x \text{ is } \textbf{stictly positive} :\Leftrightarrow x > 0, \qquad x \text{ is } \textbf{larger} \text{ than } y :\Leftrightarrow x \geq y.$$

The letters j, k, m, n, r and the Greek letter ν denote **positive integers**

$$a \vee b := \max(a,b), \quad a \wedge b := \min(a,b).$$

Iff is an abbreviation of **if and only if**. In definitions, **iff** is not used, but there the meaning of **if** is **iff** in all cases.

't is the largest integer smaller than t (i.e. the **integer part of t**), t′ is the smallest integer larger than t and $\hat{t} := ('t+t')/2$. If t is an integer then $t = 't = \hat{t} = t'$. Of course, sometimes t′, t″, ... are any numbers without connexion with t and accents are also used for derivatives. Anyway, the meaning of the accents is clear from the context.

We denote by θ a number between 0 and 1.

$$\int_{(a,b)} \equiv \int_a^b .$$

The **indicator function** 1_{Prop} of the proposition Prop equals 1 if Prop is true and 0 if Prop is false.

We recall that multiplications and divisions must be performed first, then additions and substractions, if no brackects are used. Hence, $k+1/2 \equiv k+(1/2)$.

The international notation system for Life Insurance is adopted throughout the book. Unfortunately, this system ignores stochastics, and in contradiction with Risk Theory notation, capital letters never represent random variables. For the latter, the superscript ° is used systematically in the monograph.

Chapter 1

FINANCIAL MODELS

1.1. Units

The **time unit** is the year. The **origin of time** is any instant. It may be the subscription instant of some contract or the instant at which the insurer calculates the **mathematical reserve** (to be defined later) of some contract. The **money unit** is any amount (one dollar, one Swiss Franc,...).

1.2. Constant interest rate

An isolated capital c is meaningless. Only the couple (c,t), "amount c at instant t" has a sense. We say that (c,t) and (c′,t′) are **equivalent couples** if it amounts to the same to possess the couple (c,t) or the couple (c′,t′). This equivalence is denoted as $(c,t) =_p (c',t')$. The latter relation states that capital c at time t has **present value** c′ at time t′. We now inspect how present values are connected.

Yearly interests

We assume that the relation $=_p$ satisfies the following axioms.

A1. $=_p$ is an equivalence relation, i.e.

$$(c,t) =_p (c,t) \text{ (reflexivity)},$$

$$[(c,t) =_p (c',t')] \Rightarrow [(c',t') =_p (c,t)] \text{ (symmetry)},$$

$$[(c,t) =_p (c',t') \text{ and } (c',t') =_p (c'',t'')] \Rightarrow (c,t) =_p (c'',t'') \text{ (transitivity)}.$$

A2.
$$[(c,t) =_p (c',t)] \Rightarrow [c=c'].$$

A3.
$$(c,t) =_p \left(c(1+i),t+1\right),$$

where $i > -1$ is the **annual interest rate** ($i \geq 0$ in practice).

These axioms must hold for all c, c′, c″, t, t′, t″, positive or negative.

The axioms A1 and A2 must be satisfied in any coherent model. In A3, i is the interest rate of the year [t,t+1]. It does not depend on t. A3 is replaced by another axiom in other models.

$$u := 1+i \ \ \textbf{(accumulation factor)}, \quad v := 1/(1+i) \ \textbf{(discount factor)}.$$

A useful simple relation is $iv = 1-v$.

We recall that k is a positive integer in the following Theorem and that "positive" does not exclude "zero" (see section **A Guide to Terminology and Notation**).

Theorem 1

In the model defined by the axioms A1, A2 and A3,

$$\mathbf{(c,t) =_p (cu^k,t+k),} \tag{1}$$

$$\mathbf{(c,t) =_p (cv^k,t-k).} \tag{2}$$

Proof

$$(c,t) =_p (cu,t+1) =_p (cu^2,t+2) =_p \cdots =_p (cu^k,t+k).$$

This proves (1). In order to prove (2), we observe that

$$(cv^k,t-k) =_p (cv^k.u^k,t-k+k) = (c,t)$$

by (1) applied to capital cv^k at $t-k$ •

The simple model considered hitherto does not allow to find out how (c,t) and (c′,t′) are connected if t–t′ is not an integer. The following model answers the question.

Continuous interests

We now replace A3 by the following axiom A3′.

A3′. $$(c,t) =_p \left(cf(\tau),t+\tau\right)$$

for some differentiable strictly positive function f.

The model based on axioms A1, A2 and A3′ is called the **classical financial model**, or the **financial model with constant interest rate**.

Theorem 2

In the classical financial model, a constant δ exists, such that

$$(c, t) =_p (ce^{\delta\tau}, t+\tau) \tag{3}$$

for all c, t and τ.

Proof

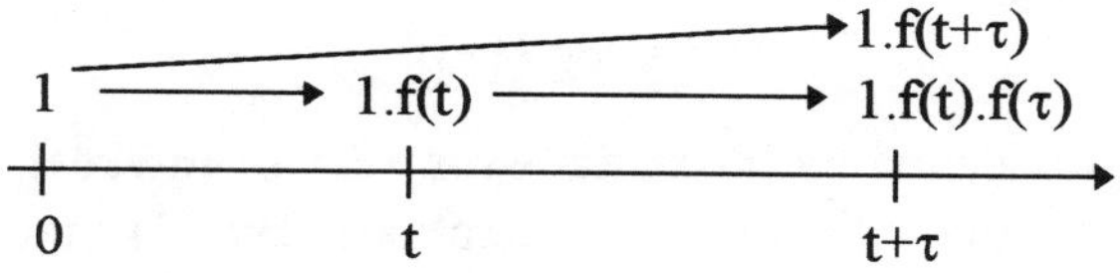

Figure 1.1. Present values (constant interest rate)

By A3′, $(1, 0) =_p (1.f(t), t) =_p (1.f(t).f(\tau), t+\tau)$,

and $(1, 0) =_p (1.f(t+\tau), t+\tau)$.

Then, by A1, $(f(t)f(\tau), t+\tau) =_p (f(t+\tau), t+\tau)$

and by A2, $f(t)f(\tau) = f(t+\tau)$.

Then $f'(t)f(\tau) = f'(t+\tau)$

by differentiation with respect to t. Then $\delta.f(\tau)=f'(\tau)$ at point $t=0$, where $\delta := f'(0)$. Hence,

$$(\log f(\tau))' = \delta, \quad \log f(\tau) = \text{const.} + \delta\tau, \quad f(\tau) = \text{const.}e^{\delta\tau}$$

and then

$$(1, t) =_p (\text{const.}e^{\delta\tau}, t+\tau)$$

by A3. For $\tau = 0$, we obtain $(1, t) =_p (\text{const.}, t)$ and then $1 = \text{const.}$ by A2. Hence, $f(\tau) = e^{\delta\tau}$ •

The two models considered hitherto are compatible. It is enough to connect i and δ by relation $1+i = e^{\delta}$. Then by (3) with $\tau = 1$, $(c, t) =_p \big(c(1+i), t+1\big)$ and this is A3. Hence, [A1, A2, A3′] $\Rightarrow$ A3.

The following Corollary of Theorem 2 is a generalization of Theorem 1.

Corollary

In the classical financial model,

$$(c,t) =_p (cu^\tau, t+\tau), \tag{4}$$

$$(c,t) =_p (cv^\tau, t-\tau) \quad \bullet \tag{5}$$

The relation $1+i=e^\delta$ implies that

$$\delta = \log(1+i).$$

The constant δ is called the **instantaneous rate of interest**. This terminology is based on the following considerations. By (3) and by the power series expansion of the exponential function,

$$(c,t) =_p \big(c(1+\delta\tau+\delta^2\tau^2/2+\ldots), t+\tau\big). \tag{6}$$

Hence, for small $\tau>0$,

$$(c,t) \approx_p (c+c\delta\tau, t+\tau).$$

This means that the interests $c\delta\tau$ produced by the capital c in the interval $[t,t+\tau]$ are proportional to c and to the duration τ, the coefficient of proportionality being δ.

1.3. Variable interest rates

Yearly interests

We here assume that the interest rate is i_k during the year $[k-1,k]$ ($k=1,2,\ldots$). Hence, we replace A3 by the following axiom A3″.

A3″. $\qquad (c,k-1) =_p (c(1+i_k),k) \quad (k=1,2,\ldots).$

We use the notations

$$u_0 := 1,\ \ u_k := (1+i_1)(1+i_2)\ldots(1+i_k),\ \ v_k := 1/u_k$$

(in the classical financial model $i=i_1=i_2=\ldots$ and then $u_k=u^k$, $v_k=v^k$).

Theorem 3

In the model defined by the axioms A1, A2 and A3″,

$$(c,0) =_p (cu_k, k), \tag{7}$$

$$(c,k) =_p (cv_k, 0). \tag{8}$$

Proof

$$(c,0) =_p \big(c(1+i_1),1\big) =_p \big(c(1+i_1)(1+i_2),2\big) =_p \ldots =_p \big(c(1+i_1)(1+i_2)\ldots(1+i_k),k\big).$$

This proves (7). For the proof of (8), we observe that

$$(cv_k,0) =_p (cv_k u_k,k) = (c,k)$$

by (7) applied to capital cv_k •

Continuous interests

We now replace A3 by the following axiom A3‴ inspired by (6).

A3‴. $$(c,0) =_p \big(cf(t),t\big) \quad (t\geq 0),$$

where f is a function such that

$$f(t+\tau) = f(t)[1 + \tau\delta_t + \tau o_t(\tau)], \tag{9}$$

o_t is such that $$\lim_{\tau\to 0} o_t(\tau) = 0 \tag{10}$$

and the function δ_t of t is a positive function on $[0,\infty[$, integrable on all bounded intervals in $[0,\infty[$.

The model based on axioms A1, A2 and A3‴ is called the **financial model with variable interest rates** in this book. The function δ_τ of $\tau\geq 0$ is called the **instantaneous interest rate function** of the model.

$$u_t := \exp(\textstyle\int_{(0,t)} \delta_\tau d\tau), \tag{11}$$

$$v_t := 1/u_t = \exp(-\textstyle\int_{(0,t)} \delta_\tau d\tau) \tag{12}$$

(in the classical financial model, $\delta_t \equiv \delta$ and then $u_t = u^t$ and $v_t = v^t$). When it is necessary to emphasize the instantaneous interest function, u_t and v_t are displayed as $u_t(\delta_\tau)$ and $v_t(\delta_\tau)$. In the latter notation, τ has a dummy character (it cannot be replaced by a numerical value).

Theorem 4

In the financial model with variable interest rates,

$$\mathbf{(c,0) =_p (cu_t,t) \quad (t\geq 0)} \tag{13}$$

$$\mathbf{(c,t) =_p (cv_t,0) \quad (t\geq 0)}. \tag{14}$$

Proof

By (9), $$[f(t+\tau)-f(t)]/\tau = f(t)[\delta_t + o_t(\tau)].$$

As $\tau \to 0$, $$f'(t) = f(t)\delta_t$$

by (10). Hence, $$\big(\log f(t)\big)' = \delta_t.$$

We integrate this relation over [0,s]:

$$\log f(s) - \log f(0) = \int_{(0,s)} \delta_t dt.$$

For t=0 in A3‴, we have $(c,0) =_p (cf(0),0)$ and then $f(0)=1$ by A2. Hence,

$$f(s) = \exp(\int_{(0,s)} \delta_t dt) = u_s$$

and then (13) follows from A3‴. By (13) applied to the capital cv_t instead of c, we have

$$(cv_t,0) =_p (cv_t u_t,t) = (c,t) \quad \bullet$$

It is easy to connect (c,t) and (c′,t′) (0≤t≤t′) via (13) and (14). Indeed,

$$(c',t') =_p (c'v_{t'},0) =_p (c'v_{t'}u_t,t), \tag{15}$$

where $$v_{t'}u_t = \exp(\int_{(t,t')} \delta_\tau d\tau).$$

Similarly, $$(c,t) =_p (cv_t,0) =_p (cv_t u_{t'},t'), \tag{16}$$

where $$v_t u_{t'} = \exp(-\int_{(t,t')} \delta_\tau d\tau).$$

Theorem 5 (Iterative relation for v_t)

In the financial model with variable interest rates,

$$\mathbf{v_{s+t}(\delta_\tau) = v_s(\delta_\tau).v_t(\delta_{s+\tau})}. \tag{17}$$

Proof

$$v_{s+t}(\delta_\tau) = \exp(-\int_{(0,s+t)} \delta_\tau d\tau) = \exp(-\int_{(0,s)} \delta_\tau d\tau).\exp(-\int_{(s,s+t)} \delta_\tau d\tau)$$
$$= \exp(-\int_{(0,s)} \delta_\tau d\tau).\exp(-\int_{(0,t)} \delta_{s+\tau} d\tau) = v_s(\delta_\tau).v_t(\delta_{s+\tau}) \quad \bullet$$

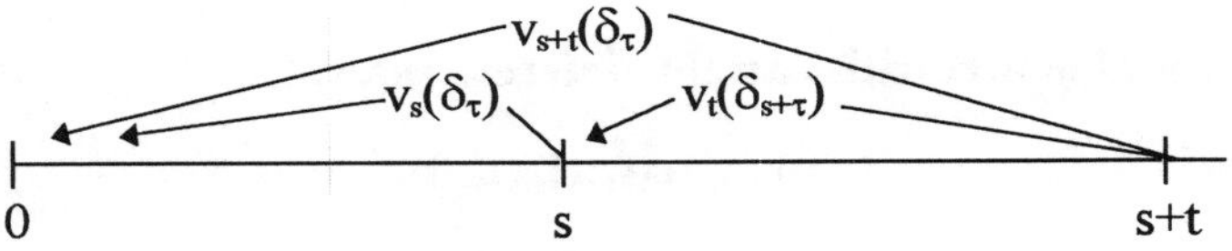

Figure 1.2. Discount factors (variable interests)

1.4. Deterministic time-capitals

A **(deterministic) time-capital** is a capital distributed over a time interval. More precisely, a time-capital is a set of couples (c,t). For instance

$$C^{\circ\circ} = (c_1,t_1) + \ldots + (c_n,t_n) \equiv \sum_{1\le k\le n} (c_k,t_k) \tag{18}$$

is a time-capital. The owner of $C^{\circ\circ}$ possesses the capital c_1 at the instant t_1 plus the capital c_2 at the instant t_2 ... plus the capital c_k at the instant t_k. The + notation in (18) is suggestive, but no sums must be performed for the moment. The notion of time-capital is a very primitive one. For instance, a new car could be paid by the time-capital

$$(20\,000\$, 0) + \sum_{1\le k\le 12} (1000\$, k/12).$$

No theory of interest is necessary in order to understand what this means.

We can consider time-capitals with positive and negative amounts c_k. Time-capitals can be multiplied by scalars α:

$$\alpha C^{\circ\circ} := (\alpha c_1,t_1) + \ldots + (\alpha c_n,t_n).$$

Sums and differences of time-capitals are obvious concepts.

In (12), n may be infinite. We also consider (theoretical) **continuous time-capitals**

$$C^{\circ\circ} = \int_{(s,s+t)} (c_\tau d\tau,\tau). \tag{19}$$

We here assume that the interval [s,s+t] is partitioned in infinitesimal intervals $[\tau,\tau+d\tau]$ and then the owner of the time-capital (19) possesses the amount $c_\tau d\tau$ in each interval $[\tau,\tau+d\tau]$.

Present value of a time-capital

From now on, only present values at time 0 are considered. The **present value of time-capital** (18) is

$$C^\circ := AC^{\circ\circ} \equiv A(C^{\circ\circ}) := c_1 v^{t_1} + \ldots + c_k v^{t_k}. \tag{20}$$

The **present value of time-capital** (19) is

$$C^{\circ} := AC^{\circ\circ} := \int_{(s,s+t)} c_\tau v^\tau d\tau. \tag{21}$$

They are calculated in the classical financial model. In the financial model with variable interest rates, v^{t_k} and v^τ must be replaced by v_{t_k} and v_τ resp. The notation for the **present value operator A** comes from the French "valeur Actuelle". **Actualizations** are evaluations of present values.

We systematically use the double superscript $^{\circ\circ}$ for time-capitals (it should suggest the distribution of a capital over a time-interval) and the single superscript $^{\circ}$ for present values (it should suggest the concentration of a capital at the origin 0).

The **time-capitals** $C_1^{\circ\circ}$ and $C_2^{\circ\circ}$ are **equivalent** if $AC_1^{\circ\circ}=AC_2^{\circ\circ}$. This equivalence is represented by the relation $C_1^{\circ\circ} =_p C_2^{\circ\circ}$.

1.5. Stochastic time-capitals

A **stochastic time-capital** is a time-capital with stochastic components. For instance, if C_k, T_k, S and T are positive random variables and if $N\geq 1$ is a positive integer random variable, then

$$C^{\circ\circ} := (C_1,T_1) + \ldots + (C_N,T_N) \tag{22}$$

and

$$C^{\circ\circ} := \int_{(S,S+T)} (c_\tau d\tau,\tau) \tag{23}$$

are stochastic time-capitals. They are defined by their realizations and the latter are obvious from the realizations of the involved random variables.

The **present value of a stochastic time-capital** is defined in the same way as in the deterministic case. For instance, if $C^{\circ\circ}$ is defined by (22), then

$$AC^{\circ\circ} := C_1 v^{T_1} + \ldots + C_N v^{T_N} \tag{24}$$

and if $C^{\circ\circ}$ is defined by (23), then

$$AC^{\circ\circ} := \int_{(S,S+T)} c_\tau v^\tau d\tau \tag{25}$$

in the classical financial model.

The present value $AC^{\circ\circ}$ of the stochastic time-capital $C^{\circ\circ}$ is a random variable. Its expectation

$$C := E(AC^{\circ\circ}) \tag{26}$$

is the **price of the stochastic time-capital** $C^{\circ\circ}$.

Of course, deterministic time-capitals are particular stochastic time-capitals. The present value of a deterministic time-capital is a constant. Hence, the price of any deterministic time-capital equals its present value.

In life insurance, the random variables are related to the remaining lifetimes X, Y, ... of persons x, y, ... A big part of life insurance theory consists in the construction of formulas allowing the evaluation of prices of stochastic time-capitals.

The adjective "stochastic" will mostly be omitted when stochastic time-capitals are mentioned.

1.6. Annuities-certain

The following time-capitals are classical **annuities-certain**.

$$ {}_{s|n}a^{\circ\circ} := \sum_{1\le k\le n} (1,s+k), \quad {}_{s|n}\ddot{a}^{\circ\circ} := \sum_{0\le k\le n-1} (1,s+k), $$

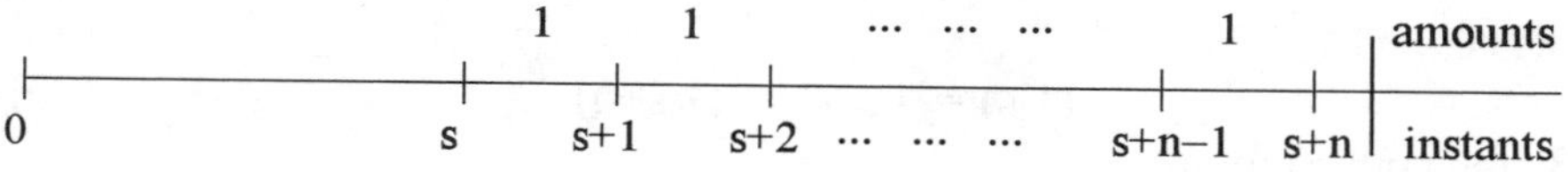

$$ {}_{s|t}\bar{a}^{\circ\circ} := \int_{(s,s+t)} (d\tau,\tau). $$

${}_{s|n}a^{\circ\circ}$ is an **annuity-immediate**, ${}_{s|n}\ddot{a}^{\circ\circ}$ an **annuity-due** and ${}_{s|t}\bar{a}^{\circ\circ}$ a **continuous annuity**. The annuities with left subscripts ${}_{s|n}$ are **s-year deferred and n-year temporary annuities**. ${}_{s|n}a^{\circ\circ}$ and ${}_{s|n}\ddot{a}^{\circ\circ}$ are time-capitals with capital distributed over the time interval [s,s+n] and with amount 1 attached to each year [s+k,s+k+1] (k=0, 1, ..., n−1). It is attached at the end of the year in case of the annuity-immediate and at the beginning of the year in case of the annuity-due. The annuity ${}_{s|t}\bar{a}^{\circ\circ}$ is a **s-year deferred and t-year temporary annuity**. Its capital is distributed uniformly over the interval [s,s+t].

s may be equal to 0 and n or t may be infinite. Then the following notations are adopted: ${}_{s|} \equiv {}_{s|\infty}$, ${}_{n} \equiv {}_{0|n}$, ${}_{t} \equiv {}_{0|t}$.

$$ a_{\overline{n|}} \equiv {}_n a , \quad \ddot{a}_{\overline{n|}} \equiv {}_n\ddot{a} , \quad \bar{a}_{\overline{t|}} \equiv {}_t\bar{a} . $$

The following prices (or present values) are easily calculated (in the classical financial model):

$$ {}_{s|n}\mathbf{a} := \mathbf{A}({}_{s|n}\mathbf{a}^{\circ\circ}) = (\mathbf{v}^s - \mathbf{v}^{s+n})/\mathbf{i}, \tag{27} $$

$$ {}_{s|n}\ddot{\mathbf{a}} := \mathbf{A}({}_{s|n}\ddot{\mathbf{a}}^{\circ\circ}) = (\mathbf{v}^s - \mathbf{v}^{s+n})/(\mathbf{iv}), \tag{28} $$

$$ {}_{s|t}\bar{\mathbf{a}} := \mathbf{A}({}_{s|t}\bar{\mathbf{a}}^{\circ\circ}) = (\mathbf{v}^s - \mathbf{v}^{s+t})/\delta. \tag{29} $$

Indeed,

$$ {}_{s|n}a = \sum_{1\le k\le n} v^{s+k} = (v^{s+1}-v^{s+n+1})/(1-v) = (v^{s+1}-v^{s+n+1})/(iv), $$

$$ {}_{s|n}\ddot{a} = \sum_{0\le k\le n-1} v^{s+k} = (v^{s}-v^{s+n})/(1-v) = (v^{s}-v^{s+n})/(iv), $$

$$ {}_{s|t}\bar{a} = \int_{(s,s+t)} v^{\tau}d\tau = -(1/\delta)\int_{(s,s+t)} dv^{\tau} = -(1/\delta)(v^{s+t}-v^{s}), $$

because $(v^{\tau})' = -\delta v^{\tau}$.

The expressions for ${}_{s|n}a$ and ${}_{s|n}\ddot{a}$ result from the elementary formula for geometric sums. They can also be obtained by a financial argument. For instance

$$ (1,s) =_p (1+i,s+1) =_p (i,s+1) + (1,s+1) $$

$$ =_p (i,s+1) + (1+i,s+2) =_p (i,s+1) + (i,s+2) + (1,s+2) $$

$$ =_p (i,s+1) + (i,s+2) + (1+i,s+3) =_p (i,s+1) + (i,s+2) + (i,s+3) + (1,s+3) $$

$$ =_p \dots \quad \dots \quad \dots =_p [(i,s+1) + \dots + (i,s+n)] + (1,s+n) =_p i\cdot{}_{s|n}a^{\circ\circ} + (1,s+n). $$

Hence,

$$ (1,s) =_p i\cdot{}_{s|n}a^{\circ\circ} + (1,s+n). \tag{30} $$

By the application of A:

$$ v^{s} = i\cdot{}_{s|n}a + v^{s+n}. \tag{31} $$

The latter relation furnishes the expression (27) for ${}_{s|n}a$.

1.7. Stochastic interests

Future interest rates can be modelled as a stochastic process and a theory of life insurance can be based on it. We refrain from such a model because it is too complicated and, essentially, because the involved parameters cannot be estimated sufficiently safely. Life insurance is particularly concerned with long term developments, but no model exists for making long term predictions. As a general rule, too realistic and too sophisticated models are mostly useless in practice: if you have to estimate the volume of the earth, you better treat our planet as a perfect sphere, rather than to take all mountains and valleys into account.

Chapter 2

MORTALITY MODELS

2.1. Life tables

A **life table** is a positive decreasing function l_ξ of $\xi \geq 0$ with $l_\infty = 0$, where of course $l_\infty := \lim_{\xi \to \infty} l_\xi = 0$. We imagine a closed group of persons with the same age, called lives, observed over time. Then l_ξ is the number of persons alive at age ξ. This is a convenient interpretation (the construction of **practical life tables** is not based on it).

In **theoretical life tables**, l_ξ is not necessarily an integer. The theoretical l_ξ is a continuous function of ξ and the derivative l_ξ' is supposed to exist whenever it is used.

2.2. Future lifetime X

We consider a **life** x aged x at the origin 0 of time. Hence x denotes the person and also her or his age. We denote the future lifetime of x by X. Hence, X is a random variable and x dies at the instant X, at age x+X.

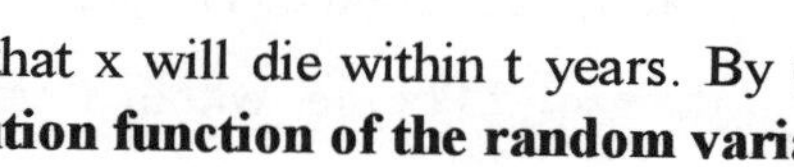

$$ {}_tp_x := P(X>t) \qquad (1)$$

denotes the probability that x will attain age x+t.

$$ {}_tq_x := P(X \leq t) \qquad (2)$$

denotes the probability that x will die within t years. By (2), **the function ${}_tq_x$ of $t \geq 0$ is the distribution function of the random variable X**.

The initial age x is always fixed. In any case, the variable is t when we speak of function ${}_tp_x$, ${}_tq_x$ or of any other function $\varphi(x,t)$,

In the **classical mortality model** adopted in this book, ${}_tp_x$ results from some theoretical life table l_ξ by the formula

$$ {}_tp_x = l_{x+t}/l_x \tag{3}$$

(we define ${}_tp_x:=0$ if l_x and then also l_{x+t} equals 0).

Life tables are only used for the calculation of probabilites ${}_tp_x$ and related functions. **The life tables l_ξ and cl_ξ, where $c>0$, must be regarded as being identical**. In other words, the initial number of lives l_0 is irrelevant.

$$ {}_tq_x = 1-{}_tp_x = (l_x-l_{x+t})/l_x. \tag{4}$$

The **iterative formula**

$$ {}_{s+t}p_x = {}_sp_x \cdot {}_tp_{x+s} \tag{5}$$

is direct via lifetable l_ξ. By elementary probability theory,

$$ {}_{s+t}p_x = P(\text{x attains age x+s+t})$$

$$ = P[(\text{x attains age x+s}) \text{ and } (\text{x attains age x+s+t})]$$

$$ = P(\text{x attains age x+s})P(\text{x attains age x+s+t / x attains age x+s}).$$

Hence

$$ {}_{s+t}p_x = {}_sp_x\, P(\text{x attains age x+s+t / x attains age x+s}). \tag{6}$$

Then by (5) and (6), assuming ${}_sp_x \neq 0$,

$$ {}_tp_{x+s} = P(\text{x attains age x+s+t / x attains age x+s}) \tag{7}$$

This intuitively obvious formula is not necessarily valid in more sophisticated models than the classical one. For instance, it is not valid in case of so-called selected life tables (see following 2.8).

2.3. Force of mortality

The **force of mortality** at age x is the number

$$\mu_x := \lim_{t\downarrow 0} {}_tq_x/t.$$

The infinitesimal version of this formula is (replace t by dt and drop lim)

$$\mu_x dt = {}_{dt}q_x = P(\text{x dies within dt years}).$$

Theorem 1

$$\mu_x = -l_x'/l_x. \qquad (8)$$

$$l_x = l_0 \exp(-\int_{(0,x)} \mu_\xi d\xi). \qquad (9)$$

Proof

$$\mu_x = \lim_{t\downarrow 0} (l_x - l_{x+t})/(t l_x) = -(1/l_x) \lim_{t\downarrow 0}(l_{x+t} - l_x)/t = -(1/l_x) l_x'$$

by the definition of the derivative. For the proof of (9), we observe that

$$-\mu_\xi = (\log l_\xi)'$$

by (8). Then

$$-\int_{(0,x)} \mu_\xi d\xi = \int_{(0,x)} (\log l_\xi)' d\xi = [\log l_\xi]_0^x = \log l_x - \log l_0 = \log(l_x/l_0)$$

and

$$\exp(-\int_{(0,x)} \mu_\xi d\xi) = \exp \log(l_x/l_0) = l_x/l_0 \quad \bullet$$

Theorem 2

The density of X is the function

$$f(t) = {}_t p_x \cdot \mu_{x+t} \quad (t \geq 0) \qquad (10)$$

Proof

The density of X is the derivative of its distribution function. Hence, it equals

$$f(t) = \partial/\partial t\ {}_t q_x = \partial/\partial t\ (1 - l_{x+t}/l_x) = -l_{x+t}'/l_x = (l_{x+t}/l_x).(-l_{x+t}'/l_{x+t}) = {}_t p_x\ \mu_{x+t} \quad \bullet$$

An intuitive argument for (10) is the following

$$f(t)dt = P(X \in dt) = P(x \text{ dies in } dt) = P[(x \text{ is alive at } t) \text{ and } (x \text{ dies in } dt)]$$

$$= P(x \text{ is alive at } t).P(x \text{ dies in } dt \,/\, x \text{ is alive at } t) = {}_t p_x \cdot \mu_{x+t} dt.$$

2.4. Decease in the middle of the year

We denote by $'X$ the largest integer before X (i.e. the integer part of X) and by X' the smallest integer after X. Hence $'X \leq X \leq X'$. We denote by $\hat{X}$ the random variable

$$\hat{X} := ('X + X')/2.$$

A **^-approximation** of an expression (a time-capital, a present value, ...) containing one or more occurrences of X, is the expression resulting from the replacement of some of them by $\hat{X}$. ^-approximations are also called **approximations by a decease in the middle of the year**.

For instance, the ^-approximation of expectation $E\varphi(X)$ is $E\varphi(\hat{X})$. It furnishes a discretization of $E\varphi(X)$:

$$E\varphi(X) \approx E\varphi(\hat{X}) = \int_{(0,\infty)} \varphi(t)d_tq_x = \sum_{0\le k\le\infty} \int_{(k,k+1)} \varphi(k+1/2)d_tq_x$$

$$= \sum_{0\le k\le\infty} \varphi(k+1/2) \int_{(k,k+1)} d_tq_x = \sum_{0\le k\le\infty} \varphi(k+1/2)\, \Delta_k q_x, \qquad (11)$$

where the difference operator is applied to the discrete variable k (x is always fixed), i.e.

$$\Delta_k q_x := {}_{k+1}q_x - {}_kq_x = {}_kp_x - {}_{k+1}p_x = (l_{x+k} - l_{x+k+1})/l_x = d_{x+k}/l_x. \qquad (12)$$

The function d_ξ is defined as $d_\xi := l_\xi - l_{\xi+1}$.

The approximation $E\varphi(X) \approx E\varphi(\hat{X})$ is excellent in life insurance practice. It can be combined with the approximation

$$\varphi(k+1/2) \approx [\varphi(k)+\varphi(k+1)]/2.$$

Then (11) becomes

$$E\varphi(X) \approx (1/2) \sum_{0\le k\le\infty} [\varphi(k)+\varphi(k+1)]\, \Delta_k q_x,. \qquad (13)$$

Of course, $\varphi(k)$ or $\varphi(k+1)$ must be replaced by $\varphi(k+)$ or $\varphi(k+1-)$ in (13) if φ is not continuous at the points k or k+1.

2.5. Expected future lifetime

$\bar{e}_x := EX$ is the **expected future lifetime at age x**. By (11), its ^-approximation is

$$\hat{e}_x := E\hat{X} = \sum_{0\le k\le\infty} (k+1/2)\, \Delta_k q_x = -\sum_{0\le k\le\infty} (k+1/2)\, \Delta_k p_x$$

$$= -[(k+1/2)\,{}_kp_x]_0^\infty + \sum_{0\le k\le\infty} {}_{k+1}p_x = 1/2 + \sum_{0\le k\le\infty} {}_{k+1}p_x$$

$$= \sum_{0\le k\le\infty} {}_kp_x - 1/2 = (l_x + l_{x+1} + \ldots)/l_x - 1/2,$$

where we have applied summation by parts. We tacitly have assumed that

$$\lim_{k\to\infty} k\, {}_kp_x = (1/l_x) \lim_{k\to\infty} k\, l_{x+k} = 0. \qquad (14)$$

It is satisfied in all practical tables (because then $l_{x+k}=0$ if k is large enough), but also in the analytical tables of the following section. Henceforth, assumptions such as (14) will be understood.

2.6. Analytic life tables

With the advent of high speed computers, the advantages of analytic life tables has decreased in recent years. But some of them remain interesting, for instance Makeham's life table. Analytical life tables are defined for all ages $x \geq 0$. In practice, they used on particular age intervals only.

de Moivre (1729)

$$l_x = (86-x) \quad (0 \leq x \leq 86),$$

(and $l_x=0$ if $x \geq 86$). Of course, this table is completely obsolete.

Gompertz (1925) $$l_x = a\, g^{c^x},$$

where $a>0$, $0<g<1$, $c>1$. In the last member, c^x must be evaluated, not g^c. Gompertz's life table results from the force of mortality function

$$\mu_\xi = \beta c^\xi,$$

by (9), after the introduction of new parameters (take s=1 in the following life table by Makeham).

Makeham (1860) $$l_x = a\, s^x g^{c^x},$$

where $a>0$, $0<s<1$, $0<g<1$, $c>1$. In the last member, c^x must be evaluated, not g^c. Makeham's life table results from the force of mortality function

$$\mu_\xi = \alpha + \beta c^\xi, \tag{15}$$

by (9), after the introduction of new parameters. Indeed,

$$\int_{(0,x)} \mu_\xi d\xi = \int_{(0,x)} (\alpha+\beta c^\xi)d\xi = \alpha x + \beta \int_{(0,x)} c^\xi d\xi$$
$$= \alpha x + \beta \int_{(0,x)} dc^\xi/\log c = \alpha x + (\beta/\log c)c^x - (\beta/\log c)$$

and then it is enough to take

$$a := l_0 e^{\beta/\log c}, \quad s := e^{-\alpha}, \quad g := e^{-\beta/\log c}.$$

By (15), the force of mortality has a constant component α (interpreted as capturing accident hazard) and a variable component βc^x (capturing the hazard of aging).

Sang (1868)

$$l_x = a + bc^x, \text{ where } a>0,\ b>0,\ 0<c<1.$$

Weibull (1939) $l_x = a\, g^{x^c}$,

where a>0, 0<g<1, c>0. In the last member, x^c must be evaluated, not g^x. Weibull's life table results from the force of mortality function

$$\mu_\xi = \beta\xi^c,$$

by (9), after the introduction of new parameters.

2.7. Restricted life tables

Life tables can be constructed for any large population group. Some of them cannot start at age 0: a life table for French actuaries can only begin at age 25, for example. A life table defined only on the age interval $[\alpha,\omega]$ is supposed not to be used outside that interval. Then it can be extended arbitrarily to the intervals $[0,\alpha[$ and $]\omega,\infty[$. Hence, without loss of generality, we may assume that the life table is defined on the complete age interval $[0,\infty[$.

2.8. Selected life tables

In a generalization of the classical mortality model, lives (x)+s aged x+s with x as **entry age** (in some population group), are considered. For instance, let x denote the age when the person bought some life annuity. It is reasonable to expect that a person who has just bought this insurance will be of better health than a person of the same age who bought a similar insurance several years ago. Hence, if x+s=y+t, then (x)+s and (y)+t cannot necessarily be treated equivalently.

A **selected life table** $l_{(\xi)+\tau}$ is a function of two variables $\xi \geq 0$ and $\tau \geq 0$. It allows to calculate the probability ${}_tp_{(x)+s}$ that (x)+s will attain age x+s+t by the formula

$${}_tp_{(x)+s} = l_{(x)+s+t}/l_{(x)+s}.$$

Formulas of the iterative type, such as (5), are not available in the model with selected life table. Most other parts of the classical model theory can obviously be adapted in case of selected tables. We will, for the sake of simplicity, use the classical model only.

2.9. Commutation functions

Commutation functions simplify the calculation of numerical values for many actuarial functions. With the advent of high speed computers, commutation functions can easily be avoided nowadays. But they are still in use in some insurance companies.

Theoretical commutation functions are defined for all ages $x \geq 0$. **Practical commutation functions** are considered for integer ages only.

Life commutation functions

$$D_x := v^x l_x,$$

$$N_x := D_x + D_{x+1} + D_{x+2} + \dots ,$$

$$S_x := N_x + N_{x+1} + N_{x+2} + \dots ,$$

where $v := 1/(1+i)$ is the discount factor of the classical financial model.

We notice that D, N, S are consonants of the word **DaNceS**, in the right order. The French mnemonic word is **DanSe**.

Decease commutation functions

$$\hat{C}_x := v^{x+1/2} d_x = v^{x+1/2} (l_x - l_{x+1}),$$

$$\hat{M}_x := \hat{C}_x + \hat{C}_{x+1} + \hat{C}_{x+2} + \dots ,$$

$$\hat{R}_x := \hat{M}_x + \hat{M}_{x+1} + \hat{M}_{x+2} + \dots .$$

We observe that C, M, R are consonants of the word **CeMeteRy**, in the right order. A French mnemonic word is **éCiMeR**.

Chapter 3

CONSTRUCTION OF LIFE TABLES

3.1. Problem description

Life tables can be constructed for any large population group. We consider such a group of individuals with ages $x \geq \alpha$, where $\alpha \geq 0$ is a fixed initial age. Let the unknown life table of the group be l_x ($x \geq \alpha$). Then

$$ {}_k p_\alpha = l_{\alpha+k}/l_\alpha $$

and

$$ l_{\alpha+k} = l_\alpha \, p_\alpha \, p_{\alpha+1} \, p_{\alpha+2} \, \ldots \, p_{\alpha+k-1}, \tag{1} $$

where

$$ p_x \equiv {}_1 p_x = l_{x+1}/l_x \; (x = \alpha, \alpha+1, \ldots, \alpha+k-1). $$

The constant $l_\alpha > 0$ is irrelevant. Hence by (1), the estimation problem of l_α, $l_{\alpha+1}$, $l_{\alpha+2}$, ..., is reduced to the estimation of the one-year probabilities p_α, $p_{\alpha+1}$, $p_{\alpha+2}$, ... The roughly estimated value of p_x (x integer) will be denoted by p_x°. We assume that the observed population group is large enough. Then no sophisticated statistical theory is necessary and p_x° is obtained as an obvious proportion of observed values (the superscript $^\circ$ can be viewed as the first letter of "Observed").

The construction of the life table can be completed (if necessary) by the fitting of a smooth curve to the discrete set p_x° ($x=\alpha, \alpha+1, \ldots, \omega$), where ω is the last age of the table. For instance, the values $p_x = p_x(c, c', c'', \ldots)$ resulting from some analytical life table with a finite number of parameters c, c', c'', ..., can be considered and then the parameters $c, c', c'', \ldots$ can be fixed in such a way that p_x is closest to p_x° ($x = \alpha, \alpha+1, \ldots, \omega$) in some sense.

National life tables (constructed by national organisms) and private tables (constructed by insurance companies) are not necessarily worked out in the same way.

3.2. National tables

The population group under consideration is visualized by a **Lexis diagram**. In this diagram, each individual of the group corresponds to a diagonal line BD, called **life line**, starting on the horizontal time axis. The abscissa of B is the instant of birth of the person. The abscissa of D is the instant of decease and the ordinate of D is the age at decease of the individual. The diagram is completed by horizontal and vertical lines with integer ordinate and abscissa. For any segment *seg*, we denote by L(*seg*) the number of life lines cutting *seg*. For any polygon *pol*, we denote by D(*pol*) the number of **decease points** D in *pol*.

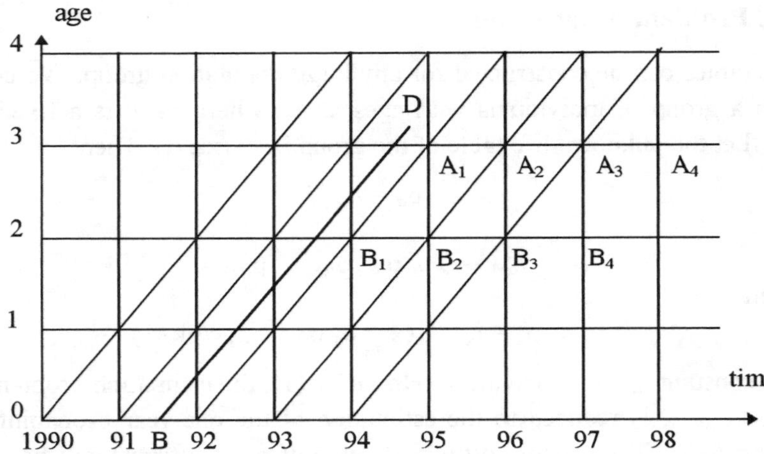

Figure 3.1. Lexis diagram

Then we can estimate p_2 for example, by

$$p_2^\circ = L(A_1A_3)/L(B_1B_3). \qquad (2)$$

because $L(B_1B_3)$ represents a number of persons aged 2 exactly and $L(A_1A_3)$ is the corresponding number of survivors reaching age 3. But

$$L(A_1A_3)=L(A_1A_2)+L(A_2A_3)= [L(A_1B_2)-D(A_1A_2B_2)]+[L(A_2B_3)-D(A_2A_3B_3)]$$

$$L(B_1B_3)=L(B_1B_2)+L(B_2B_3)= [L(A_1B_2)+D(A_1B_2B_1)]+ [L(A_2B_3)+D(A_2B_3B_2)]$$

The numbers $L(A_1B_2)$, $D(A_1A_2B_2)$, ..., $D(A_1B_2B_1)$ occurring in the last members of these relations result from national statistics. Substitution in (2) furnishes the so-called **Knapp-Zeuner formula** for p_2°.

Demographers use more explicit notations, not needed in this book, for L(*seg*) and D(*pol*). Of course, p_2 can also be estimated by $L(A_1A_4)/L(B_1B_4)$, instead of (2) and any p_x (x integer) can be treated similarly.

3.3. Private tables

The goal is the construction of a life table for a group of lives covered by some type of insurance. In order to estimate $q_x:=1-p_x$ (x integer), the company observes a subgroup of n_x lives aged x (approximatively) during one year. If the number of deaths in the subgroup is m_x, then q_x can be estimated by $q_x^\circ=m_x/n_x$. But this expression does not take new entries in the subgroup during the observation year into account. We explain how the proportion m_x/n_x must be corrected if the number of new entries equals e_x.

By linear interpolation with respect to $\theta\in[0,1]$ on the interval [0,1],

$$_\theta q_x \approx (1-\theta)\,{}_0q_x + \theta\,{}_1q_x.$$

Hence, for $\theta=1/2$,

$$_{1/2}q_x \approx (1/2)\,{}_1q_x. \tag{3}$$

because $_0q_x=0$. The relation (3) indicates that when mortality at age x is estimated, it amounts to the same to observe n lives during 1/2 year, or n/2 lives during 1 year. In practice, the new entries occur more or less uniformly over the observation year. Then it can be assumed that they all occur in the middle of the year. Hence, e_x supplementary lives are observed during 1/2 year, or equivalently, $e_x/2$ supplementary lives are observed during 1 year. The conclusion is that the denominator n_x must be replaced by $n_x+e_x/2$ in the proportion m_x/n_x. Lives leaving the subgroup during the observation period, for reasons other than death (such as policy termination), can be treated in the same way. If their number is o_x, the formula for q_x° becomes eventually

$$q_x^\circ = m_x/(n_x + e_x/2 - o_x/2). \tag{4}$$

See Ch.16.11 for an improvement of estimator q_x°.

In the foregoing section 3.2, we have implicitly assumed that immigration and emigration could be neglected. If this is not possible, similar corrections as those considered here must be introduced in the Knapp-Zeuner formulas.

3.4. Analytic least-squares graduation

We now consider some analytic expression $p_x(c,c',c'',\ldots)$ for the one-year survival probability at age x, depending on a finite number of parameters c, c′, c″, ... (x=α, α+1, ..., ω). We fix the parameters in such a way that the sum

$$Q(c,c',c'',\ldots) := \sum_{\alpha\le x\le\omega} w(x)[p_x(c,c',c'',\ldots)-p_x^\circ]^2 \tag{5}$$

is minimum. The **weight** $w(x)\ge 0$ of the observed probability p_x° is supposed to be known. It can be fixed according to several criteria. For instance, the weights may be more important on age intervals on which the table is used frequently. In the following section 3.5, we fix the weights w(x) by a statistical argument.

Nowadays, the minimum of functions such as $Q(c,c',c'',\ldots)$ can be found by numerical algorithms not necessitating the explicit analytic calculation of the partial derivatives

$$\partial/\partial c\; Q(c,c',c'',\ldots),\quad \partial/\partial c'\; Q(c,c',c'',\ldots),\quad \ldots \tag{6}$$

Most of them are based on initial approximative values c_0, c'_0, c''_0, ... of the parameters and the algorithms do not work if the initial values are not close enough to those furnishing the minimum. In 3.6 we explain how the initial values s_0, c_0, g_0 can be found in case of a fitting by a Makeham life table.

When the optimal values c, c′, c″, ... have been fixed, we have not only found the adjusted values $p_x(c,c',c'',\ldots)$ (x=α, α+1, ...,ω), but we have also automatically solved an interpolation problem because then $p_x(c,c',c'',\ldots)$ can also be considered for non integer values $x\in[\alpha,\omega]$.

3.5. Maximum likelihood graduation

We assume that the proportion p_x° (x=α, α+1, ..., ω) results from the observation of n(x) lives (with corrections $e_x/2$ and $o_x/2$ incorporated) aged x, that the number of survivals after one year equals s(x) and the number of deaths m(x) = n(x)−s(x). We assume that the true one-year probabilities are

$$p_x = p_x(c,c',c'',\ldots),\quad q_x = q_x(c,c',c'',\ldots) = 1-p_x(c,c',c'',\ldots)\quad (x=\alpha, \alpha+1, \ldots, \omega).$$

Then the probability of the sample s(x) (x=α, α+1, ..., ω) equals

$$\prod_{\alpha\le x\le\omega} n(x)![s(x)!m(x)!]^{-1}\, p_x^{s(x)}\, q_x^{m(x)} \tag{7}$$

because the binomial law can be applied to the lifes aged x and because the lives are supposed to be independent.

In the maximum likelihood method, the parameters c, c′, c″, ... are fixed by the condition that (7) is maximum. They do not occur in $n(x)![s(x)!m(x)!]^{-1}$. Hence, the condition is equivalent to the maximization of the product

$$\Pi_{\alpha\le x\le\omega}\, p_x^{\,s(x)}\, q_x^{\,m(x)} \qquad (8)$$

or to the maximization of its logarithm

$$L(c,c',c'',...) := \Sigma_{\alpha\le x\le\omega}\, [s(x)\log p_x + m(x)\log q_x]. \qquad (9)$$

Then

$$\partial/\partial c\; L(c,c',c'',..) = \Sigma_{\alpha\le x\le\omega}\, \{[s(x)/p_x]\, \partial/\partial c\; p_x + [m(x)/q_x]\, \partial/\partial c\; q_x\}$$

$$= \Sigma_{\alpha\le x\le\omega}\, [s(x)/p_x - m(x)/q_x]\, \partial/\partial c\; p_x$$

$$= \Sigma_{\alpha\le x\le\omega}\, (p_x q_x)^{-1}\, [s(x)q_x - m(x)p_x]\, \partial/\partial c\; p_x,$$

where

$$[s(x)q_x - m(x)p_x] = s(x)q_x - [n(x)-s(x)]p_x = s(x)(q_x+p_x) - n(x)p_x$$

$$= s(x) - n(x)p_x = n(x)[s(x)/n(x) - p_x] = n(x)(p_x^{\circ}-p_x).$$

Hence, the optimal c, c′, c″, ... satisfy the equation

$$0 = \partial/\partial c\; L(c,c',c'',..) = \Sigma_{\alpha\le x\le\omega}\, n(x)\, (p_x q_x)^{-1}\, (p_x^{\circ}-p_x)\, \partial/\partial c\; p_x \qquad (10)$$

and similar equations for derivatives with respect to c′, c″, ...

Let us now consider the minimization problem of

$$Q(c,c',c'',...) = \Sigma_{\alpha\le x\le\omega}\, n(x)\, (p_x^{\circ} q_x^{\circ})^{-1}\, (p_x^{\circ}-p_x)^2. \qquad (11)$$

Then the conditions

$$\partial/\partial c\; Q(c,c',c'',...) = 0, \quad \partial/\partial c'\; Q(c,c',c'',...) = 0, \quad ...$$

are the equation

$$\Sigma_{\alpha\le x\le\omega}\, n(x)\, (p_x^{\circ}q_x^{\circ})^{-1}\, (p_x^{\circ}-p_x)\, \partial/\partial c\; p_x = 0 \qquad (12)$$

and similar equations for derivatives with respect to c′, c″, ... We observe that the equations (10) and (12) differ by the coefficients $(p_x q_x)^{-1}$ and $(p_x^{\circ}q_x^{\circ})^{-1}$ only. This shows that it is practically equivalent to maximize (9) or to minimize (11) (numerical tests confirm this observation). Hence, the statistically correct weights in (5) are

$$w(x) = n(x)\, /(p_x^{\circ}q_x^{\circ}). \qquad (13)$$

3.6. Determination of initial parameters in the Makeham case

We consider the interval of ages x+r (r=0, 1, 2, ..., 4n−1) where the integers x and n are fixed. Let $l_\xi(a,s,g,c)$ be the Makeham life table with parameters a, s, g and c (Ch.2.6) and let l_{x+r}° be constructed from observed probabilities p_ξ° by formulas such as (1). Our goal is to fix the parameters a, s, g and c in such a way that

$$l_{x+r}^\circ \approx l_{x+r}(a,s,g,c) \quad (r=0, 1, 2, ..., 4n-1). \tag{14}$$

The following solution to this (not well defined) problem is furnished by the so-called **King & Hardy method**. The system (14) is replaced by the exact system

$$a_1^\circ := \Sigma_{0\le r\le n-1} \log l_{x+r}^\circ = \Sigma_{0\le r\le n-1} \log l_{x+r}(a,s,g,c),$$

$$a_2^\circ := \Sigma_{n\le r\le 2n-1} \log l_{x+r}^\circ = \Sigma_{n\le r\le 2n-1} \log l_{x+r}(a,s,g,c),$$

$$a_3^\circ := \Sigma_{2n\le r\le 3n-1} \log l_{x+r}^\circ = \Sigma_{2n\le r\le 3n-1} \log l_{x+r}(a,s,g,c),$$

$$a_4^\circ := \Sigma_{3n\le r\le 4n-1} \log l_{x+r}^\circ = \Sigma_{3n\le r\le 4n-1} \log l_{x+r}(a,s,g,c)$$

for the unknown quantities a, s, g and c, where

$$\log l_{x+r}(a,s,g,c) = \log a + (x+r) \log s + c^{x+r} \log g.$$

By the formulas for arithmetic and geometric sums, the linear system becomes

$$a_1^\circ = n \log a + [nx+n(n-1)/2] \log s + c^x[(c^n-1)/(c-1)]\log g,$$

$$a_2^\circ = n \log a + [nx+n(3n-1)/2] \log s + c^{x+n}[(c^n-1)/(c-1)]\log g,$$

$$a_3^\circ = n \log a + [nx+n(5n-1)/2] \log s + c^{x+2n}[(c^n-1)/(c-1)]\log g,$$

$$a_4^\circ = n \log a + [nx+n(7n-1)/2] \log s + c^{x+3n}[(c^n-1)/(c-1)]\log g.$$

By substractions,

$$b_1^\circ := a_2^\circ - a_1^\circ = n^2 \log s + c^x[(c^n-1)^2/(c-1)]\log g,$$

$$b_2^\circ := a_3^\circ - a_2^\circ = n^2 \log s + c^{x+n}[(c^n-1)^2/(c-1)]\log g,$$

$$b_3^\circ := a_3^\circ - a_2^\circ = n^2 \log s + c^{x+2n}[(c^n-1)^2/(c-1)]\log g.$$

By further substractions,

$$c_1^\circ := b_2^\circ - b_1^\circ = c^x[(c^n-1)^3/(c-1)] \log g,$$

$$c_2^\circ := b_3^\circ - b_2^\circ = c^{x+n}[(c^n-1)^3/(c-1)] \log g.$$

Then $c^n = c_2^\circ/c_1^\circ$. This relation furnishes c and then g, s and a results successively from the foregoing equalities.

Chapter 4

BASIC CONCEPTS OF LIVE INSURANCE MATHEMATICS

4.1. Life insurance models

The conjunction of a financial model and a mortality model is a **life insurance model**. The **classical life insurance model** is the conjunction of the classical financial model (with constant interest rate i) and the classical mortality model (with survival probabilities resulting from a continuous life table l_ξ). The classical life insurance model is adopted if nothing else is stated explicitly. Some developments have direct generalizations in case of variable interest rates: it is enough to replace the discount factor v^τ by v_τ everywhere.

The following discussion, in case of two lives, can be extended to any number of lives. Lives are denoted by x and y. Then x and y denote at the same time the persons and their ages at the origin of time. The future lifetime of x and y is the random variable X and Y resp. Hence, x dies at instant X at age x+X and y dies at instant Y at age y+Y. The life tables for x and y are l_ξ and l_η resp. They may be different (although the same l is used).

The lives x and y are **independent** if the random variables X and Y are stochastically independent. The independence assumption is not very realistic in some cases: the future lifetimes X and Y of a married couple are certainly not independent (for instance, because they use the same car simulteneously). Hence, it is assumed that the dependence can be neglected when the classical model with independent lives is used.

We use the symbol ↑ (head up) as abbreviation for "alive" and the symbol ↓ (head down) as abbreviation for "dead" (of course, no limits are involved here). Explicitly,

$$x \uparrow t \;:\Leftrightarrow\; \text{x is alive at instant t} \;\Leftrightarrow\; X > t,$$

$$x \downarrow t \;:\Leftrightarrow\; \text{x is dead at instant t} \;\Leftrightarrow\; X < t.$$

4.2. Contracts

A (mathematical) **life insurance contract** (or **policy**) is a couple ($C^{\circ\circ}$,$P^{\circ\circ}$) of time capitals $C^{\circ\circ}$ and $P^{\circ\circ}$ of which the stochastic parts are functions of future lifetimes X, Y, ..., Z of lives x, y, ..., z. The component $C^{\circ\circ}$ is the **engagement of the insurance company** (C is the first letter of "Company") to be paid to the insureds. $P^{\circ\circ}$ is the **engagement of the insureds** (P is the first letter of "Premiums"), to be paid to the insurer. One of the components $C^{\circ\circ}$ or $P^{\circ\circ}$ may be deterministic, but not both, because then ($C^{\circ\circ}$,$P^{\circ\circ}$) is a **financial contract** in which no lives are involved.

A (technically) **fair contract** is a contract satisfying the **equivalence principle** C=P, where C:=E(A$C^{\circ\circ}$) is the price of $C^{\circ\circ}$ and P:=E(A$P^{\circ\circ}$) is the price of $P^{\circ\circ}$. The equivalence principle allows to fix the premiums when the interest rate and the life tables are given. The true interest rate or the true mortality are not necessarily those used in application of the equivalence principle. Due to the differences, the insurer automatically adopts some **security loading**.

The contract ($C^{\circ\circ}$,$P^{\circ\circ}$) is called more explicitly a **net contract**. The corresponding **expense-loaded contract**, is a couple ($C^{\circ\circ}$+$E^{\circ\circ}$,$P^{\circ\circ}$+$L^{\circ\circ}$), where $E^{\circ\circ}$ is a time-capital covering the expenses (acquisition, administration, collection) of the insurance company and $L^{\circ\circ}$ is a corresponding loading to be paid by the insureds.

One of the goals of life insurance mathematics is the study of pure and expense-loaded contracts and of their evolution with time. It starts with the investigation of the components $C^{\circ\circ}$, $P^{\circ\circ}$, $E^{\circ\circ}$ and $L^{\circ\circ}$. We use the notation $Q^{\circ\circ}$ (Q is the first letter of the French "Quelconque") for any time capital. In the comments, we assume that $Q^{\circ\circ}$ is paid by the insurer to the insureds.

4.3. Ruin problems in portfolios

A **life insurance portfolio** is a collection of life insurance contracts. What is the probability that the risk reserve of the insurer, completed with the present value of the premiums to be collected by the insurer in the future, is larger than the present value of the sums to be paid by the insurer ? This ruin problem is solved in Ch.10 under normal assumptions.

4.4. Validity level of relations

Let $Q_1^{\circ\circ}$ and $Q_2^{\circ\circ}$ be time-capitals. The relations $Q_1^{\circ\circ}=Q_2^{\circ\circ}$, $Q_1^{\circ}=Q_2^{\circ}$ and $Q_1=Q_2$ are valid at the **time-capital level**, at the **present value level** and at the **price level** resp.

If a relation is valid at the time-capital level, then it is valid at the present value level because we can apply the operator A. If a relation is valid at the present value level, then it is valid at the price level because we can apply the operator E. In many cases, we display two proofs at different levels of the same relation. Then one of the proofs is superfluous but it may nevertheless be interesting and instructive.

We make use of the following device in order to simplify the typography of relations. Let $s_1, s_2, \ldots, s_k$ be symbols such as

$$^{\circ}\ ,\ ^{\circ\circ}\ ,\ _{m|n}\ ,\ ^{-}\ ,\ ^{\cdot\cdot}\ ,\ ^{(r)}\ ,\ c_\tau\ ,\ \delta_\tau. \qquad (1)$$

If some relation is completed by the indication $[s_1, s_2, \ldots, s_k]$, then it can be completed everywhere by one or more symbols $s_1, s_2, \ldots, s_k$ if the corresponding relations are meaningful. For instance, the unique relation

$$a_{\overline{xy}} = a_x + a_y - a_{xy} \quad [^{\circ}, ^{\circ\circ}, _{m|n}, ^{-}, ^{\cdot\cdot}, ^{(r)}, c_\tau, \delta_\tau] \qquad (2)$$

is an abbreviation of 160 relations such as

$$a_{\overline{xy}}^{\circ\circ} = a_x^{\circ\circ} + a_y^{\circ\circ} - a_{xy}^{\circ\circ},$$

$$_{m|n}a_{\overline{xy}}^{\circ} = {}_{m|n}a_x^{\circ} + {}_{m|n}a_y^{\circ} - {}_{m|n}a_{xy}^{\circ},$$

$$_{m|n}a^{(r)}_{\overline{xy}}(c_\tau) = {}_{m|n}a^{(r)}_x(c_\tau) + {}_{m|n}a^{(r)}_y(c_\tau) - {}_{m|n}a^{(r)}_{xy}(c_\tau).$$

A relation not included in (1) is

$$\bar{a}^{(r)}_{\overline{xy}} = \bar{a}^{(r)}_x + \bar{a}^{(r)}_y - \bar{a}^{(r)}_{xy}$$

because $\bar{a}^{(r)}_{\overline{xy}}$, $\bar{a}^{(r)}_x$, $\bar{a}^{(r)}_y$, $\bar{a}^{(r)}_{xy}$ will not be defined.

4.5. Approximations

Ages x, y, ..., z are approximated by integers in the practical applications of the theoretical formulas, Instants s can be reduced to integer instants by linear interpolations. Let $s=m+\theta$ $(0<\theta<1)$. Then f(s) results from the values f(m) and f(m+1) by the formula

$$f(m+\theta) \approx (1-\theta)\, f(m) + \theta\, f(m+1).$$

f(m) or f(m+1) must be replaced by f(m+) or f(m+1−) if f is not continuous at point m or at point m+1.

Discretizations of integrals such as $\int_{(m,m+n)} f(\tau)\ d\ {}_{\tau}q_x$ are performed as follows:

$$\int_{(m,m+n)} f(\tau)\ d\ {}_{\tau}q_x = \sum_{m\le k\le m+n-1} \int_{(k,k+1)} f(\tau)\ d\ {}_{\tau}q_x$$

$$\approx \sum_{m\le k\le m+n-1} \int_{(k,k+1)} f(k+1/2)\ d\ {}_{\tau}q_x = \sum_{m\le k\le m+n-1} f(k+1/2)\ \Delta\ {}_{k}q_x$$

or

$$\int_{(s,s+n)} f(\tau)\ d\ {}_{\tau}q_x = \sum_{m\le k\le m+n-1} \int_{(k,k+1)} f(\tau)\ d\ {}_{\tau}q_x$$

$$\approx \sum_{m\le k\le m+n-1} \int_{(k,k+1)} [f(k+)+f(k+1-)]/2\ d\ {}_{\tau}q_x$$

$$= \sum_{m\le k\le m+n-1}[f(k+)+f(k+1-)]/2\ \ \Delta\ {}_{k}q_x,$$

where $\Delta\ {}_{k}q_x = -\ \Delta\ {}_{k}p_x = d_{x+k}/l_x$.

4.6. Null events

A **null event** is an event of which the probability equals 0. For instance, the events

$$X = t,\quad X \text{ is an integer},\quad X = Y,$$

are null events because the random variables X and Y have a density (Ch.2. Th.2) and because they are independent. Two events are regarded as identical if they differ by a null event. For instance, a couple of identical events is

$$X < t,\ X \le t$$

and another couple is

$$X < Y,\ X \le Y.$$

'k=k', but the relation X'='X+1 is nevertheless regarded as exact (it holds almost surely because the probability that X is an integer equals 0).

Chapter 5

LIFE ANNUITIES (ONE LIFE)

5.1. Deferred life capital

The **s-years deferred life capital** (or **pure endowment of duration s**) on the life x is the time-capital

$${}_sE_x^{\circ\circ} := (1_{x\uparrow s},\ s).$$

Hence, the insurer pays 1 at instant s if x is alive at s. The present value of ${}_sE_x^{\circ\circ}$ is

$${}_sE_x^{\circ} = A({}_sE_x^{\circ\circ}) = 1_{x\uparrow s}\, v^s.$$

The price of ${}_sE_x^{\circ\circ}$ is

$${}_sE_x = E({}_sE_x^{\circ}) = E(1_{x\uparrow s}v^s) = E1_{x\uparrow s}.v^s = P(x\uparrow s)v^s = {}_sp_x\ v^s,$$

because the expectation of the indicator function of an event equals the probability of that event. Hence

$${}_sE_x = {}_sp_x\ v^s$$

is the price of 1 unit at s contingent on survival of x at s. Then $c.{}_sE_x$ is the price of c at s contingent on survival.

Iterative relation

$${}_{s+t}E_x = {}_sE_x\ {}_tE_{x+s}. \tag{1}$$

This iterative relation is direct from the iterative relation Ch.2.(5) for survival probabilities. Indeed,

$${}_{s+t}E_x = {}_{s+t}p_x\ v^{s+t} = {}_sp_x\ v^s\ .{}_tp_{x+s}\ v^t = {}_sE_x\ {}_tE_{x+s}.$$

Formula (1) can be interpreted as follows. The amount of 1 at s+t contingent on survival at s+t can be insured in one step (then the price is ${}_{s+t}E_x$) or in two steps. In the latter case, the price at s of 1 at s+t contingent on survival at s+t is ${}_tE_{x+s}$, because x is aged x+s at s and because then the duration is t years.

The price at 0 of the amount ${}_tE_{x+s}$ at s contingent on survival at s, is ${}_tE_{x+s}\cdot{}_sE_x$. The insurance in one step is equivalent to the insurance in two steps. Hence, (1) must hold.

Commutation functions

$${}_mE_x = {}_mp_x\, v^m = (l_{x+m}/l_x)v^m = l_{x+m}v^{x+m}/(l_xv^x) = D_{x+m}/D_x.$$

By linear interpolation,

$${}_{m+\theta}E_x \approx (1-\theta)\, {}_mE_x + \theta\, {}_{m+1}E_x.$$

General capital-function

Let c_τ be a function, called **capital-function**, at least defined at the point τ=s. Then

$${}_sE_x(c_\tau)^{\circ\circ} := (c_s 1_{x\uparrow s}, s) = c_s\, {}_sE_x^{\circ\circ}.$$

Variable interest rates

The time capital ${}_sE_x(\delta_\tau)^{\circ\circ}$ is the same as ${}_sE_x^{\circ\circ}$, but now the notation (δ_τ) indicates that its present value ${}_sE_x(\delta_\tau)^{\circ}$ will be calculated in the model with instantaneous interest rate function δ_τ. Hence,

$${}_sE_x(\delta_\tau)^{\circ} = 1_{X>s}, \quad {}_sE_x(\delta_\tau) = {}_sp_x\, v_s.$$

By Ch.1.(17), ${}_{s+t}E_x(\delta_\tau) = {}_{s+t}p_x\, v_{s+t}(\delta_\tau) = {}_sp_x\, v_s(\delta_\tau).\ {}_tp_{x+s}\, v_t(\delta_{s+\tau})$.

Hence, the iterative formula (1) becomes

$${}_{s+t}E_x(\delta_\tau) = {}_sE_x(\delta_\tau)\, {}_tE_{x+s}(\delta_{s+\tau}). \tag{2}$$

More generally, the time-capital ${}_sE_x(c_\tau,\delta_\tau)^{\circ\circ}$ is the same as ${}_sE_x(c_\tau)^{\circ\circ}$, but its present value is calculated in the model with variable interest rates.

5.2. Constant life annuities

The following time-capitals are classical **constant life annuities on x**.

$${}_{s|n}a_x^{\circ\circ} := \sum_{1\le k\le n} (1_{x\uparrow s+k}, s+k),$$

$${}_{s|n}\ddot{a}_x^{\circ\circ} := \sum_{0\le k\le n-1} (1_{x\uparrow s+k}, s+k),$$

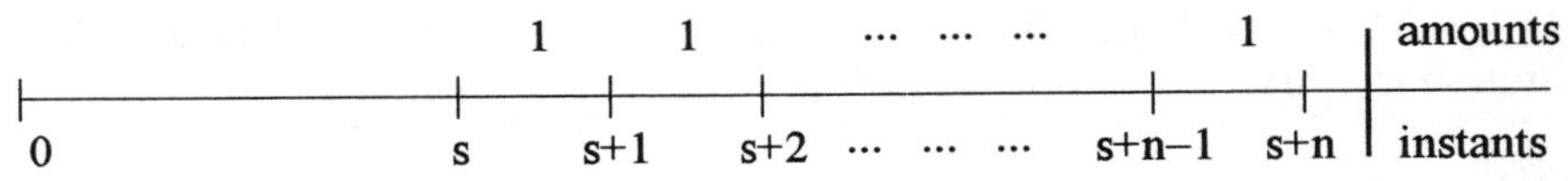

$$ {}_{s|t}\bar{a}_x{}^{\circ\circ} := \int_{(s,s+t)} (1_x\uparrow_\tau d\tau, \tau). $$

${}_{s|n}a_x{}^{\circ\circ}$ is an **annuity-immediate**, ${}_{s|n}\ddot{a}_x{}^{\circ\circ}$ an **annuity-due** and ${}_{s|t}\bar{a}_x{}^{\circ\circ}$ a **continuous annuity**. Annuities with left-sided subscript ${}_{s|n}$ are **s-year deferred and n-year temporary annuities**. The annuity ${}_{s|t}a_x{}^{\circ\circ}$ is a **s-year deferred and t-year temporary annuity**. Hence, the terminology is the same as in case of annuities-certain (Ch.1.6). The payments are also the same, but in case of life annuities they are contingent on survival of x at the considered instants.

s may be equal to 0 and n or t may be infinite. Then the following notations are adopted: ${}_{s|} \equiv {}_{s|\infty}$, ${}_{n} \equiv {}_{0|n}$, ${}_{t} \equiv {}_{0|t}$.

Important particular cases are the (non deferred) **temporary life annuities**

$$ a_{x\,\overline{n|}}{}^{\circ\circ} \equiv {}_n a_x{}^{\circ\circ}, \quad \ddot{a}_{x\,\overline{n|}}{}^{\circ\circ} \equiv {}_n\ddot{a}_x{}^{\circ\circ}, \quad \bar{a}_{x\,\overline{t|}}{}^{\circ} \equiv {}_t\bar{a}_x{}^{\circ\circ}, $$

the **deferred whole life annuities**

$$ {}_{s|}a_x{}^{\circ\circ} \equiv {}_{s|\infty}a_x{}^{\circ\circ}, \quad {}_{s|}\ddot{a}_x{}^{\circ\circ} \equiv {}_{s|\infty}\ddot{a}_x{}^{\circ\circ}, \quad {}_{s|}\bar{a}_x{}^{\circ\circ} \equiv {}_{s|\infty}\bar{a}_x{}^{\circ\circ} $$

and the (non deferred) **whole life annuities**

$$ a_x{}^{\circ\circ} \equiv {}_{0|\infty}a_x{}^{\circ\circ}, \quad \ddot{a}_x{}^{\circ\circ} \equiv {}_{0|\infty}\ddot{a}_x{}^{\circ\circ}, \quad \bar{a}_x{}^{\circ\circ} \equiv {}_{0|\infty}\bar{a}_x{}^{\circ\circ}. $$

We notice that

$$ {}_{s|n}a_x{}^{\circ\circ} = \sum_{1\le k\le n} {}_{s+k}E_x{}^{\circ\circ}, \tag{3} $$

$$ {}_{s|n}\ddot{a}_x{}^{\circ\circ} = \sum_{0\le k\le n-1} {}_{s+k}E_x{}^{\circ\circ}, \tag{4} $$

$$ {}_{s|t}\bar{a}_x{}^{\circ\circ} = \int_{(s,s+t)} {}_\tau E_x{}^{\circ\circ}\, d\tau. \tag{5} $$

These relations are valid at the time-capital level and hence, at the lower present value and price levels (i.e. we may replace $^{\circ\circ}$ by $^{\circ}$ and we may also suppress $^{\circ\circ}$ everywhere). Hence,

$$ {}_{s|n}a_x = \sum_{1\le k\le n} {}_{s+k}E_x = \sum_{1\le k\le n} v^{s+k}\, {}_{s+k}p_x, \tag{6} $$

$$ {}_{s|n}\ddot{a}_x = \sum_{0\le k\le n-1} {}_{s+k}E_x = \sum_{0\le k\le n-1} v^{s+k}\, {}_{s+k}p_x, \tag{7} $$

$$ {}_{s|t}\bar{a}_x = \int_{(s,s+t)} {}_\tau E_x\, d\tau = \int_{(s,s+t)} v^\tau\, {}_\tau p_x\, d\tau. \tag{8} $$

These prices can be displayed at once as follows. Let us first consider the time-capital ${}_{s|n}a_x{}^{\circ\circ}$. At each instant s+k ($1\le k\le n$), the insurer pays the amount 1, with present value v^{s+k} and he pays it with a probability ${}_{s+k}p_x$.

Then (3) follows. Formula (4) is obtained in the same way. For (5) the argument is: in each interval $d\tau$ ($s \leq \tau \leq s+t$), the insurer pays the amount $d\tau$, with present value $v^\tau d\tau$ and he pays it with a probability ${}_\tau p_x$.

Relations between annuities-immediate and annuities-due

The last member of (3) completed with term ${}_sE_x{}^{oo}$ is the same as the last member of (4) completed with term ${}_{s+n}E_x{}^{oo}$. Hence,

$$ {}_sE_x{}^{oo} + {}_{s|n}a_x{}^{oo} = {}_{s|n}\ddot{a}_x{}^{oo} + {}_{s+n}E_x{}^{oo}. $$

The following are particular cases at price level.

s=0: $$1 + {}_na_x = {}_n\ddot{a}_x + {}_nE_x,$$

n=∞: $${}_sE_x + {}_{s|}a_x = {}_{s|}\ddot{a}_x,$$

s=0 and n=∞: $$1 + a_x = \ddot{a}_x.$$

Iterative relations

$$ {}_{s|n}a_x = {}_sE_x\ {}_na_{x+s} \quad [\ddot{\ },\ \bar{\ }]. \tag{9} $$

(in the continuous case n can be replaced by any positive number t; we will not repeat this remark in similar situations hereafter). These relations result from (3), (4), (5) and from the iterative relation for the deferred life capital. They can also be obtained by an intuitive argument based on an insurance in two steps. We consider the case of ${}_{s|n}a_x{}^{oo}$. At s, the price of the (non-deferred) n-years temporary life annuity-immediate is ${}_na_{x+s}$ because x is aged x+s at s. The price at 0 of the amount ${}_na_{x+s}$ at s contingent on survival at s is ${}_na_{x+s}\cdot{}_sE_x$. The insurance in one step is equivalent to the insurance in two steps.

Commutation functions

$$ {}_{m|n}a_x = \Sigma_{m+1\leq k\leq m+n}\ {}_kE_x = (\Sigma_{m+1\leq k<\infty} - \Sigma_{m+n+1\leq k<\infty})\ D_{x+k}/D_x $$
$$ = (N_{x+m+1} - N_{x+m+n+1})/D_x, $$
$$ {}_{m|n}\ddot{a}_x = \Sigma_{m\leq k\leq m+n-1}\ {}_kE_x = (\Sigma_{m\leq k<\infty} - \Sigma_{m+n\leq k<\infty})\ D_{x+k}/D_x $$
$$ = (N_{x+m} - N_{x+m+n})/D_x. $$

The following are particular cases.

m=0: $${}_{n}a_x = (N_{x+1} - N_{x+n+1})/D_x,$$
$${}_{n}\ddot{a}_x = (N_x - N_{x+n})/D_x.$$

n=∞: $${}_{m|}a_x = N_{x+m+1}/D_x,$$
$${}_{m|}\ddot{a}_x = N_{x+m}/D_x.$$

m=0 and n=∞: $$a_x = N_{x+1}/D_x,$$
$$\ddot{a}_x = N_x/D_x.$$

We notice that N is the first letter of "Numerator" and D the first letter of "Denominator". **The expressions for the annuities-immediate result from those for the annuities-due by the replacement of x by x+1 in the numerator**. This is a general rule for formulas with commutation functions.

$\bar{a}_x$ *versus* $\bar{a}_{\overline{EX}|}$

The capital of $\bar{a}_x^{\circ\circ}$ is distributed uniformly on the interval [0,X]. Hence,

$$\bar{a}_x^{\circ\circ} = \bar{a}_{\overline{X}|}^{\circ\circ} \tag{10}$$

and then it is natural to compare $\bar{a}_x$ with $\bar{a}_{\overline{EX}|}$. By (10),

$$\bar{a}_x^{\circ} = \bar{a}_{\overline{X}|}^{\circ} = (1-v^X)/\delta$$

and then

$$\bar{a}_x = \mathrm{E}\,\bar{a}_{\overline{X}|}^{\circ} = (1-\mathrm{E}v^X)/\delta,$$

whereas

$$\bar{a}_{\overline{EX}|} = (1-v^{EX})/\delta.$$

v^τ is a convex function of $\tau \geq 0$. Hence, by Jensen's formula (App.C), $v^{EX} \leq \mathrm{E}v^X$. Then

$$\bar{a}_x \leq \bar{a}_{\overline{EX}|}. \tag{11}$$

5.3. Partitioned life annuities

In case of the **r-period partitioned life annuities** ${}_{s|m}a_x^{(r)\circ\circ}$ and ${}_{s|m}\ddot{a}^{(r)\circ\circ}$, each year [s+k,s+k+1] (k=0, 1, ..., n−1) is partitioned in r **periods**

$$[s+k+\nu/r, s+k+(\nu+1)/r] \quad (\nu=0,1,\ldots,r-1),$$

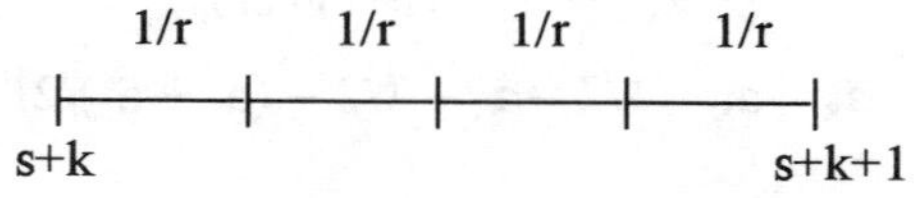

and the amount 1/r is attached at each of these periods. It is attached at the end of the period in case of the partitioned annuity-immediate ${}_{s|m}a_x^{(r)oo}$ and at the beginning of the period in case of the partitioned annuity-due ${}_{s|m}\ddot{a}^{(r)oo}$. The amount attached at an instant is paid by the insurer if x is alive at that instant. Hence,

$$ {}_{s|n}a_x^{(r)oo} := (1/r) \textstyle\sum_{1\le v\le nr} (1_{x\uparrow s+v/r}, s+v/r), $$

$$ {}_{s|n}\ddot{a}_x^{(r)\,oo} := (1/r) \textstyle\sum_{0\le v\le nr-1} (1_{x\uparrow s+v/r}, s+v/r) $$

The price of the partitioned annuities is

$$ {}_{s|n}a_x^{(r)} = (1/r) \textstyle\sum_{1\le v\le nr}\ {}_{s+v/r}E_x, \tag{12} $$

$$ {}_{s|n}\ddot{a}_x^{(r)} = (1/r) \textstyle\sum_{0\le v\le nr-1}\ {}_{s+v/r}E_x. \tag{13} $$

The iterative relation (9) remains valid in case of partitioned life annuities. Hence (9) can be completed as follows:

$$ {}_{s|n}a_x = {}_sE_x\ {}_na_{x+s} \quad [\ddot{},\ \bar{},\ {}^{(r)}]. \tag{14} $$

By App.B.Th.3 with the function $f_\tau = {}_\tau E_x$,

$$ {}_{s|n}a_x^{(r)} \approx {}_{s|n}a_x + ({}_sE_x - {}_{s+n}E_x).(r-1)/(2r), \tag{15} $$

$$ {}_{s|n}\ddot{a}_x^{(r)} \approx {}_{s|n}\ddot{a}_x - ({}_sE_x - {}_{s+n}E_x).(r-1)/(2r), \tag{16} $$

$$ {}_{s|n}\bar{a}_x \approx {}_{s|n}a_x + ({}_sE_x - {}_{s+n}E_x)/2 = {}_{s|n}\ddot{a}_x - ({}_sE_x - {}_{s+n}E_x)/2 = ({}_{s|n}a_x + {}_{s|n}\ddot{a}_x)/2. \tag{17} $$

The continuous case is a limit case of both discrete cases as $r\uparrow\infty$. The following are particular cases of (15), (16) and (17).

s=0:

$$ {}_na_x^{(r)} \approx {}_na_x + (1 - {}_nE_x).(r-1)/(2r), $$

$$ {}_n\ddot{a}_x^{(r)} \approx {}_n\ddot{a}_x - (1 - {}_nE_x).(r-1)/(2r), $$

$$ {}_n\bar{a}_x \approx {}_na_x + (1 - {}_nE_x)/2 = {}_n\ddot{a}_x - (1 - {}_nE_x)/2 = ({}_na_x + {}_n\ddot{a}_x)/2. $$

n=∞:

$$ {}_{s|}a_x^{(r)} \approx {}_{s|}a_x + {}_sE_x\ .(r-1)/(2r), $$

$$ {}_{s|}\ddot{a}_x^{(r)} \approx {}_{s|}\ddot{a}_x - {}_sE_x\ .(r-1)/(2r), $$

$$ {}_{s|}\bar{a}_x \approx {}_{s|}a_x + {}_sE_x\,/2 = {}_{s|}\ddot{a}_x - {}_sE_x\,/2 = ({}_{s|}a_x + {}_{s|}\ddot{a}_x)/2. $$

s=0 and n=∞:

$$ a_x^{(r)} \approx a_x + (r-1)/(2r), $$

$$ \ddot{a}_x^{(r)} \approx \ddot{a}_x - (r-1)/(2r), $$

$$ \bar{a}_x \approx a_x + 1/2 = \ddot{a}_x - 1/2 = (a_x + \ddot{a}_x)/2. $$

By App.B.(12),

$$ {}_{s|n}a_x \le {}_{s|n}a_x^{(r)} \le {}_{s|n}\bar{a}_x \le {}_{s|n}\ddot{a}_x^{(r)} \le {}_{s|n}\ddot{a}_x. \tag{18}$$

We recall that for each annuity occurring in (18) the amount 1 (partitioned in r parts in case of the partitioned annuities) is attached to each year [s+k,s+k+1] (k=0, 1, ..., n−1), as follows (we take r=4 in the representations).

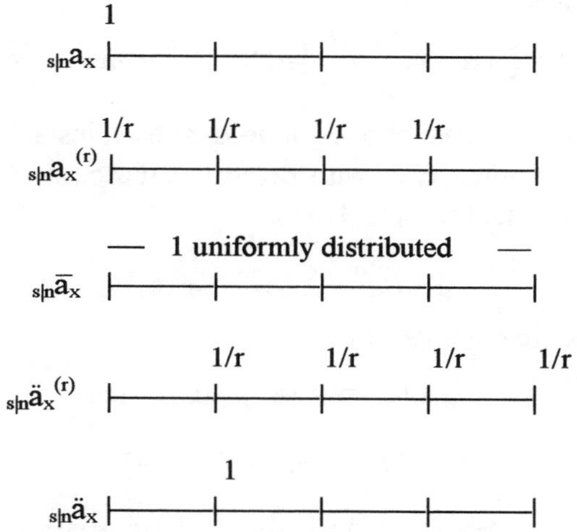

Then (18) is obvious from these representations because the price of the time-capital $(c1_{x\uparrow\tau}, \tau)$ equals $c\,{}_\tau E_x$ and because $_\tau E_x$ is a decreasing function of τ.

5.4. General variable life annuities

We now consider the following **variable life annuities** with general **capital-function** c_τ $(s \le \tau \le s+n)$,

$$ {}_{s|n}a_x(c_\tau)^{oo} := \textstyle\sum_{1\le k\le n} (c_{s+k-}\, 1_{x\uparrow s+k},\ s+k), $$

$$ {}_{s|n}\ddot{a}_x(c_\tau)^{oo} := \textstyle\sum_{0\le k\le n-1} (c_{s+k+}\, 1_{x\uparrow s+k},\ s+k), $$

$$ {}_{s|t}\bar{a}_x(c_\tau)^{oo} := \textstyle\int_{(s,s+t)} (c_\tau\, 1_{x\uparrow\tau} d\tau, \tau), $$

$$ {}_{s|n}a_x^{(r)}(c_\tau)^{oo} := (1/r) \textstyle\sum_{1\le \nu\le nr} (c_{s+\nu/r-}\, 1_{x\uparrow s+\nu/r},\ s+\nu/r), $$

$$ {}_{s|n}\ddot{a}_x^{(r)}(c_\tau)^{oo} := (1/r) \textstyle\sum_{0\le \nu\le nr-1} (c_{s+\nu/r+}\, 1_{x\uparrow s+\nu/r},\ s+\nu/r). $$

The value of the capital-function c_τ at the points τ=s, s+1, ..., s+n is irrelevant because the left-sided and right-sided limits $c_{\tau-}$ and $c_{\tau+}$ are considered at these points and because the value of an integral does not change when the integrand is modified at isolated points. The present value of time-capital $_{s|n}a_x(c_\tau)^{\circ\circ}$ is

$$_{s|n}a_x(c_\tau)^\circ = \sum_{1\le k\le n} c_{s+k-}\, v^{s+k}\, 1_{x\uparrow s+k}$$

and its price equals

$$_{s|n}a_x(c_\tau) = \sum_{1\le k\le n} c_{s+k-}\, v^{s+k}\, E1_{x\uparrow s+k} = \sum_{1\le k\le n} c_{s+k-}\, v^{s+k}\, {}_{s+k}p_x.$$

This price can be displayed at once. Indeed, at each instant s+k (1≤k≤n), the insurer pays the amount c_{s+k-} with present value $c_{s+k-}\, v^{s+k}$ and he pays it with a probability equal to $_{s+k}p_x$. Hence,

$$_{s|n}a_x(c_\tau) = \sum_{1\le k\le n} c_{s+k-}\, {}_{s+k}E_x. \tag{19}$$

The other prices are obtained similarly:

$$_{s|n}\ddot{a}_x(c_\tau) = \sum_{0\le k\le n-1} c_{s+k+}\, {}_{s+k}E_x, \tag{20}$$

$$_{s|t}\bar{a}_x(c_\tau) = \int_{(s,s+t)} c_\tau\, {}_\tau E_x\, d\tau, \tag{21}$$

$$_{s|n}a_x^{(r)}(c_\tau) = (1/r) \sum_{1\le v\le nr} c_{s+v/r-}\, {}_{s+v/r}E_x, \tag{22}$$

$$_{s|n}\ddot{a}_x^{(r)}(c_\tau) = (1/r) \sum_{0\le v\le nr-1} c_{s+v/r+}\, {}_{s+v/r}E_x. \tag{23}$$

The iterative relations are

$$_{s|n}a_x(c_\tau) = {}_sE_x\, {}_na_x(c_{s+\tau}) \quad [\,\ddot{}\,,\ ^{(r)}\,,\ \bar{}\,]. \tag{24}$$

By App.B.Th.2 with $f_\tau := c_\tau\, {}_\tau E_x$ (s≤τ≤s+n),

$$_{s|n}a_x^{(r)}(c_\tau) \approx {}_{s|n}a_x(c_\tau) + [{}_{s|n}\ddot{a}_x(c_\tau) - {}_{s|n}a_x(c_\tau)].(r-1)/(2r), \tag{25}$$

$$_{s|n}\ddot{a}_x^{(r)}(c_\tau) \approx {}_{s|n}\ddot{a}_x(c_\tau) - [{}_{s|n}\ddot{a}_x(c_\tau) - {}_{s|n}a_x(c_\tau)].(r-1)/(2r), \tag{26}$$

$$_{s|n}\bar{a}_x(c_\tau) \approx [{}_{s|n}\ddot{a}_x(c_\tau) + {}_{s|n}a_x(c_\tau)]/2. \tag{27}$$

Succint form: $a_x^{(r)} \approx a_x + (\ddot{a}_x - a_x).(r-1)/(2r) \quad [{}_{s|n}, c_\tau]$, (28)

$$\ddot{a}_x^{(r)} \approx \ddot{a}_x - (\ddot{a}_x - a_x).(r-1)/(2r) \quad [{}_{s|n}, c_\tau], \tag{29}$$

$$\bar{a}_x \approx (\ddot{a}_x + a_x)/2 \quad [{}_{s|n}, c_\tau]. \tag{30}$$

If c_τ is a continuous function of τ, then $f_\tau := c_\tau\ {}_\tau E_x$ is a continuous function of τ. Then by App.B.Th.3,

$$ {}_{s|n}a_x^{(r)}(c_\tau) \approx {}_{s|n}a_x(c_\tau) + [{}_sE_x(c_\tau) - {}_{s+n}E_x(c_\tau)].(r-1)/(2r), \tag{31}$$

$$ {}_{s|n}\ddot{a}_x^{(r)}(c_\tau) \approx {}_{s|n}\ddot{a}_x(c_\tau) - [{}_sE_x(c_\tau) - {}_{s+n}E_x(c_\tau)].(r-1)/(2r), \tag{32}$$

$$ {}_{s|n}\bar{a}_x(c_\tau) \approx {}_{s|n}a_x(c_\tau) + [{}_sE_x(c_\tau) - {}_{s+n}E_x(c_\tau)]/2 $$

$$ = {}_{s|n}\ddot{a}_x(c_\tau) - [{}_sE_x(c_\tau) - {}_{s+n}E_x(c_\tau)]/2 = [{}_{s|n}\ddot{a}_x(c_\tau) + {}_{s|n}a_x(c_\tau)]/2, \tag{33}$$

because

$$ c_s\ {}_sE_x = {}_sE_x(c_\tau),\quad c_{s+n}\ {}_{s+n}E_x = {}_{s+n}E_x(c_\tau). $$

We observe that (31), (32) and (33) are exactly the relations (15), (16) and (17) completed everywhere by c_τ.

5.5. Classical variable life annuities

a. $$ {}_{s|n}(Ia)_x^{\circ\circ} := {}_{s|n}a_x(c_\tau)^{\circ\circ},\ {}_{s|n}(I\ddot{a})_x^{\circ\circ} := {}_{s|n}\ddot{a}_x(c_\tau)^{\circ\circ}, $$

$$ {}_{s|n}(Ia)_x^{(r)\circ\circ} := {}_{s|n}a_x^{(r)}(c_\tau)^{\circ\circ},\ {}_{s|n}(I\ddot{a})_x^{(r)\circ\circ} := {}_{s|n}\ddot{a}_x^{(r)}(c_\tau)^{\circ\circ}, $$

where c_τ is defined on [s,s+n] as follows:

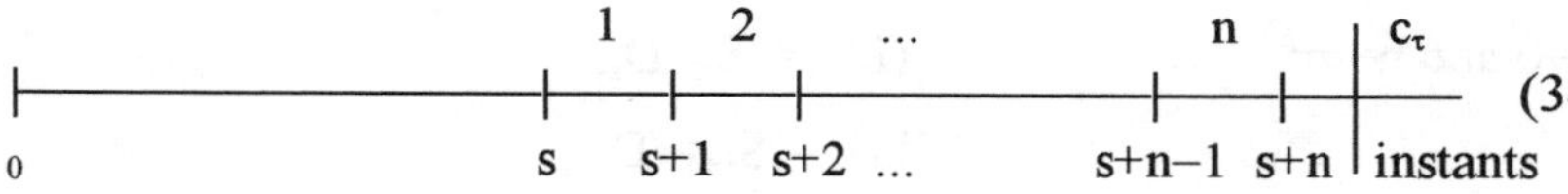

(34)

Of course, this representation signifies that $c_\tau \equiv k$ on $(s+k-1,s+k)$ $(1 \le k \le n)$.

By the foregoing formulas,

$$ {}_{s|n}(I\ddot{a})_x = \sum_{0\le k\le n-1} (k+1)\ {}_{s+k}E_x = {}_sE_x + \sum_{1\le k\le n-1} (k+1)\ {}_{s+k}E_x, \tag{35}$$

$$ {}_{s|n}(Ia)_x = \sum_{1\le k\le n} k\ {}_{s+k}E_x = \sum_{1\le k\le n-1} k\ {}_{s+k}E_x + n\ {}_{s+n}E_x. \tag{36}$$

Hence,

$$ {}_{s|n}(I\ddot{a})_x - {}_{s|n}(Ia)_x = {}_sE_x + \sum_{1\le k\le n-1} {}_{s+k}E_x - n\ {}_{s+n}E_x = {}_{s|n}\ddot{a}_x - n\ {}_{s+n}E_x. \tag{37}$$

and by (25) and (26),

$$ {}_{s|n}(Ia)_x^{(r)} \approx {}_{s|n}(Ia)_x + [{}_{s|n}\ddot{a}_x - n\ {}_{s+n}E_x].(r-1)/(2r), \tag{38}$$

$$ {}_{s|n}(I\ddot{a})_x^{(r)} \approx {}_{s|n}(I\ddot{a})_x - [{}_{s|n}\ddot{a}_x - n\ {}_{s+n}E_x].(r-1)/(2r). \tag{39}$$

By (29) and by a summation by parts (App.A),

$$D_x\, {}_{m|n}(I\ddot{a})_x = \Sigma_{0\le k\le n-1}\,(k+1)\, D_{x+m+k} = -\,\Sigma_{0\le k\le n-1}\,(k+1)\,\Delta N_{x+m+k}$$

$$= -[(k+1)N_{x+m+k}]_0^{\,n} + \Sigma_{0\le k\le n-1}\, N_{x+m+k+1}$$

$$= N_{x+m} - (n+1)N_{x+m+n} + \Sigma_{0\le k\le n-1}\, N_{x+m+k+1}$$

$$= N_{x+m} + N_{x+m+1} + \ldots + N_{x+m+n} - (n+1)N_{x+m+n}$$

$$= N_{x+m} + \ldots + N_{x+m+n-1} - n\, N_{x+m+n} = (\Sigma_{k\ge m} - \Sigma_{k\ge m+n})N_{x+k} - nN_{x+m+n}$$

$$= S_{x+m} - S_{x+m+n} - nN_{x+m+n}.$$

Hence,

$${}_{m|n}(I\ddot{a})_x = (S_{x+m} - S_{x+m+n} - nN_{x+m+n})/D_x. \qquad (40)$$

In the same way,

$${}_{m|n}(Ia)_x = (S_{x+m+1} - S_{x+m+n+1} - nN_{x+m+n+1})/D_x. \qquad (41)$$

The following are particular cases.

m=0: $${}_{n}(I\ddot{a})_x = (S_x - S_{x+n} - nN_{x+n})/D_x,$$

$${}_{n}(Ia)_x = (S_{x+1} - S_{x+n+1} - nN_{x+n+1})/D_x.$$

n=∞: $${}_{m}(I\ddot{a})_x = S_{x+m}\,/D_x,$$

$${}_{m}(Ia)_x = S_{x+m+1}\,/D_x.$$

m=0 and n=∞: $$(I\ddot{a})_x = S_x\,/D_x,$$

$$(Ia)_x = S_{x+1}\,/D_x.$$

b. $$(I_{\overline{n|}}a)_x^{\circ\circ} := a_x(c_\tau)^{\circ\circ},\ (I_{\overline{n|}}\ddot{a})_x^{\circ\circ} := \ddot{a}_x(c_\tau)^{\circ\circ},$$

$$(I_{\overline{n|}}a)_x^{(r)\circ\circ} := a_x^{(r)}(c_\tau)^{\circ\circ},\ (I_{\overline{n|}}\ddot{a})_x^{(r)\circ\circ} := \ddot{a}_x^{(r)}(c_\tau)^{\circ\circ},$$

where the capital-function c_τ is defined on [0,∞[as follows:

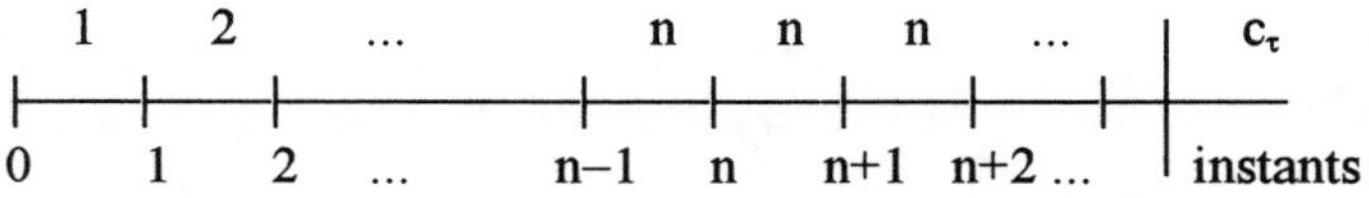

(42)

The capital-function of the annuities $_{n|}(Ia)_x^{\circ\circ}$ $[\ddot{\ },^{(r)}]$ is defined on $[0,\infty[$ as follows

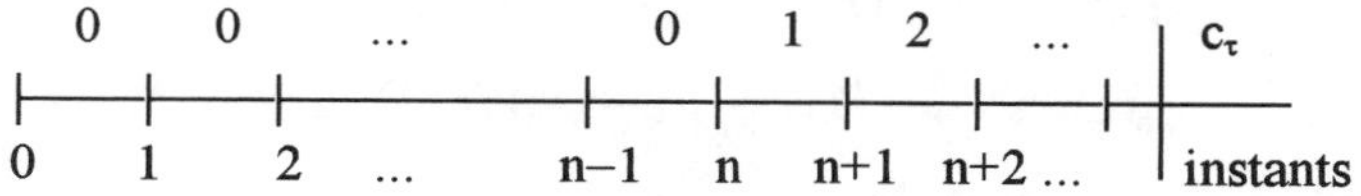

(43)

and the capital-function of the annuities $(Ia)_x^{\circ\circ}$ $[\ddot{\ },^{(r)}]$ is defined on $[0,\infty[$ as follows

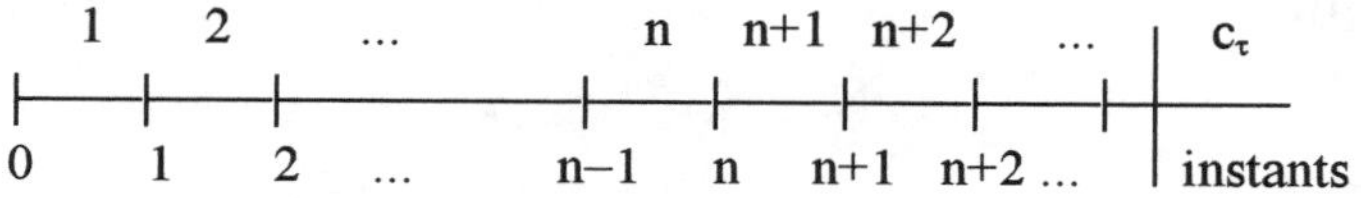

(44)

Hence,

$$(I_{\overline{n}|}\, a)_x^{\circ\circ} + {}_{n|}(Ia)_x^{\circ\circ} = (Ia)_x^{\circ\circ}\ [\ddot{\ },^{(r)}]. \tag{45}$$

Then

$$\begin{aligned}&(I_{\overline{n}|}\ddot{a})_x - (I_{\overline{n}|}\, a)_x\\ &= [(I\ddot{a})_x - (Ia)_x] - [{}_{n|}(I\ddot{a})_x - {}_{n|}(Ia)_x]\\ &= \ddot{a}_x - {}_{n|}\ddot{a}_x = {}_n\ddot{a}_x.\end{aligned} \tag{46}$$

and

$$(I_{\overline{n}|}\, a)_x^{(r)} \approx (I_{\overline{n}|}\, a)_x + {}_n\ddot{a}_x.(r-1)/(2r), \tag{47}$$

$$(I_{\overline{n}|}\ddot{a})_x^{(r)} \approx (I_{\overline{n}|}\ddot{a})_x - {}_n\ddot{a}_x.(r-1)/(2r). \tag{48}$$

By (45) and (40)

$$(I_{\overline{n}|}\ddot{a})_x = (I\ddot{a})_x - {}_{n|}(I\ddot{a})_x = (S_x - S_{x+n})/D_x \tag{49}$$

and by (41)

$$(I_{\overline{n}|}a)_x = (Ia)_x - {}_{n|}(Ia)_x = (S_{x+1} - S_{x+n+1})/D_x. \tag{50}$$

c. $\quad {}_n(Da)_x^{\circ\circ} := {}_{0|n}a_x(c_\tau)^{\circ\circ},\ {}_n(D\ddot{a})_x^{\circ\circ} := {}_{0|n}\ddot{a}_x(c_\tau)^{\circ\circ},$

$${}_n(Da)_x^{(r)\circ\circ} := {}_{0|n}a_x^{(r)}(c_\tau)^{\circ\circ},\ {}_n(D\ddot{a})_x^{(r)\circ\circ} := {}_{0|n}\ddot{a}_x^{(r)}(c_\tau)^{\circ\circ},$$

where c_τ is defined on $[0,n]$ as follows:

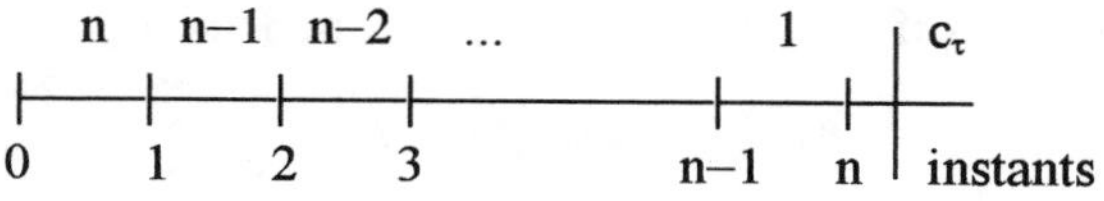

(51)

Then

$${}_n(D\ddot{a})_x = \textstyle\sum_{0\le k\le n-1} (n-k)\, {}_kE_x = n + \sum_{1\le k\le n-1} (n-k)\, {}_kE_x, \tag{52}$$

$${}_n(Da)_x = \textstyle\sum_{1\le k\le n} (n-k+1)\, {}_kE_x = \sum_{1\le k\le n-1} (n-k+1)\, {}_kE_x + {}_nE_x, \tag{53}$$

$${}_n(D\ddot{a})_x - {}_n(Da)_x = n - \textstyle\sum_{1\le k\le n-1} {}_kE_x - {}_nE_x = n - {}_na_x. \tag{54}$$

Then by (25) and (26),

$$ {}_n(Da)_x^{(r)} \approx {}_n(Da)_x + (n - {}_na_x).(r-1)/(2r), \tag{55}$$

$$ {}_n(D\ddot{a})_x^{(r)} \approx {}_n(D\ddot{a})_x - (n - {}_na_x).(r-1)/(2r). \tag{56}$$

By (52) and by a summation by parts,

$$D_x\ {}_n(D\ddot{a})_x = \Sigma_{0\le k\le n-1}\ (n-k)\ D_{x+k} = -\ \Sigma_{0\le k\le n-1}\ (n-k)\ \Delta N_{x+k}$$

$$= -[(n-k)N_{x+k}]_0^n - \Sigma_{0\le k\le n-1}\ N_{x+k+1} = nN_x - (\Sigma_{k\ge 0} - \Sigma_{k\ge n})N_{x+k+1}$$

$$= nN_x - S_{x+1} + S_{x+n+1}.$$

Hence,

$$ {}_n(D\ddot{a})_x = (nN_x - S_{x+1} + S_{x+n+1})/D_x \tag{57}$$

and in the same way,

$$ {}_n(Da)_x = (nN_{x+1} - S_{x+2} + S_{x+n+2})/D_x. \tag{58}$$

5.6. Annuities on status x|

Let x be a life. The corresponding artificial life x|, called a **status**, is defined by the equivalences

$$x|\uparrow t\ :\Leftrightarrow\ x\downarrow t,$$

$$x|\downarrow t\ :\Leftrightarrow\ x\uparrow t.$$

Hence, x| is dead on the interval [0,X[and alive on the interval]X,∞[.

In the foregoing definitions of the time-capitals ${}_sE_x{}^{oo}$, ${}_sE_x(c_\tau)^{oo}$ and annuities

$$a_x{}^{oo}\quad [{}_{s|n}\,,\,^{-}\,,\,^{\cdot\cdot}\,,\,^{(r)}\,,\,c_\tau],$$

we can replace x by x| everywhere.

Two examples:

$${}_sE_{x|}{}^{oo} := (1_{x|\uparrow s},\ s).$$

The insurer pays 1 at s if x| is alive at s, i.e. if x is dead at s.

$$a_{x|}{}^{oo} := \Sigma_{k\ge 1}\ (1_{x|\uparrow k},\ k).$$

The insurer pays 1 at k=1,2,... if x| is alive at k, i.e. if x is dead at k.

In iterative formulas, x cannot be replaced by x|. In all other foregoing formulas in which no commutation functions occur, x can be replaced everywhere by x|. We notice that ${}_sp_{x|} = {}_sq_x$.

The relation $1_{x|\uparrow\tau} + 1_{x\uparrow\tau} = 1$ implies that

$$_{s}E_{x|}{}^{oo} + {}_{s}E_{x}{}^{oo} = {}_{s}E^{oo} \quad [c_\tau], \tag{59}$$

where $_{s}E:=(1,s)$ and $_{s}E(c_\tau):=(c_s,s)$. It also implies that

$$a_{x|}{}^{oo} + a_{x}{}^{oo} = a^{oo} \quad [_{s|n}\, ,\ddot{}\, ,^{(r)}, \bar{}\, , c_\tau]. \tag{60}$$

Of course, these relations are valid at price level also. For instance, by (60) at price level, we have

$$_{n}a_{x|} = {}_{n}a - {}_{n}a_{x} = (1-v^n)/i - {}_{n}a_{x}.$$

The remark is general: **the price of any annuity on x| is the difference of the price of the corresponding annuity-certain and the price of the corresponding annuity on x**.

5.7. Variable interest rates

All present values can be calculated in the model with variable interest rates. Then the indication δ_τ is mentioned in brackets. It is enough to replace the discount factor v^τ by v_τ everywhere. Most formulas remain valid in that case. For instance, the formulas (28), (29) and (30) can be completed as

$$a_x^{(r)} \approx a_x + (\ddot{a}_x - a_x).(r-1)/(2r) \quad [_{s|n}, c_\tau, \delta_\tau, {}_{|}\,], \tag{61}$$

$$\ddot{a}_x^{(r)} \approx \ddot{a}_x - (\ddot{a}_x - a_x).(r-1)/(2r) \quad [_{s|n}, c_\tau, \delta_\tau, {}_{|}\,], \tag{62}$$

$$\overline{a}_x \approx (\ddot{a}_x + a_x)/2 \quad [_{s|n}, c_\tau, \delta_\tau, {}_{|}\,], \tag{63}$$

where the indication $_{|}$ means that $_x$ can be replaced everywhere by $_{x|}$.

The formulas (31), (32) and (33) may be completed as follows:

$$_{s|n}a_x^{(r)} \approx {}_{s|n}a_x + ({}_{s}E_x - {}_{s+n}E_x).(r-1)/(2r) \quad [\text{continuous } c_\tau, \delta_\tau, {}_{|}\,], \tag{64}$$

$$_{s|n}\ddot{a}_x^{(r)} \approx {}_{s|n}\ddot{a}_x - ({}_{s}E_x - {}_{s+n}E_x).(r-1)/(2r) \quad [\text{continuous } c_\tau, \delta_\tau, {}_{|}\,], \tag{65}$$

$$_{s|n}\overline{a}_x \approx {}_{s|n}a_x + ({}_{s}E_x - {}_{s+n}E_x)/2 = {}_{s|n}\ddot{a}_x - ({}_{s}E_x - {}_{s+n}E_x)/2$$

$$= ({}_{s|n}\ddot{a}_x + {}_{s|n}a_x)/2 \quad [\text{continuous } c_\tau, \delta_\tau, {}_{|}\,]. \tag{66}$$

We notice that v_τ is continuous in any case, even when δ_τ is not.

The iterative relations (24) become

$$_{s|n}a_x(c_\tau,\delta_\tau) = {}_{s}E_x(\delta_\tau)\, {}_{n}a_x(c_{s+\tau},\delta_{s+\tau}) \quad [\ddot{}\, , ^{(r)}, \bar{}\,]. \tag{67}$$

Chapter 6

LIFE INSURANCES (ONE LIFE)

6.1. Constant life insurances

The **s-year deferred, t-year temporory life insurance** on the life x is the time-capital

$$ {}_{s|t}\bar{A}_x^{\circ\circ} := (1_{s<X\le s+t},\ X). \qquad (1)$$

The **m-year deferred, n-year temporary life insurance payable in the middle of the year of death** is the time-capital

$$ {}_{m|n}\hat{A}_x^{\circ\circ} := (1_{m<X\le m+n},\ \hat{X}). \qquad (2)$$

Hence, the time-capital (2) is a ^-approximation of (1). Of course the theoretical time-capital ${}_{m|n}\hat{A}_x^{\circ\circ}$ is not practical because the insurer ignores at time k+1/2 that X will die or not between k+1/2 and k+1.

The time-capitals

$$ {}_{m|n}A_x^{\circ\circ} := (1_{m<X\le m+n},\ X') $$

(the insurer pays 1 at the end of the year of death of x) and

$$ {}_{m|n}\ddot{A}_x^{\circ\circ} := (1_{m<X\le m+n},\ {}'X) $$

(the insurer pays 1 at the beginning of the year of death of x) are only briefly considered in this monograph.

A generalization of time-capital (2) is

$$ {}_{s|n}\hat{A}_x^{\circ\circ} := \sum_{0\le k\le n-1} (1_{s+k<X\le s+k+1},\ s+k+1/2), \qquad (3)$$

because s is not necessarily an integer. The definitions (2) and (3) coincide if s is an integer m.

s or m may be equal to 0 and n or t may be infinite. Then the following notations are adopted: ${}_{s|} \equiv {}_{s|\infty}$, ${}_{n} \equiv {}_{0|n}$, ${}_{t} \equiv {}_{0|t}$.

Important particular cases are the (non deferred) **temporary life insurances**

$$\overline{A}^{\,1}_{x\,\overline{t}|}{}^{oo} \equiv {}_{t}\overline{A}_{x}{}^{oo}\,, \quad \hat{A}^{\,1}_{x\,n}{}^{oo} \equiv {}_{n}\hat{A}_{x}{}^{oo},$$

the **deferred whole life insurances**

$${}_{s|}\overline{A}_{x}{}^{oo} \equiv {}_{s|\infty}\overline{A}_{x}{}^{oo}\,, \quad {}_{s|}\hat{A}_{x}{}^{oo} \equiv {}_{s|\infty}\hat{A}_{x}{}^{oo},$$

and the (non deferred) **whole life insurances**

$$\overline{A}_{x}{}^{oo} \equiv {}_{0|\infty}\overline{A}_{x}{}^{oo}\,, \quad \hat{A}_{x}{}^{oo} \equiv {}_{0|\infty}\hat{A}_{x}{}^{oo},$$

The bizarre notations $\overline{A}^{\,1}_{x\,\overline{t}|}$, $\hat{A}^{\,1}_{x\,\overline{n}|}$ are justified in Ch.11.6.

Present values and prices

$${}_{s|t}\overline{A}_{x}{}^{o} = 1_{s<X\leq s+t}\, v^{X}, \tag{4}$$

$${}_{s|t}\overline{A}_{x} = E(1_{s<X\leq s+t}\, v^{X}) = \int_{(s,s+t)} v^{\tau} d\, {}_{\tau}q_{x} \tag{5}$$

because the function ${}_{\tau}q_x$ of τ is the distribution function of X. The price expressed by the last member of (5) results from the following consideration. In the interval $d\tau$ ($s<\tau<s+t$), the insurer pays the amount 1, with present value v^{τ} and he pays it with a probability equal to $d\, {}_{\tau}q_x$ (the probability that x deceases in $d\tau$). By (3),

$${}_{s|n}\hat{A}_{x}{}^{o} := \sum_{0\leq k\leq n-1} 1_{s+k<X\leq s+k+1}\, v^{s+k+1/2} \tag{6}$$

and then

$${}_{s|n}\hat{A}_{x} := \sum_{0\leq k\leq n-1} E(1_{s+k<X\leq s+k+1})\, v^{s+k+1/2}$$

$$= \sum_{0\leq k\leq n-1} P(s+k<X\leq s+k+1)\, v^{s+k+1/2} = \sum_{0\leq k\leq n-1} v^{s+k+1/2}\, \Delta\, {}_{s+k}q_x\,, \tag{7}$$

where Δ must of course be applied to the discrete variable k. We notice that

$$\Delta\, {}_{s+k}q_x = {}_{s+k+1}q_x - {}_{s+k}q_x = P(X\leq s+k+1) - P(X\leq s+k) = P(s+k<X\leq s+k). \tag{8}$$

Hence $\Delta_{s+k}q_x$ is the probability that x will decease in interval $]s+k,s+k+1]$.

The price expressed by the last member of (7) results from the following consideration. At $s+k+1/2$ ($0\leq k\leq n-1$), the insurer pays the amount 1, with present value $v^{s+k+1/2}$ and he pays it with a probability equal to $\Delta\, {}_{s+k}q_x$.

From (6) with s=m and similar expressions for ${}_{m|n}A_x{}^{\circ}$ and ${}_{m|n}\ddot{A}_x{}^{\circ}$ results that

$${}_{m|n}\ddot{A}_x{}^{\circ} = u^{1/2}\ {}_{m|n}\hat{A}_x{}^{\circ} = u\ {}_{m|n}A_x{}^{\circ},\quad {}_{m|n}\ddot{A}_x = u^{1/2}\ {}_{m|n}\hat{A}_x = u\ {}_{m|n}A_x\ .$$

These relations are obvious because the same amounts are paid in case of ${}_{m|n}\ddot{A}_x{}^{\circ\circ}$ (at the beginning of the year), ${}_{m|n}\hat{A}_x{}^{\circ\circ}$ (in the middle of the year) and ${}_{m|n}A_x{}^{\circ\circ}$ (at the end of the year).

Iterative relations

We first prove the following iterative relation for $d\ {}_{s+\tau}q_x$ (where d must be applied to the variable τ):

$$d\ {}_{s+\tau}q_x = {}_sp_x\ d\ {}_\tau q_{x+s}. \tag{9}$$

Indeed,

$$d\ {}_{s+\tau}q_x = -\ d\ {}_{s+\tau}p_x = -\ d(l_{x+s+\tau}/l_x)$$
$$= -(l_{x+s}/l_x)\ d(l_{x+s+\tau}/l_{x+s}) = -\ {}_sp_x\ d\ {}_\tau p_{x+s} = {}_sp_x\ d\ {}_\tau q_{x+s}.$$

(9) has the following interpretation

$$d\ {}_{s+\tau}q_x = P(x \text{ deceases in } s+d\tau) = P(x{\uparrow}s \text{ and } x \text{ deceases in } s+d\tau)$$
$$= P(x{\uparrow}s)P(x \text{ deceases in } s+d\tau\ /\ x{\uparrow}s) = {}_sp_x\ d\ {}_\tau q_{x+s}.$$

In the discrete case, (9) becomes

$$\Delta\ {}_{s+k}q_x = {}_sp_x\ \Delta\ {}_kq_{x+s}. \tag{10}$$

Then

$${}_{s|n}\bar{A}_x = {}_sE_x\ {}_n\bar{A}_{x+s}\ ,\quad {}_{s|n}\hat{A}_x = {}_sE_x\ {}_n\hat{A}_{x+s}\ , \tag{11}$$

by (5) and (7). For instance,

$${}_{s|t}\bar{A}_x = \int_{(s,s+t)} v^\tau d\ {}_\tau q_x = \int_{(0,t)} v^{s+\tau} d\ {}_{s+\tau}q_x = v^s\ {}_sp_x \int_{(0,t)} v^\tau d\ {}_\tau q_{x+s} = {}_sE_x\ {}_t\bar{A}_{x+s}.$$

The two relations (11) are direct by an interpretation based on an insurance in two steps.

By a ^-approximation,

$${}_n\bar{A}_x = E(1_{0\le X\le n}\ v^X) \approx E(1_{0\le X\le n}\ v^{\hat{X}}) = {}_n\hat{A}_x \tag{12}$$

and then

$${}_{s|n}\bar{A}_x = {}_sE_x\ {}_n\bar{A}_{x+n} \approx {}_sE_x\ {}_n\hat{A}_{x+n} = {}_{s|n}\hat{A}_x\ . \tag{13}$$

Commutation functions

We notice that

$$\Delta\ {}_{m+k}q_x = -\Delta\ {}_{m+k}p_x = {}_{m+k}p_x - {}_{m+k+1}p_x = (l_{x+m+k} - l_{x+m+k+1})/l_x = d_{x+m+k}/l_x.$$

By (7),

$$ {}_{m|n}\hat{A}_x = \sum_{0\le k\le n-1} v^{m+k+1/2}\,\Delta\,{}_{m+k}q_x = \sum_{0\le k\le n-1} v^{m+k+1/2}\, d_{x+m+k}/l_x $$
$$ = \sum_{0\le k\le n-1} (v^{x+m+k+1/2}\, d_{x+m+k})/(v^x\, l_x) = (1/D_x) \sum_{0\le k\le n-1} \hat{C}_{x+m+k} $$
$$ = (1/D_x)\left(\sum_{k\ge 0} - \sum_{k\ge n}\right) \hat{C}_{x+m+k} = (\hat{M}_{x+m} - \hat{M}_{x+m+n})/D_x. $$

Hence

$$ {}_{m|n}\hat{A}_x = (\hat{M}_{x+m} - \hat{M}_{x+m+n})/D_x\,. \tag{14} $$

In particular, for

m=0: $\quad {}_{n}\hat{A}_x = (\hat{M}_x - \hat{M}_{x+n})/D_x\,,$

n=∞: $\quad {}_{m|}\hat{A}_x = \hat{M}_{x+m}\,/D_x\,,$

m=0 and n=∞: $\quad \hat{A}_x = \hat{M}_x\,/D_x\,.$

6.2. General variable life insurances

Let c_τ be a capital-function defined on [s,s+t]. Then

$$ {}_{s|t}\overline{A}_x(c_\tau)^{\circ\circ} := (c_X\, 1_{s<X\le s+t}\,,\, X). \tag{15} $$

Let c_τ be a capital-function defined on [s,s+n]. Then

$$ {}_{s|n}\hat{A}_x(c_\tau)^{\circ\circ} := \sum_{0\le k\le n-1} (c_{s+k+1/2}\, 1_{s+k<X\le s+k+1},\ s+k+1/2). \tag{16} $$

If s is an integer m, then an equivalent definition is

$$ {}_{m|n}\hat{A}_x(c_\tau)^{\circ\circ} := (c_{\hat{X}}\, 1_{m<X\le m+n}\,,\, \hat{X}). \tag{17} $$

We say that c_τ is a **staircase capital-function** on [s,s+n] if c_τ is constant on each interval]s+k,s+k+1[(0≤k≤n−1). The value of c_τ at the points s+k (k=0, 1, 2, ..., n−1) is irrelevant. The classical capital-functions considered hereafter and already considered in Ch.5.5, are staircase capital-functions.

Present values and prices

$$ {}_{s|n}\hat{A}_x(c_\tau)^{\circ} = \sum_{0\le k\le n-1} c_{s+k+1/2}\, 1_{s+k<X\le s+k+1}\, v^{s+k+1/2} \tag{18} $$

and then

$$ {}_{s|n}\hat{A}_x(c_\tau) = \sum_{0\le k\le n-1} c_{s+k+1/2}\, E(1_{s+k<X\le s+k+1})\, v^{s+k+1/2} $$
$$ = \sum_{0\le k\le n-1} c_{s+k+1/2}\, P(s+k<X\le s+k+1)\, v^{s+k+1/2} $$
$$ = \sum_{0\le k\le n-1} c_{s+k+1/2}\, v^{s+k+1/2}\,\Delta\,{}_{s+k}q_x. \tag{19} $$

$$ {}_{s|t}\overline{A}_x(c_\tau) = E(1_{s<X\le s+t}\, c_X\, v^X) = \int_{(s,s+t)} c_\tau\, v^\tau d\,{}_\tau q_x. \tag{20} $$

Iterative relations

The generalization of (11) is

$$ {}_{s|n}\overline{A}_x(c_\tau) = {}_sE_x\, {}_n\overline{A}_{x+s}(c_{s+\tau}), \qquad {}_{s|n}\hat{A}_x(c_\tau) = {}_sE_x\, {}_n\hat{A}_{x+s}(c_{s+\tau}). \tag{21} $$

By a ^-approximation

$$ {}_s\overline{A}_x(c_\tau) = E(1_{s<X\le s+n}\, c_X\, v^X) \approx E(1_{s<X\le s+n}\, c_{\hat{X}}\, v^{\hat{X}}) = {}_n\hat{A}_x(c_\tau), \tag{22} $$

and then

$$ {}_{s|n}\overline{A}_x(c_\tau) = {}_sE_x\, {}_n\overline{A}_{x+s}(c_{s+\tau}) \approx {}_sE_x\, {}_n\hat{A}_{x+s}(c_{s+\tau}) = {}_{s|n}\hat{A}_x(c_\tau). \tag{23} $$

Commutation functions

By (19),

$$ {}_{m|n}\hat{A}_x(c_\tau) = \textstyle\sum_{0\le k\le n-1} c_{m+k+1/2}\, v^{m+k+1/2}\, \Delta\, {}_{m+k}q_x. $$

$$ = \textstyle\sum_{0\le k\le n-1} c_{m+k+1/2}\, v^{m+k+1/2}\, d_{x+m+k}/l_x $$

$$ = \textstyle\sum_{0\le k\le n-1} c_{m+k+1/2}\, (v^{x+m+k+1/2}\, d_{x+m+k})/(v^x\, l_x). $$

Hence,

$$ {}_{m|n}\hat{A}_x(c_\tau) = (1/D_x) \textstyle\sum_{0\le k\le n-1} c_{m+k+1/2}\, \hat{C}_{x+m+k}\,. \tag{24} $$

6.3. Classical variable life insurances

a.

$$ {}_{s|n}(I\hat{A})_x^{\circ\circ} := {}_{s|n}\hat{A}_x(c_\tau)^{\circ\circ}, $$

$$ {}_{s|n}(I\overline{A})_x^{\circ\circ} := {}_{s|n}\overline{A}_x(c_\tau)^{\circ\circ}, $$

where c_τ is the staircase capital-function defined on [s,s+n] as follows:

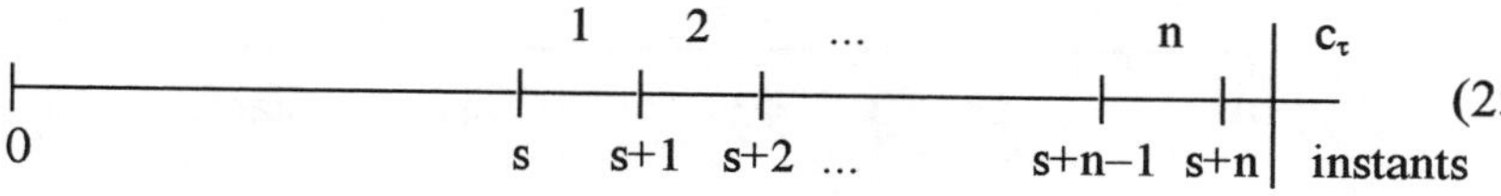

(25)

By (24)

$$ {}_{m|n}(I\hat{A})_x = (1/D_x) \textstyle\sum_{0\le k\le n-1} (k+1)\, \hat{C}_{x+m+k}. \tag{26} $$

By Ch.5.(35),

$$ {}_{m|n}(I\ddot{a})_x = \textstyle\sum_{0\le k\le n-1} (k+1)\, {}_{m+k}E_x = (1/D_x) \sum_{0\le k\le n-1} (k+1)\, D_{x+m+k}. \tag{27} $$

The commutation functions D, N and S are connected in the same way as $\hat{C}$, $\hat{M}$ and $\hat{R}$. Hence, the comparison of the last member of (26) with the last member of (27) and the relations Ch.5.(40) allows to conclude that

$$ {}_{m|n}(I\hat{A})_x = (\hat{R}_{x+m} - \hat{R}_{x+m+n} - n\hat{M}_{x+m+n})/D_x\,. \tag{28} $$

Particular cases:

m=0: $${}_n(I\hat{A})_x = (\hat{R}_x - \hat{R}_{x+n} - n\hat{M}_{x+n})/D_x ,$$

n=∞: $${}_{m|}(I\hat{A})_x = \hat{R}_{x+m} /D_x ,$$

m=0 and n=∞: $$(I\hat{A})_x = \hat{R}_x /D_x .$$

b. $$(I_{\overline{n}|}\hat{A})_x^{\circ\circ} := \hat{A}_x(c_\tau)^{\circ\circ},$$

$$(I_{\overline{n}|}\bar{A})_x^{\circ\circ} := \bar{A}_x(c_\tau)^{\circ\circ},$$

where the staircase capital-function c_τ is defined on $[0,\infty[$ as follows:

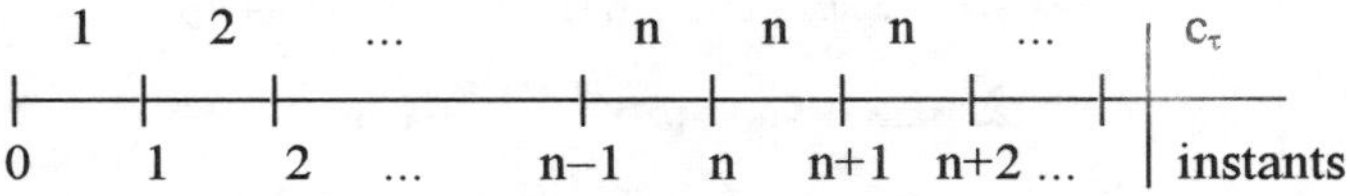

(29)

By comparison with Ch.5.(49)

$$(I_{\overline{n}|}\hat{A})_x = (\hat{R}_x - \hat{R}_{x+n})/D_x . \tag{30}$$

c. $${}_n(D\hat{A})_x^{\circ\circ} := {}_{0|n}\hat{A}_x(c_\tau)^{\circ\circ},$$

$${}_n(D\bar{A})_x^{\circ\circ} := {}_{0|n}\bar{A}_x(c_\tau)^{\circ\circ},$$

where c_τ is the staircase capital-function defined on $[0,n]$ as follows:

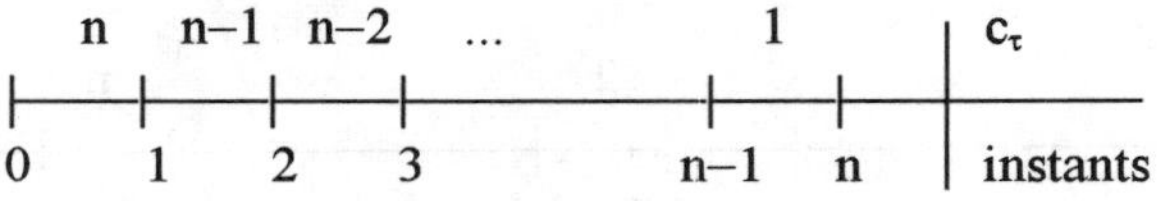

(31)

By comparison with Ch.5.(57),

$${}_n(D\hat{A})_x = (n\hat{M}_x - \hat{R}_{x+1} + \hat{R}_{x+n+1})/D_x . \tag{32}$$

6.4. Endowments

Endowment insurances are time-capitals

$$\alpha\ {}_t\bar{A}_x^{\circ\circ} + \beta\ {}_tE_x^{\circ\circ}\ (\alpha\geq 0,\ \beta>0). \tag{33}$$

The insurer pays α at the moment of death if this occurs before t, otherwise he pays β at t. Thes case $\alpha=0$ is a **pure endowment**. In case $\alpha=\beta=1$, a special notation (justified in Ch.11.6) is used:

$$ {}_t\bar{A}_x^{\circ\circ} + {}_tE_x^{\circ\circ} =: \bar{A}_{x\overline{t|}}^{\circ\circ}. \tag{34}$$

6.5. Insurance of a remaining debt at death

The insured is indebted to the deterministic time-capital

$$(\alpha_1,t_1) + (\alpha_2,t_2) + \ldots \tag{35}$$

at the origin 0, where $0<t_1<t_2<\ldots$ At the instant τ, the present value of the remaining debt equals

$$c_\tau = \sum_{t_k>\tau} \alpha_k \, (v')^{t_k-\tau},$$

where $v':=1/(1+i')$ and i' is the yearly interest used in the calculation of present values concerning (35). The insurer pays the amount c_τ at the moment τ of death of the insured. The price of this insurance is $\bar{A}_x(c_\tau)$.

Let us now assume that the interest rate i' equals the interest rate i used by the insurer. Then at the death of x, the insurer can also pay the remaining amounts α_k at t_k. The latter insurance is the time-capital

$$\sum_{k\geq 1} (\alpha_k \, 1x{\downarrow}t_k \, , \, t_k)$$

Its price is

$$\sum_{k\geq 1} \alpha_k \, v^{t_k} P(x{\downarrow}t_k) = \sum_{k\geq 1} \alpha_k \, v^{t_k} \, {}_{t_k}q_x. \tag{36}$$

Let us verify that the latter price equals $\bar{A}_x(c_\tau)$. In practice the number of terms of the time-capital (35) is finite, i.e. we assume that $\alpha_k=0$ if k is large enough (then no convergence problems do occur).

$$\bar{A}_x(c_\tau) = \int_{(0,\infty)} c_\tau \, v^\tau \, d \, {}_\tau q_x = \int_{(0,\infty)} \Big(\sum_{t_k>\tau} \alpha_k \, v^{t_k}\Big) d \, {}_\tau q_x$$

$$= \sum_{n\geq 0} \int_{(t_n,t_{n+1})} \Big(\sum_{k\geq n+1} \alpha_k \, v^{t_k}\Big) \, d \, {}_\tau q_x \qquad \text{(with } t_0:=0\text{)}$$

$$= \sum_{0\leq n\leq \infty} \Big(\sum_{k\geq n+1} \alpha_k \, v^{t_k}\Big) \, \Delta \, {}_{t_n}q_x \qquad \text{(with } \Delta \text{ applied to n)}$$

$$= -\sum_{0\leq n\leq \infty} {}_{t_{n+1}}q_x \, \Delta\Big(\sum_{k\geq n+1} \alpha_k \, v^{t_k}\Big) \quad \text{(summation by parts)}$$

$$= -\sum_{0\leq n\leq \infty} {}_{t_{n+1}}q_x \, (-\alpha_{n+1} \, v^{t_{n+1}}) = \sum_{1\leq n\leq \infty} {}_{t_n}q_x \, \alpha_n \, v^{t_n}.$$

In practice, the time-capital (35) is some classical annuity-certain in most cases.

6.6. Variable interest rates.

The notations are completed with the indication δ_τ in brackets, if present values are calculated in the financial model with instantaneous interest rate function δ_τ. Then the discount factor v^τ must be replaced by v_τ everywhere.

The iterative formulas (21) become

$$_{s|n}\bar{A}_x(c_\tau,\delta_\tau) = {}_sE_x(\delta_\tau)\ {}_n\bar{A}_{x+s}(c_{s+\tau},\delta_{s+\tau}), \tag{37}$$

$$_{s|n}\hat{A}_x(c_\tau,\delta_\tau) = {}_sE_x(\delta_\tau)\ {}_n\hat{A}_{x+s}(c_{s+\tau},\delta_{s+\tau}). \tag{38}$$

Chapter 7

RELATIONS BETWEEN LIFE ANNUITIES AND LIFE INSURANCES (ONE LIFE)

7.1. Constant annuities and insurances. Price level

By an integration by parts,

$$_{s|t}\bar{A}_x = \int_{(s,s+t)} v^\tau \, d\, _\tau q_x = -\int_{(s,s+t)} v^\tau \, d\, _\tau p_x$$

$$= -[v^\tau {}_\tau p_x]_s^{s+t} + \int_{(s,s+t)} {}_\tau p_x \, dv^\tau = v^s {}_s p_x - v^{s+t} {}_{s+t} p_x - \delta \int_{(s,s+t)} {}_\tau p_x \, v^\tau \, d\tau.$$

Hence,

$$\mathbf{_{s|t}\bar{A}_x = {}_sE_x - {}_{s+t}E_x - \delta \, {}_{s|t}\bar{a}_x} \,. \tag{1}$$

Particular cases:

s=0: $\mathbf{_t\bar{A}_x = 1 - {}_tE_x - \delta \, {}_t\bar{a}_x}$,

t=∞: $\mathbf{_{s|}\bar{A}_x = {}_sE_x - \delta \, {}_{s|}\bar{a}_x}$,

s=0 and t=∞: $\mathbf{\bar{A}_x = 1 - \delta \, \bar{a}_x}$.

By a summation by parts,

$$_{m|n}\hat{A}_x = \sum_{m\le k\le m+n-1} v^{k+1/2} \, \Delta \, _k q_x = -\sum_{m\le k\le m+n-1} v^{k+1/2} \, \Delta \, _k p_x$$

$$= -[v^{k+1/2} {}_k p_x]_m^{m+n} + \sum_{m\le k\le m+n-1} {}_{k+1}p_x \, \Delta v^{k+1/2}$$

$$= v^{m+1/2} {}_m p_x - v^{m+n+1/2} {}_{m+n} p_x - iv \sum_{m\le k\le m+n-1} {}_{k+1}p_x \, v^{k+1/2}$$

$$= v^{1/2}(v^m {}_m p_x - v^{m+n} {}_{m+n} p_x - iv \sum_{m\le k\le m+n-1} {}_{k+1}p_x \, v^k).$$

Hence,

$$\mathbf{u^{1/2} \, {}_{m|n}\hat{A}_x = {}_mE_x - {}_{m+n}E_x - i \, {}_{m|n}a_x} \,. \tag{2}$$

Particular cases:

m=0: $\mathbf{u^{1/2} \, {}_n\hat{A}_x = 1 - {}_nE_x - i \, {}_na_x}$,

n=∞: $\mathbf{u^{1/2} \, {}_{m|}\hat{A}_x = {}_mE_x - i \, {}_{m|}a_x}$,

m=0 and n=∞: $\mathbf{u^{1/2} \, \hat{A}_x = 1 - i \, a_x}$.

The last member of (2) can be transformed as follows:

$$ {}_mE_x - {}_{m+n}E_x - i\ {}_{m|n}a_x = {}_mE_x - {}_{m+n}E_x - i({}_{m|n}\ddot{a}_x - {}_mE_x + {}_{m+n}E_x). $$

$$ = u({}_mE_x - {}_{m+n}E_x) - i\ {}_{m|n}\ddot{a}_x = u({}_mE_x - {}_{m+n}E_x - iv\ {}_{m|n}\ddot{a}_x). \tag{3} $$

Hence by (2),

$$ \mathbf{v^{1/2}\ {}_{m|n}\hat{A}_x = {}_mE_x - {}_{m+n}E_x - iv\ {}_{m|n}\ddot{a}_x}\,. \tag{4} $$

Particular cases:

m=0: $\mathbf{v^{1/2}\ {}_n\hat{A}_x = 1 - {}_nE_x - iv\ {}_n\ddot{a}_x}$,

n=∞: $\mathbf{v^{1/2}\ {}_{m|}\hat{A}_x = {}_mE_x - iv\ {}_m\ddot{a}_x}$.

m=0 and n=∞: $\mathbf{v^{1/2}\ \hat{A}_x = 1 - iv\ \ddot{a}_x}$.

7.2. Constant annuities and insurances. Present value level

The foregoing relations are valid at the present value level. Let us first consider the annuity ${}_{s|t}\bar{a}_x^{\circ\circ}$. If $s<X\le s+t$, the insurer pays the annuity ${}_{s|X-s}\bar{a}^{\circ\circ}$. If $s+t<X$, he pays the annuity ${}_{s|t}a^{\circ\circ}$. Hence,

$$ {}_{s|t}\bar{a}_x^{\circ\circ} = 1_{s<X\le s+t}\ {}_{s|X-s}\bar{a}^{\circ\circ} + 1_{s+t<X}\ {}_{s|t}\bar{a}^{\circ\circ}. \tag{5} $$

Then

$$ {}_{s|t}\bar{a}_x^{\circ} = 1_{s<X\le s+t}\ {}_{s|X-s}\bar{a}^{\circ} + 1_{s+t<X}\ {}_{s|t}\bar{a}^{\circ} $$

$$ = 1_{s<X\le s+t}\,(v^s - v^X)/\delta + 1_{s+t<X}\,(v^s - v^{s+t})/\delta, $$

$$ \delta\ {}_{s|t}\bar{a}_x^{\circ} = 1_{s<X\le s+t}\,(v^s - v^X) + 1_{s+t<X}\,(v^s - v^{s+t}) $$

$$ = (1_{s<X\le s+t} + 1_{s+t<X})v^s - 1_{s+t<X}\,v^{s+t} - 1_{s<X\le s+t}\,v^X $$

$$ = 1_{s+t<X}\,v^s - 1_{s+t<X}\,v^{s+t} - 1_{s<X\le s+t}\,v^X = {}_sE_x^{\circ} - {}_{s+t}E_x^{\circ} - {}_{s|t}\bar{A}_x^{\circ}. $$

Hence,

$$ \mathbf{{}_{s|t}\bar{A}_x^{\circ} = {}_sE_x^{\circ} - {}_{s+t}E_x^{\circ} - \delta\ {}_{s|t}\bar{a}_x^{\circ}}. \tag{6} $$

We now consider the annuity ${}_{m|n}a_x^{\circ\circ}$. As above, it equals

$$ {}_{m|n}a_x^{\circ\circ} = 1_{m<X\le m+n}\ {}_{m|'X-m}a^{\circ\circ} + 1_{m+n<X}\ {}_{m|n}a^{\circ\circ} \tag{7} $$

and its present value equals

$$ {}_{m|n}a_x^{\circ} = 1_{m<X\le m+n}\ {}_{m|'X-m}a^{\circ} + 1_{m+n<X}\ {}_{m|n}a^{\circ} $$

$$ = 1_{m<X\le m+n}\,(v^m - v^{'X})/i + 1_{m+n<X}\,(v^m - v^{m+n})/i. $$

Then

$$ i\ {}_{m|n}a_x^{\circ} = (1_{m<X\le m+n} + 1_{m+n<X})v^m - 1_{m+n<X}\,v^{m+n} - 1_{m<X\le m+n}\,v^{'X} $$

$$ = 1_{m<X}\,v^m - 1_{m+n<X}\,v^{m+n} - u\ 1_{m<X\le m+n}\,v^{\hat{X}-1/2} $$

$$ = 1_{m<X}\,v^m - 1_{m+n<X}\,v^{m+n} - u^{1/2}\ 1_{m<X\le m+n}\,v^{\hat{X}} = {}_mE_x^{\circ} - {}_{m+n}E_x^{\circ} - u^{1/2}\ {}_{m|n}\hat{A}_x^{\circ}. $$

Hence,

$$\mathbf{u^{1/2}\ {}_{m|n}\hat{A}_x{}^{\circ} = {}_{m}E_x{}^{\circ} - {}_{m+n}E_x{}^{\circ} - i\ {}_{m|n}a_x{}^{\circ}}. \tag{8}$$

The relations (3) are valid at the present value level. Then by (8),

$$\mathbf{v^{1/2}\ {}_{m|n}\hat{A}_x{}^{\circ} = {}_{m}E_x{}^{\circ} - {}_{m+n}E_x{}^{\circ} - iv\ {}_{m|n}\ddot{a}_x{}^{\circ}}. \tag{9}$$

7.3. Variable annuities and insurances. General discrete case

In the constant case,

$${}_{m}E_x{}^{\circ} - {}_{m+n}E_x{}^{\circ} = {}_{m|n}\ddot{a}_x{}^{\circ} - {}_{m|n}a_x{}^{\circ}.$$

Hence, (6), (8) and (9) are particular cases of the following general Theorem. We observe that s is not necessarily an integer. The relations of the Theorem are valid, at the present value level, for any staircase capital-functions.

Theorem 1

$$\mathbf{\bar{A}_x = (\ddot{a}_x - a_x) - \delta\ \bar{a}_x \quad [{}^{\circ},\ {}_{s|n}\ ,\ staircase\ c_\tau]}, \tag{10}$$

$$\mathbf{u^{1/2}\ \hat{A}_x = (\ddot{a}_x - a_x) - i\ a_x \quad [{}^{\circ},\ {}_{s|n}\ ,\ staircase\ c_\tau]}, \tag{11}$$

$$\mathbf{v^{1/2}\ \hat{A}_x = (\ddot{a}_x - a_x) - iv\ \ddot{a}_x \quad [{}^{\circ},\ {}_{s|n}\ ,\ staircase\ c_\tau]}. \tag{12}$$

Proof

We start with the proof of (11).

$$u^{1/2}\ {}_{s|n}\hat{A}_x(c_\tau)^{\circ} = u^{1/2} \sum_{0\le k\le n-1} 1_{s+k<X\le s+k+1}\ c_{s+k+1/2}\ v^{s+k+1/2}$$

$$= \sum_{0\le k\le n-1} (1_{s+k<X} - 1_{s+k+1<X})\ c_{s+k+1/2}\ v^{s+k}$$

$$= \sum_{0\le k\le n-1} 1_{s+k<X}\ c_{s+k+}\ v^{s+k} - u \sum_{0\le k\le n-1} 1_{s+k+1<X}\ c_{s+k+1-}\ v^{s+k+1}$$

$$= {}_{s|n}\ddot{a}_x(c_\tau)^{\circ} - u\ {}_{s|n}a_x(c_\tau)^{\circ} \tag{13}$$

$$= [{}_{s|n}\ddot{a}_x(c_\tau)^{\circ} - {}_{s|n}a_x(c_\tau)^{\circ}] + i\ {}_{s|n}a_x(c_\tau)^{\circ}.$$

For the proof of (12), we multiply (11) by v and we notice that

$$v(\ddot{a}_x - a_x) - iv\ a_x = (v-1+1)(\ddot{a}_x - a_x) - iv\ a_x$$

$$= (1-iv)(\ddot{a}_x - a_x) - iv\ a_x = (\ddot{a}_x - a_x) - iv\ \ddot{a}_x. \tag{14}$$

For the proof of (10), we notice that

$${}_{s+k|1}\bar{A}_x{}^{\circ} = {}_{s+k}E_x{}^{\circ} - {}_{s+k+1}E_x{}^{\circ} - \delta\ {}_{s+k|1}\bar{a}_x{}^{\circ}$$

by (6).

We multiply that relation by $c_{s+k+1/2} = c_{s+k+} = c_{s+k+1-}$ and we sum over k=0, 1, ..., n−1:

$$\sum_{0\leq k\leq n-1} c_{s+k+1/2}\ {}_{s+k|1}\bar{A}_x{}^{\circ}$$

$$= \sum_{0\leq k\leq n-1} c_{s+k+}\ {}_{s+k}E_x{}^{\circ} - \sum_{0\leq k\leq n-1} c_{s+k+1-}\ \ {}_{s+k+1}E_x{}^{\circ} - \delta\sum_{0\leq k\leq n-1} c_{s+k+1/2}\ {}_{s+k|1}\bar{a}_x{}^{\circ},$$

$${}_{s|n}\bar{A}_x(c_\tau)^{\circ} = [{}_{s|n}\ddot{a}_x(c_\tau)^{\circ} - {}_{s|n}a_x(c_\tau)^{\circ}] - \delta\ {}_{s|n}\bar{a}_x(c_\tau)^{\circ} \quad \bullet \qquad (15)$$

7.4. Variable annuities and insurances. General continuous case

C_τ and c_τ are **associated capital-functions** on the interval [s,s+t] if

$$\int_{(s,\tau)} c_\sigma v^\sigma\, d\sigma = C_s v^s - C_\tau v^\tau \quad (s\leq\tau\leq s+t). \qquad (16)$$

Hence, C_τ and c_τ are associated iff $-C_\tau v^\tau$ is any indefinite integral of $c_\tau v^\tau$. The function C_τ is necessarily continuous. If c_τ is given, C_τ can be defined by the relation

$$C_\tau v^\tau = \text{const.} - \int_{(\alpha,\tau)} c_\sigma v^\sigma\, d\sigma, \qquad (17)$$

where const. and α are any constants. By differentiation of (16) with respect to τ,

$$c_\tau v^\tau = -(C_\tau v^\tau)'. \qquad (18)$$

Hence, if C_τ is given, then c_τ results from (18) under classical conditions (it is sufficient that C_τ is continuous, with piecewise continuous derivative). The relation (18) is equivalent to

$$c_\tau = \delta\, C_\tau - C_\tau'. \qquad (19)$$

Theorem 2

Let C_τ and c_τ be associated capital-functions on [s,s+t]. Then

$${}_{s|t}\bar{A}_x(C_\tau)^{\circ} = {}_sE_x(C_\tau)^{\circ} - {}_{s+t}E_x(C_\tau)^{\circ} - {}_{s|t}\bar{a}_x(c_\tau)^{\circ}. \qquad (20)$$

Proof

$${}_{s|t}\bar{a}_x(c_\tau)^{\circ} = 1_{s<X\leq s+t} \int_{(s,X)} c_\tau v^\tau\, d\tau + 1_{s+t<X} \int_{(s,s+t)} c_\tau v^\tau\, d\tau$$

$$= 1_{s<X\leq s+t}\,(C_s v^s - C_X v^X) + 1_{s+t<X}\,(C_s v^s - C_{s+t} v^{s+t})$$

$$= (1_{s<X\leq s+t} + 1_{s+t<X})\, C_s v^s - 1_{s+t<X}\, C_{s+t} v^{s+t} - 1_{s<X\leq s+t}\, C_X v^X$$

$$= 1_{s<X}\, C_s v^s - 1_{s+t<X}\, C_{s+t} v^{s+t} - 1_{s<X\leq s+t}\, C_X v^X$$

$$= {}_sE_x(C_\tau)^{\circ} - {}_{s+t}E_x(C_\tau)^{\circ} - {}_{s|t}\bar{A}_x(C_\tau)^{\circ} \quad \bullet$$

7.5. Classical variable annuities and insurances

We consider the classical variable life annuities and life insurances already introduced in Ch.5 and Ch.6 and moreover the following time-capitals.

$$ {}_{s|t}(\bar{I}\bar{A})_x^{oo} := {}_{s|t}\bar{A}_x(C_\tau)^{oo}, \tag{21}$$

where $C_\tau := \tau - s$ on $[s, s+t]$. Then $c_\tau = \delta(\tau - s) - 1$ by (19).

$$ (\bar{I}_{\overline{t|}}\,\bar{A})_x^{oo} := {}_{s|t}\bar{A}_x(C_\tau)^{oo}, \tag{22}$$

where $C_\tau := \tau$ on $[0,t]$ and $C_\tau := t$ on $[t, \infty[$. Then $c_\tau = \delta\tau - 1$ on $[0,t]$ and $c_\tau = \delta t$ on $[t, \infty[$.

$$ {}_s(\bar{D}\bar{A})_x^{oo} := {}_s\bar{A}_x(C_\tau)^{oo}, \tag{23}$$

where $C_\tau := (s - \tau)$ on $[0,s]$. Then $c_\tau = \delta(s - \tau) + 1$.

$$ {}_{s|t}(\bar{I}\bar{a})_x^{oo} := {}_{s|t}\bar{a}_x(c_\tau)^{oo}, \tag{24}$$

where $c_\tau := \tau - s$ on $[s, s+t]$.

$$ (\bar{I}_{\overline{t|}}\,\bar{a})_x^{oo} := {}_{s|t}\bar{a}_x(c_\tau)^{oo}, \tag{25}$$

where $c_\tau := \tau$ on $[0,t]$ and $c_\tau := t$ on $[t, \infty[$.

$$ {}_s(\bar{D}\bar{a})_x^{oo} := {}_s\bar{a}_x(c_\tau)^{oo}, \tag{26}$$

where $c_\tau := (s - \tau)$ on $[0,s]$.

The following relations are enunciated at price level, but they are valid at present value level. Indeed, they are based on Th.1, Th.2 and on the relations (37), (46) and (54) of Ch.5. Obviously, the latter relations are valid at present value level (with identical proofs).

a.

$$ {}_{s|n}(I\bar{A})_x = {}_{s|n}\ddot{a}_x - n\,{}_{s+n}E_x - \delta\,{}_{s|n}(I\bar{a})_x, $$

$$ u^{1/2}\,{}_{s|n}(IA)_x = {}_{s|n}\ddot{a}_x - n\,{}_{s+n}E_x - i\,{}_{s|n}(Ia)_x, $$

$$ v^{1/2}\,{}_{s|n}(IA)_x = {}_{s|n}\ddot{a}_x - n\,{}_{s+n}E_x - iv\,{}_{s|n}(I\ddot{a})_x, $$

$$ {}_{s|t}(\bar{I}\bar{A})_x = {}_{s|t}\bar{a}_x - t\,{}_{s+t}E_x - \delta\,{}_{s|t}(\bar{I}\bar{a})_x. $$

b.

$$ (I_{\overline{n|}}\,\bar{A})_x = {}_n\ddot{a}_x - \delta\,(I_{\overline{n|}}\,\bar{a})_x, $$

$$ u^{1/2}\,(I_{\overline{n|}}\,A)_x = {}_n\ddot{a}_x - i\,(I_{\overline{n|}}\,a)_x, $$

$$ v^{1/2}\,(I_{\overline{n|}}\,A)_x = {}_n\ddot{a}_x - iv\,(I_{\overline{n|}}\,\ddot{a})_x, $$

$$ (\bar{I}_{\overline{t|}}\,\bar{A})_x = {}_t\bar{a}_x - \delta\,(\bar{I}_{\overline{t|}}\,\bar{a})_x. $$

c.
$$_n(D\bar{A})_x = n - {}_n a_x - \delta\, {}_n(D\bar{a})_x,$$
$$u^{1/2}\, {}_n(DA)_x = n - {}_n a_x - i\, {}_n(Da)_x,$$
$$v^{1/2}\, {}_n(DA)_x = n - {}_n a_x - iv\, {}_n(D\ddot{a})_x,$$
$$_t(\bar{D}\bar{A})_x = t - {}_t\bar{a}_x - \delta\, {}_t(\bar{D}\bar{a})_x.$$

Of course, the time-capital $_{s|n}(I\bar{a})_x{}^{\circ\circ}$ (see last term of first relation of a) is $_{s|n}\bar{a}_x(c_\tau)^{\circ\circ}$, where c_τ is defined by Ch.5.(34). Similarly, the last term of the first relation of b. and of c. results from c_τ defined by Ch.5.(42) and by Ch.5.(51) resp.

Chapter 8

DECOMPOSITIONS OF TIME-CAPITALS (ONE LIFE)

8.1. Reserves of a time-capital

Let $Q^{\circ\circ}$ be a general time-capital on the life x. It is a linear combination of deferred capitals, life annuities, life insurances and perhaps other components. We assume that the life insurance components are payable at death (see 8.6).

We denote by ${}_{s|t}Q^{\circ\circ}$ the **restriction of $Q^{\circ\circ}$ to interval [s,s+t[** defined in the obvious way: all payments outside that interval are suppressed. The usual abbreviations are adopted: ${}_{0|t} \equiv {}_{t}$, ${}_{s|\infty} \equiv {}_{s|}$. For instance, if $Q^{\circ\circ}:=\overline{A}_x(c_\tau)^{\circ\circ}$, then ${}_{s|t}Q^{\circ\circ}={}_{s|t}\overline{A}_x(c_\tau)^{\circ\circ}$. If $Q^{\circ\circ}:=a_x(c_\tau)^{\circ\circ}$, then ${}_{s|}Q^{\circ\circ} = {}_{s'|}\ddot{a}_x(c_\tau)^{\circ\circ}$ (s>0).

We denote by ${}_{\bullet s|t}Q^{\circ\circ}$ the restricted time-capital ${}_{s|t}Q^{\circ\circ}$ with s as a new origin of time. We call ${}_{\bullet s|t}Q^{\circ\circ}$ a **restricted re-actualized time-capital**.

We denote by ${}_{\bullet s|t}Q_x{}^{\circ\circ}$ the time-capital ${}_{\bullet s|t}Q^{\circ\circ}$ evaluated under the assumption that x is alive at s and by ${}_{\bullet s|t}Q_{x|}{}^{\circ\circ}$ the time-capital ${}_{\bullet s|t}Q^{\circ\circ}$ evaluated under the assumption that x is dead at s. The time-capitals ${}_{\bullet s|t}Q_x{}^{\circ\circ}$ and ${}_{\bullet s|t}Q_{x|}{}^{\circ\circ}$ are **conditional restricted re-actualized time-capitals**. The life x is alive at 0.

Hence, $${}_{t}Q^{\circ\circ} \equiv {}_{0|t}Q^{\circ\circ} \equiv {}_{\bullet 0|t}Q^{\circ\circ} \equiv {}_{\bullet 0|t}Q_x{}^{\circ\circ},$$

but ${}_{\bullet 0|t}Q_{x|}{}^{\circ\circ}$ is meaningless.

The price ${}_{\bullet t|}Q_x$ is the (mathematical) **reserve of $Q^{\circ\circ}$ at t when x is alive at t** and ${}_{\bullet t|}Q_{x|}$ is the (mathematical) **reserve of $Q^{\circ\circ}$ at t when x is dead at t**. The **reserve of $Q^{\circ\circ}$ at t** is the reserve at t when x is alive, if nothing is specified. We say that $Q^{\circ\circ}$ **vanishes with x** if ${}_{\bullet t|}Q_{x|}=0$ for all t>0.

Examples

a. Let $Q^{\circ\circ}:=(1,s)$. Then

$${}_{\bullet t|}Q_x = {}_{\bullet t|}Q_{x|} = v^{s-t}\ (t\le s),\quad {}_{\bullet t|}Q_x = {}_{\bullet t|}Q_{x|} = 0\ \ (s<t).$$

$Q^{\circ\circ}$ does not depend on x and of course it does not vanish with x.

b. Let $Q^{\circ\circ}:={}_sE_x{}^{\circ\circ}$. Then

$${}_{\bullet t|}Q_x = {}_{s-t}E_{x+t}\ \ (0\le t<s),\quad {}_{\bullet s|}Q_x = 1,\quad {}_{\bullet t|}Q_x = 0\ \ (s<t),\quad {}_{\bullet t|}Q_{x|} = 0\ \ (0<t).$$

$Q^{\circ\circ}$ vanishes with x.

c. Let $Q^{\circ\circ}:={}_sE_{x|}{}^{\circ\circ}$. Then

$${}_{\bullet t|}Q_x = {}_{s-t}E_{x+t|}\ \ (0\le t<s),\quad {}_{\bullet s|}Q_x = 0,\quad {}_{\bullet t|}Q_x = 0\ \ (s<t),$$

$${}_{\bullet t|}Q_{x|} = v^{s-t}\ \ (0\le t<s),\quad {}_{\bullet s|}Q_{x|} = 1,\quad {}_{\bullet t|}Q_{x|} = 0\ \ (s<t).$$

$Q^{\circ\circ}$ does not vanish with x.

d. Let $Q^{\circ\circ}:={}_{m|n}\ddot{a}_x{}^{\circ\circ}$. Then

$${}_{\bullet k|}Q_x = {}_{m-k|n}\ddot{a}_{x+k}\ \ (0\le k\le m),\ {}_{\bullet k|}Q_x = {}_{m+n-k}\ddot{a}_{x+k}\ \ (m<k\le m+n),\ {}_{\bullet k|}Q_x = 0\ \ (m+n<k),$$

$${}_{\bullet t|}Q_x = {}_{m-t|n}\ddot{a}_{x+t}\ \ (0\le t\le m),\ {}_{\bullet t|}Q_x = {}_{t'-t|m+n-t'}\ddot{a}_{x+t}\ \ (m<t\le m+n),\ {}_{\bullet t|}Q_x = 0\ \ (m+n\le t),$$

$${}_{\bullet t|}Q_{x|} = 0\ \ (0<t).$$

$Q^{\circ\circ}$ vanishes with x.

e. Let $Q^{\circ\circ}:={}_{m|n}\ddot{a}_{x|}{}^{\circ\circ}$. Then

$${}_{\bullet k|}Q_x = {}_{m-k|n}\ddot{a}_{x+k|}\ \ (0\le k\le m),\ {}_{\bullet k|}Q_x = {}_{m+n-k}\ddot{a}_{x+k|}\ \ (m<k\le m+n),\ {}_{\bullet k|}Q_x = 0\ \ (m+n<k),$$

$${}_{\bullet t|}Q_x = {}_{m-t|n}\ddot{a}_{x+t|}\ \ (0\le t\le m),\ {}_{\bullet t|}Q_x = {}_{t'-t|m+n-t'}\ddot{a}_{x+k|}\ \ (m<t\le m+n),\ {}_{\bullet t|}Q_x = 0\ \ (m+n\le t),$$

$${}_{\bullet k|}Q_{x|} = {}_{m-k|n}\ddot{a}\ \ (0<k\le m),\ {}_{\bullet k|}Q_{x|} = {}_{m+n-k}\ddot{a}\ \ (m<k\le m+n),\ {}_{\bullet k|}Q_{x|} = 0\ \ (m+n<k),$$

$${}_{\bullet t|}Q_{x|} = {}_{m-t|n}\ddot{a}\ \ (0\le t\le m),\ {}_{\bullet t|}Q_{x|} = {}_{t'-t|m+n-t'}\ddot{a}\ \ (m<t\le m+n),\ {}_{\bullet t|}Q_{x|} = 0\ \ (m+n\le t).$$

$Q^{\circ\circ}$ does not vanish with x.

f. Let $Q^{\circ\circ}:={}_{m|n}\ddot{a}_x(c_\tau)^{\circ\circ}$. Then

$${}_{\bullet k|}Q_x = {}_{m-k|n}\ddot{a}_{x+k}(c_{k+\tau})\ \ (0\le k\le m),\quad {}_{\bullet k|}Q_x = {}_{m+n-k}\ddot{a}_{x+k}(c_{k+\tau})\ \ (m<k\le m+n),$$

$${}_{\bullet t|}Q_x = {}_{m-t|n}\ddot{a}_{x+t}(c_{t+\tau})\ \ (0\le t\le m),\quad {}_{\bullet t|}Q_x = {}_{t'-t|m+n-t'}\ddot{a}_{x+t}(c_{t+\tau})\ \ (m<t\le m+n),$$

$${}_{\bullet t|}Q_x = 0\ \ (m+n\le t),\quad {}_{\bullet t|}Q_{x|} = 0\ \ (0<t).$$

$Q^{\circ\circ}$ vanishes with x.

g. Let $Q^{\circ\circ} := (Ia)_x^{\circ\circ}$. Then

$${}_{\bullet k|}Q_x = k\,\ddot{a}_{x+k} + (I\ddot{a})_{x+k} \quad (k>0), \quad {}_{\bullet t|}Q_x = t'\,{}_{t'-t|}\ddot{a}_{x+t} + {}_{t'-t|}(I\ddot{a})_{x+t} \quad (t>0),$$

$${}_{\bullet t|}Q_{x|} = 0 \quad (0<t).$$

$Q^{\circ\circ}$ vanishes with x.

h. Let $Q^{\circ\circ} := {}_{m|n}\bar{A}_x^{\circ\circ}$. Then

$${}_{\bullet t|}Q_x = {}_{m-t|n}\bar{A}_{x+t} \quad (0\le t\le m), \quad {}_{\bullet t|}Q_x = {}_{m+n-t}\bar{A}_{x+t} \quad (m<t\le m+n), \quad {}_{\bullet t|}Q_x = 0 \quad (m+n<t),$$

$${}_{\bullet t|}Q_{x|} = 0 \quad (0<t).$$

$Q^{\circ\circ}$ vanishes with x.

i. Let $Q^{\circ\circ} := {}_{m|n}\bar{A}_x^{\circ\circ}(c_\tau)$. Then

$${}_{\bullet t|}Q_x = {}_{m-t|n}\bar{A}_{x+t}(c_{t+\tau}) \quad (0\le t\le m), \quad {}_{\bullet t|}Q_x = {}_{m+n-t}\bar{A}_{x+t}(c_{t+\tau}) \quad (m<t\le m+n),$$

$${}_{\bullet t|}Q_x = 0 \quad (m+n<t), \quad {}_{\bullet t|}Q_{x|} = 0 \quad (0<t).$$

$Q^{\circ\circ}$ vanishes with x.

j. Let $Q^{\circ\circ} := (I\bar{A})_x^{\circ\circ}$. Then

$${}_{\bullet t|}Q_x = t\,\bar{A}_{x+t} + (I\bar{A})_{x+t} \quad (0<t), \quad {}_{\bullet t|}Q_{x|} = 0 \quad (0<t).$$

$Q^{\circ\circ}$ vanishes with x.

8.2. The decomposition formula

Theorem 1

$$\mathbf{Q = {}_{0|t}Q_x + {}_tE_x\,{}_{\bullet t|}Q_x + {}_tE_{x|}\,{}_{\bullet t|}Q_{x|}}\,. \tag{1}$$

If $Q^{\circ\circ}$ vanishes with x,

$$\mathbf{Q = {}_{0|t}Q_x + {}_tE_x\,{}_{\bullet t|}Q_x}\,. \tag{2}$$

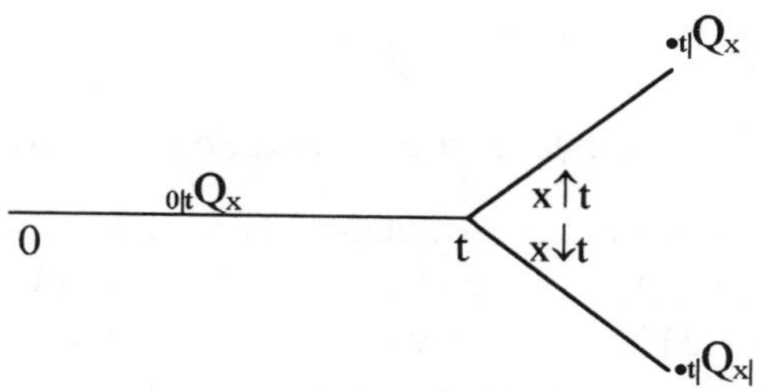

Figure 8.1. Decomposition of a time-capital

Proof

$$Q^\circ = {}_tQ^\circ + {}_{t|}Q^\circ = {}_tQ^\circ + v^t\, {}_{\bullet t|}Q^\circ$$

and then
$$E(Q^\circ) = E({}_tQ^\circ) + v^t\, E({}_{\bullet t|}Q^\circ)$$

$$= {}_tQ + v^t\, P(x{\uparrow}t)\, E({}_{\bullet t|}Q^\circ / x{\uparrow}t) + v^t\, P(x{\downarrow}t)\, E({}_{\bullet t|}Q^\circ / x{\downarrow}t)$$

$$= {}_tQ + v^t\, {}_tp_x\, {}_{\bullet t|}Q_x + v^t\, {}_tp_{x|}\, {}_{\bullet t|}Q_{x|} = {}_tQ + {}_tE_x\, {}_{\bullet t|}Q_x + {}_tE_{x|}\, {}_{\bullet t|}Q_{x|} \quad \bullet$$

Corollary

Let $0<s<t$. Then

$$\mathbf{{}_{\bullet s|}Q_x = {}_{\bullet s|t-s}Q_x + {}_{t-s}E_{x+s}\, {}_{\bullet t|}Q_x + {}_{t-s}E_{x+s|}\, {}_{\bullet t|}Q_{x|}}, \tag{3}$$

$$\mathbf{{}_{\bullet s|}Q_{x|} = {}_{\bullet s|t-s}Q_{x|} + v^{t-s}\, {}_{\bullet t|}Q_{x|}}, \tag{4}$$

If $Q^{\circ\circ}$ vanishes with x, then

$$\mathbf{{}_{\bullet s|}Q_x = {}_{\bullet s|t-s}Q_x + {}_{t-s}E_{x+s}\, {}_{\bullet t|}Q_x}\,. \tag{5}$$

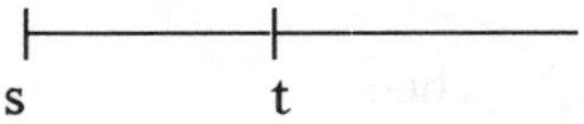

Proof
(3) and (5) result from the application of the Theorem at s to the time-capital ${}_{\bullet s|}Q_x^{\circ\circ}$. Relation (4) is obvious (it is valid already at the present value level) •

The formulas (1)–(5) are **decomposition formulas**. For instance, (1) results from a double decomposition: a decomposition of time interval $[0,\infty[$ in $[0,t[$ and $[t,\infty[$ and at point t, a decomposition of the truth in the two events $x{\uparrow}t$ and $x{\downarrow}t$. (1) and (2) are **decomposition formulas 0—t—** (this suggestive notation indicates that $[0,\infty[$ is partitioned in $[0,t[$ and $[t,\infty[$). (3), (4) and (5) are **decomposition formulas s—t—** (corresponding to the partition of $[s,\infty[$ in $[s,t[$ and $[t,\infty[$).

8.3. Evaluation of a reserve at a non-integer instant

It is convenient to reduce the evaluation of ${}_{\bullet k+\theta|}Q_x$ and ${}_{\bullet k+\theta|}Q_{x|}$ to the evaluations of ${}_{\bullet k|}Q_x$, ${}_{\bullet k+1|}Q_x$, ${}_{\bullet k|}Q_{x|}$ and ${}_{\bullet k+1|}Q_{x|}$. Then the following formulas (6) and (7), based on (3) and (4), may be useful. After a justification of the formulas, we will indicate how they are used in practice.

$$\mathbf{{}_{\bullet k+\theta|}Q_x \approx (1-\theta)\,{}_{\bullet k|}Q_x + \theta\,{}_{\bullet k+1|}Q_x - [(1-\theta)\,{}_{\bullet k|1}Q_x - {}_{\bullet k+\theta|1-\theta}Q_x]}, \tag{6}$$

$$\mathbf{{}_{\bullet k+\theta|}Q_{x|} \approx (1-\theta)\,{}_{\bullet k|}Q_{x|} + \theta\,{}_{\bullet k+1|}Q_{x|} - [(1-\theta)\,{}_{\bullet k|1}Q_{x|} - {}_{\bullet k+\theta|1-\theta}Q_{x|}]}. \tag{7}$$

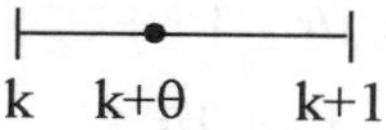

For the justification of (6), we use the decomposition formula k+θ—k+1— and we apply two linear interpolations:

$${}_{\bullet k+\theta|}Q_x = {}_{\bullet k+\theta|1-\theta}Q_x + {}_{1-\theta}E_{x+k+\theta}\,{}_{\bullet k+1|}Q_x + {}_{1-\theta}E_{x+k+\theta|}\,{}_{\bullet k+1|}Q_{x|}$$

$$\approx {}_{\bullet k+\theta|1-\theta}Q_x + [(1-\theta)\,{}_1E_{x+k} + \theta.1]\,{}_{\bullet k+1|}Q_x + [(1-\theta)\,{}_1E_{x+k|} + \theta.0]\,{}_{\bullet k+1|}Q_{x|}$$

$$= {}_{\bullet k+\theta|1-\theta}Q_x + \theta\,{}_{\bullet k+1|}Q_x + (1-\theta)[{}_1E_{x+k}\,{}_{\bullet k+1|}Q_x + {}_1E_{x+k|}\,{}_{\bullet k+1|}Q_{x|}]. \tag{8}$$

By the decomposition formula k—k+1—,

$${}_{\bullet k|}Q_x = {}_{\bullet k|1}Q_x + [{}_1E_{x+k}\,{}_{\bullet k+1|}Q_x + {}_1E_{x+k|}\,{}_{\bullet k+1|}Q_{x|}].$$

Hence, $[{}_1E_{x+k}\,{}_{\bullet k+1|}Q_x + {}_1E_{x+k|}\,{}_{\bullet k+1|}Q_{x|}] = {}_{\bullet k|}Q_x - {}_{\bullet k|1}Q_x$

and then ${}_{\bullet k+\theta|}Q_x = {}_{\bullet k+\theta|1-\theta}Q_x + \theta\,{}_{\bullet k+1|}Q_x + (1-\theta)({}_{\bullet k|}Q_x - {}_{\bullet k|1}Q_x)$.

by (8). We proceed in a similar way for the justification of (7),. By the decomposition formula k+θ—k+1— applied to x|,

$${}_{\bullet k+\theta|}Q_{x|} = {}_{\bullet k+\theta|1-\theta}Q_{x|} + v^{1-\theta}\,{}_{\bullet k+1|}Q_{x|}$$

$$\approx {}_{\bullet k+\theta|1-\theta}Q_{x|} + [(1-\theta)\,v + \theta.1]\,{}_{\bullet k+1|}Q_{x|}$$

$$= {}_{\bullet k+\theta|1-\theta}Q_{x|} + \theta\,{}_{\bullet k+1|}Q_{x|} + (1-\theta)\,[v\,{}_{\bullet k+1|}Q_{x|}]. \tag{9}$$

By the decomposition formula k—k+1— applied to x|

$${}_{\bullet k|}Q_x = {}_{\bullet k|1}Q_x + [v\,{}_{\bullet k+1|}Q_{x|}].$$

Hence, $[v\,{}_{\bullet k+1|}Q_{x|}] = {}_{\bullet k|}Q_x - {}_{\bullet k|1}Q_x$

and then ${}_{\bullet k+\theta|}Q_{x|} = {}_{\bullet k+\theta|1-\theta}Q_{x|} + \theta\,{}_{\bullet k+1|}Q_{x|} + (1-\theta)({}_{\bullet k|}Q_{x|} - {}_{\bullet k|1}Q_{x|})$.

by (9). This justifies (7).

In the last member of (6), the **main terms** $(1-\theta){}_{\bullet k|}Q_x+\theta{}_{\bullet k+1|}Q_x$ result from ${}_{\bullet k+\theta|}Q_x$ by a linear interpolation on $\theta\in[0,1]$. The terms in square brackets must be regarded as a **correction** due the discontinuity of ${}_{\bullet t|}Q_x$ at the points t=k and t=k+1.

Numerically, the correction is small as compared with the main terms and it may be evaluated rather loosely. For instance, let $Q^{\circ\circ} := \ddot{a}_x^{\circ\circ}$. then

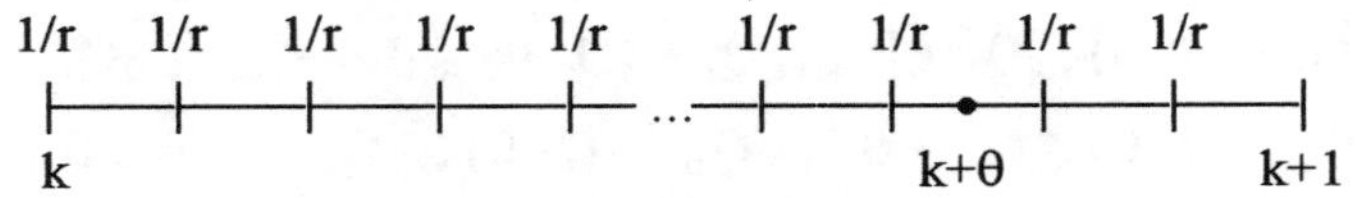

$${}_{\bullet k|1}Q_x \approx 1/r + 1/r + \ldots + 1/r = 1,$$

and
$${}_{\bullet k+\theta|1-\theta}Q_x \approx 1/r + 1/r + \ldots + 1/r = n/r,$$

where n is the number of amounts $1/r$ attached to the interval $[k+\theta, k+1[$ ($n=2$ in case of the figure). The general rule is that actualizations (i.e. evaluations of present values) and probabilizations are neglected in the evaluation of the correction.

In case of life insurances (supposed to be payable at death), ${}_{\bullet t|}Q_x$ and ${}_{\bullet s|t}Q_x$ are continuous functions of s and t and then the correction vanishes. Indeed, by a linear interpolation on $\theta \in [0,1]$,

$${}_{\bullet k+\theta|1-\theta}Q_x \approx (1-\theta)\ {}_{\bullet k|1}Q_x + \theta\ {}_{\bullet k|0}Q_x = (1-\theta)\ {}_{\bullet k|1}Q_x.$$

A similar discussion can be applied to formula (7).

8.4. Fouret's formula

Theorem 2

Let $Q^{\circ\circ}$ be a time-capital vanishing with x. Then

$$\mathbf{{}_{\bullet k+1|}Q_x = ({}_{\bullet k|}Q_x - {}_{\bullet k|1}Q_x)/{}_1E_{x+k}\quad (k=0,1,2,\ldots).} \tag{10}$$

Proof

By the decomposition formula k—k+1—,

$${}_{\bullet k|}Q_x = {}_{\bullet k|1}Q_x + {}_1E_{x+k}\ {}_{\bullet k+1|}Q_x \quad \bullet$$

By (10), ${}_{\bullet 1|}Q_x$, ${}_{\bullet 2|}Q_x$, ... can be calculated successively from ${}_{\bullet 0|}Q_x \equiv Q$ and ${}_{\bullet 0|1}Q_x$, ${}_{\bullet 1|1}Q_x$, ${}_{\bullet 2|1}Q_x$, ...

8.5. Thiele's formula

Theorem 3

Let $Q^{\circ\circ}$ be a time-capital vanishing with x. Then

$$\partial/\partial t\ {}_{\bullet t|}Q_x = {}_{\bullet t|}Q_x\,(\delta + \mu_{x+t}) - \lim_{\varepsilon\downarrow 0}\ {}_{\bullet t|\varepsilon}Q_x/\varepsilon. \tag{11}$$

if the derivative exists.

Proof

By the decomposition formula t—t+ε— (ε>0),

$$_{\bullet t|}Q_x = {}_{\bullet t|\varepsilon}Q_x + {}_{\varepsilon}E_{x+t}\ {}_{\bullet t+\varepsilon|}Q_x.$$

Then $$_{\bullet t+\varepsilon|}Q_x - {}_{\bullet t|}Q_x = -\,({}_{\varepsilon}E_{x+t} - {}_{0}E_{x+t})\ {}_{\bullet t+\varepsilon|}Q_x - {}_{\bullet t|\varepsilon}Q_x$$

because ${}_{0}E_{x+t}=1$. Hence,

$$[{}_{\bullet t+\varepsilon|}Q_x - {}_{\bullet t|}Q_x]/\varepsilon = -\,[({}_{\varepsilon}E_{x+t} - {}_{0}E_{x+t})/\varepsilon]\ {}_{\bullet t+\varepsilon|}Q_x - [{}_{\bullet t|\varepsilon}Q_x/\varepsilon].$$

As $\varepsilon\downarrow 0$, we obtain (11) by the very definition of a derivative. We observe that the limit of the first expression in square brackets of the last member is the derivative with respect to ε of

$${}_{\varepsilon}E_{x+t} = v^{\varepsilon}\ l_{x+t+\varepsilon}/l_{x+t}$$

at the point ε=0. It equals

$$-\delta\ v^{\varepsilon}\ l_{x+t+\varepsilon}/l_{x+t} + v^{\varepsilon}\ l'_{x+t+\varepsilon}/l_{x+t}$$

$$= -\delta\ v^{\varepsilon}\ l_{x+t+\varepsilon}/l_{x+t} + v^{\varepsilon}\ (l'_{x+t+\varepsilon}/l_{x+t+\varepsilon}).(l_{x+t+\varepsilon}/l_{x+t})$$

$$= -\delta\ v^{\varepsilon}\ l_{x+t+\varepsilon}/l_{x+t} - v^{\varepsilon}\ \mu_{x+t+\varepsilon}\ (l_{x+t+\varepsilon}/l_{x+t})$$

at the point ε=0, i.e.

$$-(\delta + \mu_{x+t}) \quad \bullet$$

As a first illustration of (11), let $Q^{\circ\circ} := \overline{A}_x(c_\tau)$. Then

$${}_{\bullet t|}Q_x = \overline{A}_{x+t}(c_{t+\tau}),$$

$${}_{\bullet t|\varepsilon}Q_x = {}_{\varepsilon}\overline{A}_{x+t}(c_{t+\tau}) = \int_{(0,\varepsilon)} c_{t+\tau}\ v^{\tau}\ d\ {}_{\tau}q_{x+t} = \int_{(0,\varepsilon)} c_{t+\tau}\ v^{\tau}\ {}_{\tau}p_{x+t}\ \mu_{x+t+\tau}\ d\tau$$

and $$\lim_{\varepsilon\downarrow 0}\ {}_{\bullet t|\varepsilon}Q_x/\varepsilon = c_{t+0}\ v^0\ {}_{0}p_{x+t}\ \mu_{x+t+0} = c_t\ \mu_{x+t}.$$

Hence $$\partial/\partial t\ \overline{A}_{x+t}(c_{t+\tau}) = \overline{A}_{x+t}(c_{t+\tau})\ (\delta + \mu_{x+t}) - c_t\ \mu_{x+t}.$$

For $c_\tau \equiv 1$, $$\partial/\partial t\ \overline{A}_{x+t} = \overline{A}_{x+t}\ (\delta + \mu_{x+t}) - \mu_{x+t}$$

and for t=0 $$\partial/\partial x\ \overline{A}_x = \overline{A}_x\ (\delta + \mu_x) - \mu_x.$$

As a second illustration of (11), let $Q^{\circ\circ} := \overline{a}_x(c_\tau)$. Then

$${}_{\bullet t|}Q_x = \overline{a}_{x+t}(c_{t+\tau}),$$

$${}_{\bullet t|\varepsilon}Q_x = {}_{\varepsilon}\overline{a}_{x+t}(c_{t+\tau}) = \int_{(0,\varepsilon)} c_{t+\tau}\ v^{\tau}\ {}_{\tau}p_{x+t}\, d\tau$$

and $$\lim_{\varepsilon\downarrow 0}\ {}_{\bullet t|\varepsilon}Q_x/\varepsilon = c_{t+0}\ v^0\ {}_{0}p_{x+t} = c_t.$$

Hence $$\partial/\partial t\ \overline{a}_{x+t}(c_{t+\tau}) = \overline{a}_{x+t}(c_{t+\tau})\ (\delta + \mu_{x+t}) - c_t.$$

For $c_\tau \equiv 1$, $$\partial/\partial t\ \overline{a}_{x+t} = \overline{a}_{x+t}\ (\delta + \mu_{x+t}) - 1$$

and for $t=0$ $$\partial/\partial x\ \overline{a}_x = \overline{a}_x\ (\delta + \mu_x) - 1.$$

8.6. Insurances payable in the middle of the year of death

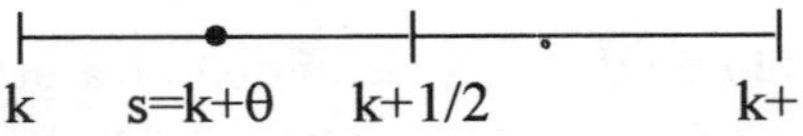

The theoretical life insurance $Q^{\circ\circ} := \hat{A}_x^{\circ\circ}$ has been excluded in this Chapter (see 8.1), because some reserves are not clearly defined for such time-capitals. For instance, let $s=k+\theta$, $0<\theta<1/2$, $x\downarrow s$, i.e. $X<k+\theta$. If $k<X<k+\theta$, the insurer must pay 1 at $k+1/2$. If $X<k$ he must pay nothing. Hence, ${}_{\bullet s|}Q_{x|}^{\circ\circ}$ is not defined univoquely from the information that x is dead at s. But ${}_{\bullet k|}Q_{x|}^{\circ\circ}$ is well defined.

The definitions of 8.1 and relations (1)–(5) and (10) are still valid for time-capitals $Q^{\circ\circ} := {}_{m|n}\hat{A}_x^{\circ\circ}(c_\tau)$ if only integer instants s and t are considered.

For instance, by the decomposition formula 0—1— applied to $\hat{A}_x^{\circ\circ}$,

$$\hat{A}_x = {}_{0|1}A_x + {}_1E_x\ \hat{A}_{x+1} = {}_1q_x\ v^{1/2} + {}_1p_x\ \hat{A}_{x+1}.$$

Chapter 9

LIFE INSURANCE CONTRACTS (ONE LIFE)

9.1. Life insurance contracts

A **life insurance contract** on the life x is a couple $(C^{\circ\circ}, P^{\circ\circ})$ of time-capitals $C^{\circ\circ}$ and $P^{\circ\circ}$ depending on x. The time-capital $C^{\circ\circ}$ is the **engagement of the insurer** to be paid to x and $P^{\circ\circ}$ is the **engagement of the insured** x to be paid to the insurance company (see Ch.4.2). For the moment no expense-loadings are taken into account, i.e. only **net contracts are considered**. In practice, $C^{\circ\circ}$ and $P^{\circ\circ}$ are **positive time-capitals**, i.e. time-capitals with positive amounts.

In a case of a **single premium contract** the insured pays a single premium P at the subscription time 0. Hence, then $P^{\circ\circ} := (P,0)$. We use the notation $(C^{\circ\circ}, P)$, instead of $(C^{\circ\circ}, (P,0))$ for single premium contracts. Very often

$$P^{\circ\circ} := p\ {}_n\ddot{a}_x^{\circ\circ} \quad \text{or} \quad P^{\circ\circ} := p\ {}_n\ddot{a}_x^{(r)\circ\circ}$$

and then p is a **temporary yearly life premium** or a **temporary yearly partitioned life premium**.

A **fair contract** is a contract satisfying the **equivalence principle** C=P. This principle allows to fix the premiums. All contracts are supposed to be fair.

Examples of contracts

a. $$((1,n),\ p\ {}_n\ddot{a}_x^{\circ\circ}).$$

The insurer pays 1 at n, whatever happens to x. By the equivalence principle

$$v^n = p\ {}_n\ddot{a}_x\,, \quad p = v^n / {}_n\ddot{a}_x$$

b. $({}_nE_x{}^{\circ\circ}, P)$.

The insurer pays 1 at n if x is alive at n. By the equivalence principle, $P = {}_nE_x$.

c. $({}_n\bar{A}_x{}^{\circ\circ}, p\ {}_m\ddot{a}_x{}^{(r)\circ\circ})$, where $m \le n$.

The insurer pays 1 at the moment of death of x if it occurs before n. The insured pays a temporary yearly partitioned premium p.

$$p = {}_n\bar{A}_x / {}_m\ddot{a}_x{}^{(r)}.$$

d. $(\alpha\ {}_n\bar{A}_x{}^{\circ\circ} + \beta\ {}_nE_x{}^{\circ\circ}, p\ {}_n\ddot{a}_x{}^{\circ\circ})$.

$$p = (\alpha\ {}_n\bar{A}_x + \beta\ {}_nE_x) / {}_n\ddot{a}_x.$$

e. $({}_{n|}a_x{}^{\circ\circ}, p\ {}_m\ddot{a}_x{}^{\circ\circ})$, where $m \le n+1$.

$$p = {}_{n|}a_x / {}_m\ddot{a}_x.$$

f. $({}_nE_x{}^{\circ\circ} + P\ {}_n\bar{A}_x{}^{\circ\circ}, P)$.

The insurer pays 1 if x is alive at n. If x dies before n, he returns the single premium P at the moment of death.

$$P = {}_nE_x / (1 - {}_n\bar{A}_x).$$

g. $({}_nE_x{}^{\circ\circ} + p\ {}_n(I\bar{A})_x{}^{\circ\circ}, p\ {}_n\ddot{a}_x{}^{\circ\circ})$.

The insurer pays 1 if x is alive at n. If x deceases before n, he returns the yearly premiums already received at the moment of death.

$$p = {}_nE_x / ({}_n\ddot{a}_x - {}_n(I\bar{A})_x).$$

9.2. Reserves of a contract

We consider a contract $(C^{\circ\circ}, P^{\circ\circ})$ on x and we define the **reserve time-capital** $V^{\circ\circ} := C^{\circ\circ} - P^{\circ\circ}$. We notice that $V=0$, because the contract is supposed to be fair: $C=P$.

${}_{\bullet t|}V_x$ is the (mathematical) **reserve of the contract at t when x is alive at t** and ${}_{\bullet t|}V_{x|}$ is the (mathematical) **reserve of the contract at t when x is dead at t**. The **reserve of the contract at t** is the reserve at t when x is alive, if nothing is specified. We say that **the contract vanishes with x** if both $C^{\circ\circ}$ and $P^{\circ\circ}$ vanish with x (see Ch.8.1).

The foregoing contracts b, c, d, e, f and g vanish with x. The contracts a does not.

The following Theorem holds for all values of $t \geq 0$ if the life insurance components of $C^{\circ\circ}$ are payable at death. It is valid for components $_{m|n}\hat{A}_x(c_\tau)^{\circ\circ}$ if t is an integer (see Ch.8.6).

Theorem 1

Let $(C^{\circ\circ}, P^{\circ\circ})$ be a contract on the life x.

a. (Prospective expression of reserves)

$$_{\bullet t|}V_x = {}_{\bullet t|}C_x - {}_{\bullet t|}P_x \quad (t \geq 0), \tag{1}$$

$$_{\bullet t|}V_{x|} = {}_{\bullet t|}C_{x|} - {}_{\bullet t|}P_{x|} \quad (t > 0). \tag{2}$$

b. (Retrospective expression of reserve)

If the contract vanishes with x,

$$_{\bullet t|}V_x = ({}_{\bullet 0|t}P_x - {}_{\bullet 0|t}C_x)/{}_tE_x\,. \tag{3}$$

c. (Recurrent expression of reserve or Fouret's formula)

If the contract vanishes with x,

$$_{\bullet k+1|}V_x = ({}_{\bullet k|}V_x + {}_{\bullet k|1}P_x - {}_{\bullet k|1}C_x)/{}_1E_{x+k} \quad (k=0,1,2,\ldots), \tag{4}$$

where $_{\bullet 0|}V_x = V = 0$.

d. (Mixed expression of reserve)

If the contract vanishes with x,

$$_{\bullet t|}V_x = ({}_{\bullet 0|t}P_x \; {}_{\bullet t|}C_x - {}_{\bullet 0|t}C_x \; {}_{\bullet t|}P_x)/P. \tag{5}$$

Proof

a. results from the definition of $V^{\circ\circ}$. Formula (3) results from the decomposition formula 0—t—

$$0 = V = {}_{\bullet 0|t}V_x + {}_tE_x \; {}_{\bullet t|}V_x$$

and from the definition of $V^{\circ\circ}$. Formula (4) results from Ch.8.4.Th.2. For the proof of (5), we multiply (1) by $_{\bullet 0|t}P_x$, (3) by $_tE_x \; {}_{\bullet t|}P_x$, we sum up and we use the relation $P := {}_{\bullet 0|t}P_x + {}_tE_x \; {}_{\bullet t|}P_x$ •

9.3. Practical constraints on contracts

The reserve ${}_{\bullet t|}V_x$ at t is the difference between the expected value $E({}_{\bullet t|}C^\circ)$ of the future engagements of the insurer and the expected value $E({}_{\bullet t|}P^\circ)$ of the engagements of the insured. Hence ${}_{\bullet t|}V_x$ is the amount due at t by the insurer to the insured for all future engagements and $-{}_{\bullet t|}V_x$ is the amount due at t by the insured to the insurer for all future engagements. The initial fairness of the contract disappears if one subscriber interrupts his engagements. Let us assume that ${}_{\bullet t|}V_x<0$ at some fixed instant t and that x stops the payment of premiums at t. Then, by foregoing discussion, the insurance company is cheated because it will never receive the strictly positive amount $-{}_{\bullet t|}V_x$. Hence, **contracts with strictly negative reserves at some instant t**, when x is alive or dead at t, **are never considered in practice**.

By this rule, the following theoretical contracts $(C^{\circ\circ},P^{\circ\circ})$ are excluded in practice:

a. Contracts such that the engagement $P^{\circ\circ}$ of the insured is spread over a strictly larger interval [0,m] than the engagement, say on [0,n], of the insurer. For instance, the contract $({}_{10}\bar{A}_x^{\circ\circ},\ p\ {}_{20}\ddot{a}_x)$ is not considered, because

$$ {}_{\bullet 15|}V_x = -p\ {}_5\ddot{a}_{x+15} < 0. $$

b. Insurances with non-deferred engagement of the insurance company, payable by annuities-immediate. For instance, let us consider the theoretical contract $(\bar{A}_x^{\circ\circ},\ p\ a_x^{\circ\circ})$ vanishing with x. Then by (3), if $\theta\in]0,1]$,

$$ {}_{\bullet\theta|}V_x = ({}_{\bullet 0|\theta}P_x - {}_{\bullet 0|\theta}C_x)/{}_\theta E_x = -{}_\theta\bar{A}_x/{}_\theta E_x < 0. $$

In this theoretical contract, the insurer has no engagement on [0,1[, but he is nevertheless covered by a life insurance on that interval.

The reserves of single premium contracts $(C^{\circ\circ}, P)$ are always positive. Indeed, then

$$ {}_{\bullet t|}V_x = {}_{\bullet t|}C_x - {}_{\bullet t|}P_x = {}_{\bullet t|}C_x \ge 0 \quad (t>0), $$

$$ {}_{\bullet t|}V_{x|} = {}_{\bullet t|}C_{x|} - {}_{\bullet t|}P_{x|} = {}_{\bullet t|}C_{x|} \ge 0 \quad (t>0). $$

The reserves of contract $(C^{\circ\circ},\ p\ {}_n\ddot{a}_x)$ are positive if n is small enough. Indeed, in the extreme case n=1, the contract becomes a single premium contract.

9.4. Contracts with partitioned premiums

By an approximation explained hereafter, contract

$$(C^{\circ\circ}, p^{(r)}\ {}_{m}\ddot{a}_{x}^{(r)\circ\circ}) \tag{6}$$

is reduced to contract

$$(C^{\circ\circ}, p\ {}_{m}\ddot{a}_{x}^{\circ\circ}) \tag{7}$$

with yearly non-partitioned premiums and with the same engagement $C^{\circ\circ}$ of the insurer. By the equivalence principle

$$p^{(r)}\ {}_{m}\ddot{a}_{x}^{(r)} = C = p\ {}_{m}\ddot{a}_{x}\,,$$

$$p^{(r)}/p = {}_{m}\ddot{a}_{x}/{}_{m}\ddot{a}_{x}^{(r)}. \tag{8}$$

The last member of (8) can be evaluated by the formulas of Ch.5. In practice, it is approximated by a number not depending on x or m. For instance, the following approximations have been used in Belgium,

$$p^{(2)} \approx 1.02\ p,\quad p^{(4)} \approx 1.03\ p,\quad p^{(12)} \approx 1.04\ p^{(12)}.$$

At integer instants k, the reserves of contract (6) are approximated by those of contract (7) in practice:

$$_{\bullet k|}V_{x}^{(r)} \approx {}_{\bullet k|}V_{x}\,,\quad {}_{\bullet k|}V_{x|}^{(r)} \approx {}_{\bullet k|}V_{x|}\,.$$

Then the general approximations of Ch.8.3 are used at non-integer instants $k+\theta$.

9.5. Risk and savings premiums

We consider contract $(C^{\circ\circ},P^{\circ\circ})$ where $C^{\circ\circ}$ is any time-capital vanishing with x for the moment and

$$P^{\circ\circ} := \Sigma_{k\geq 0}\ \pi_{k}\ {}_{k}E_{x}^{\circ\circ}.$$

Hence, the insurer pays π_k at k if he is alive at that moment.

We assume that x is alive at time k. The insurer owns the amount $_{\bullet k|}V_x$ at k and he receives the premium π_k at k. He decomposes π_k in two parts π_k^s and π_k^r, where the **savings premium** π_k^s is defined by the relation

$$({}_{\bullet k|}V_{x} + \pi_{k}^{s})u = {}_{\bullet k+1|}V_{x}. \tag{9}$$

Hence, the present value at k+1 of the reserve $_{\bullet k|}V_x$ at k completed by π_k^s equals the reserve $_{\bullet k+1|}V_x$. By (9),

$$\pi_{k}^{s} = v\ {}_{\bullet k+1|}V_{x} - {}_{\bullet k|}V_{x}. \tag{10}$$

By the decomposition formula k—k+1—,

$$ {}_{\bullet k|}V_x = {}_{\bullet k|1}V_x + {}_1E_{x+k}\ {}_{\bullet k+1|}V_x = {}_{\bullet k|1}C_x - {}_{\bullet k|1}P_x + {}_1E_{x+k}\ {}_{\bullet k+1|}V_x. $$

Hence,

$$ {}_{\bullet k|}V_x + \pi_k = {}_{\bullet k|1}C_x + {}_1E_{x+k}\ {}_{\bullet k+1|}V_x\,. \tag{11} $$

The interpretation of (11) is the following: The reserve ${}_{\bullet k|}V_x$ and the premium π_k at k must allow to cover the engagement ${}_{\bullet k|1}C_x$ of the insurer on [k,k+1[and to constitute the reserve ${}_{\bullet k+1|}V_x$ at k+1 if x is alive at that moment.

By (10) and (11)

$$ (v\ {}_{\bullet k+1|}V_x - \pi_k^s) + \pi_k = {}_{\bullet k|1}C_x + {}_1E_{x+k}\ {}_{\bullet k+1|}V_x\,, $$

$$ v\ {}_{\bullet k+1|}V_x + \pi_k^r = {}_{\bullet k|1}C_x + v\ {}_1p_{x+k}\ {}_{\bullet k+1|}V_x\,, $$

$$ \pi_k^r = {}_{\bullet k|1}C_x - v\ {}_1q_{x+k}\ {}_{\bullet k+1|}V_x. \tag{12} $$

Let us assume now that C^{oo} is defined as follows: the insurer pays $c_{k+1/2}$ at k+1/2 if x dies between k and k+1 (of course, in practice the capital is paid at the moment of death).

$$ {}_{\bullet k|1}C_x = c_{k+1/2}\ {}_1\hat{A}_{x+k} = c_{k+1/2}\ v^{1/2}\ {}_1q_{x+k} \tag{13} $$

and (12) becomes

$$ \pi_k^r = c_{k+1/2}\ {}_1\hat{A}_{x+k} - v^{1/2}\ v^{1/2}\,{}_1q_{x+k}\ {}_{\bullet k+1|}V_x = c_{k+1/2}\ {}_1\hat{A}_{x+k} - v^{1/2}\ {}_1\hat{A}_{x+k}\ {}_{\bullet k+1|}V_x. $$

Hence

$$ \pi_k^r = (c_{k+1/2} - v^{1/2}\ {}_{\bullet k+1|}V_x)\ {}_1\hat{A}_{x+k}. \tag{14} $$

π_k^r is the **risk premium** of a one-year term insurance allowing to cover the **amount at risk** $c_{k+1/2}-v^{1/2}\ {}_{\bullet k+1|}V_x$. Let us assume that the first insurer buys this insurance from a reinsurer (this may happen in practice). Let us consider the following possibilities a. and b. In any case, the reserve ${}_{\bullet k|}V_x$ and the savings premium π_k^s at k furnish the reserve ${}_{\bullet k+1|}V_x$ at k+1.

a. x is alive at k+1.

Then the first insurer looses the risk premium π_k^r, but he still owns the reserve ${}_{\bullet k+1|}V_x$ needed at k+1.

b. x dies during year [k,k+1].

Then the first insurer recovers the amount $c_{k+1/2}-v^{1/2}\ {}_{\bullet k+1|}V_x$ from the reinsurer at k+1/2. The reserve ${}_{\bullet k+1|}V_x$ at k+1 equals $v^{1/2}\,{}_{\bullet k+1|}V_x$ at k+1/2. Hence, at k+1/2 the first insurer owns the amount

$$(c_{k+1/2} - v^{1/2}\ {}_{\bullet k+1|}V_x) + v^{1/2}\ {}_{\bullet k+1|}V_x = c_{k+1/2}$$

necessary to pay the inheritors of the insured.

In this discussion it is, of course, implicitly assumed that the risk and savings premiums are positive.

9.6. Illustration: general endowment insurance

We consider contract

$$(\alpha\ {}_n\overline{A}_x^{\circ\circ} + \beta\ {}_nE_x^{\circ\circ},\ \overline{p}\ {}_n\ddot{a}_x^{\circ\circ}). \tag{15}$$

It vanishes with x. For the calculation of reserves at integer instants k, it is replaced by the theoretical contract

$$(\alpha\ {}_n\hat{A}_x^{\circ\circ} + \beta\ {}_nE_x^{\circ\circ},\ p\ {}_n\ddot{a}_x^{\circ\circ}) \tag{16}$$

with which we pursue.

Premium

By the equivalence principle,

$$p = (\alpha\ {}_n\hat{A}_x + \beta\ {}_nE_x)/{}_n\ddot{a}_x, \tag{17}$$

Prospective reserve

$${}_{\bullet k|}V_x = \alpha\ {}_{n-k}\hat{A}_{x+k} + \beta\ {}_{n-k}E_{x+k} - p\ {}_{n-k}\ddot{a}_{x+k}\quad (k=0,1,2,\ldots,n). \tag{18}$$

In particular, $\quad {}_{\bullet n|}V_x = \beta.$

Of course $\quad {}_{\bullet t|}V_x = 0\quad (t>n).$

Retrospective reserve

$${}_{\bullet k|}V_x = (p\ {}_k\ddot{a}_x - \alpha\ {}_k\hat{A}_x)/{}_kE_x\quad (k=0,1,2,\ldots,n). \tag{19}$$

Recurrent reserve

$${}_{\bullet k+1|}V_x = ({}_{\bullet k|}V_x + p - \alpha\ v^{1/2}\ q_{x+k})/{}_1E_{x=k}\quad (k=0,1,2,\ldots,n-1), \tag{20}$$

because $\quad {}_{\bullet k|1}P_x = p,\ \ {}_{\bullet k|1}C_x = \alpha\ {}_1\hat{A}_{x+k} = \alpha\ v^{1/2}\ q_{x+k}.$

Mixed reserve

The mixed expression of the reserve is not interesting in practice. It is used hereafter in theoretical considerations. We assume that $k \leq n$.

$P = p\ {}_n\ddot{a}_x$ and then by (5),

$${}_n\ddot{a}_x\ {}_{\bullet k|}V_x = B\ {}_k\ddot{a}_x - C\ {}_{n-k}\ddot{a}_{x+k}\ ,$$

where $\quad B := \alpha\ {}_{n-k}\hat{A}_{x+k} + \beta\ {}_{n-k}E_{x+k}$

and $$C := \alpha\ {}_{k}\hat{A}_{x}\,.$$

By Ch.7.(4), $$B = \alpha\, u^{1/2}\,(1 - {}_{n-k}E_{x+k} - iv\ {}_{n-k}\ddot{a}_{x+k}) + \beta\ {}_{n-k}E_{x+k}$$
$$= \alpha\, u^{1/2}\,(1 - iv\ {}_{n-k}\ddot{a}_{x+k}) + (\beta - \alpha\, u^{1/2})\ {}_{n-k}E_{x+k}\,,$$
$$C = \alpha\, u^{1/2}\,(1 - {}_{k}E_{x} - iv\ {}_{k}\ddot{a}_{x})$$

and then $${}_{n}\ddot{a}_{x}\ {}_{\bullet k|}V_{x}$$
$$= [\alpha\, u^{1/2}\,(1 - iv\ {}_{n-k}\ddot{a}_{x+k}) + (\beta - \alpha\, u^{1/2})\ {}_{n-k}E_{x+k}]\ {}_{k}\ddot{a}_{x} - \alpha\, u^{1/2}\,(1 - {}_{k}E_{x} - iv\ {}_{k}\ddot{a}_{x})\ {}_{n-k}\ddot{a}_{x+k}$$
$$= [\alpha\, u^{1/2} + (\beta - \alpha\, u^{1/2})\ {}_{n-k}E_{x+k}]\ {}_{k}\ddot{a}_{x} - \alpha\, u^{1/2}\,(1 - {}_{k}E_{x})\ {}_{n-k}\ddot{a}_{x+k}$$
$$= \alpha\, u^{1/2}[{}_{k}\ddot{a}_{x} + {}_{k}E_{x}\ {}_{n-k}\ddot{a}_{x+k}] + (\beta - \alpha\, u^{1/2})\ {}_{n-k}E_{x+k}\ {}_{k}\ddot{a}_{x} - \alpha\, u^{1/2}\ {}_{n-k}\ddot{a}_{x+k}\,,$$

where the sum in square brackets equals ${}_{n}\ddot{a}_{x}$. Hence,

$${}_{n}\ddot{a}_{x}\ {}_{\bullet k|}V_{x} = \alpha\, u^{1/2}\ {}_{n}\ddot{a}_{x} - \alpha\, u^{1/2}\ {}_{n-k}\ddot{a}_{x+k} + (\beta - \alpha\, u^{1/2})\ {}_{n-k}E_{x+k}\ {}_{k}\ddot{a}_{x}\quad (k \le n). \tag{21}$$

Case of payments at the end of the year of death

For the reserves ${}_{\bullet k|}V_{x}$ of the theoretical contract

$$(\alpha\ {}_{n}A_{x}^{\circ\circ} + \beta\ {}_{n}E_{x}^{\circ\circ},\ p\ {}_{n}\ddot{a}_{x}^{\circ\circ}) \tag{22}$$

relation

$${}_{n}\ddot{a}_{x}\ {}_{\bullet k|}V_{x} = \alpha\ {}_{n}\ddot{a}_{x} - \alpha\ {}_{n-k}\ddot{a}_{x+k} + (\beta - \alpha)\ {}_{n-k}E_{x+k}\ {}_{k}\ddot{a}_{x}\quad (k \le n) \tag{23}$$

holds. Indeed, $\hat{A}$ must be replaced by $A = v^{1/2}\hat{A}$ in the foregoing developments and then the factors $u^{1/2}$ disappear in the expressions of B and C.

9.7. Positive reserves (analytic proofs)

Theorem 2

Let $$(\mathbf{C}^{\circ\circ},\ \mathbf{p}\textstyle\sum_{k\ge 0} \pi_{k}\ {}_{k}\mathbf{E}_{x}^{\circ\circ}) \tag{24}$$

and $$(\mathbf{C}^{\circ\circ},\ \mathbf{p}'\textstyle\sum_{k\ge 0} \pi'_{k}\ {}_{k}\mathbf{E}_{x}^{\circ\circ}) \tag{25}$$

be contracts such that

$$\mathbf{p} > 0,\ \ \mathbf{p}' > 0,\ \pi_{k} \ge 0,\ \ \pi'_{k} \ge 0\ (k=1,2,\ldots)$$

and $$\pi'_{0}/\pi_{0} \ge \pi'_{1}/\pi_{1} \ge \pi'_{2}/\pi_{2} \ge \ldots \tag{26}$$

(with 0/0:=0). Then $\ {}_{\bullet k|}\mathbf{V}'_{x} \ge {}_{\bullet k|}\mathbf{V}_{x}\ \ (k=0,1,2,\ldots)$**,**

where ${}_{\bullet k|}\mathbf{V}_{x}$ and ${}_{\bullet k|}\mathbf{V}'_{x}$ are reserves of contract (24) and (25) resp.

Proof
The time-capital $C^{\circ\circ}$ is the same in (24) and (25). Then

$$p\ \Sigma_{\alpha\geq 0}\ \pi_\alpha\ {}_\alpha E_x = p'\ \Sigma_{\alpha\geq 0}\ \pi'_\alpha\ {}_\alpha E_x,$$

i.e.
$$B := p\ \Sigma_{\alpha\geq 0}\ \pi_\alpha\ D_{x+\alpha} = p'\ \Sigma_{\alpha\geq 0}\ \pi'_\alpha\ D_{x+\alpha}$$

and
$$_{\bullet k|}V'_x - {}_{\bullet k|}V_x = p\ \Sigma_{\beta\geq k}\ \pi_\beta\ {}_{\beta-k}E_{x+k} - p'\ \Sigma_{\beta\geq k}\ \pi'_\beta\ {}_{\beta-k}E_{x+k},$$

i.e.
$$D_{x+k}[{}_{\bullet k|}V'_x - {}_{\bullet k|}V_x] = p\ \Sigma_{\beta\geq k}\ \pi_\beta\ D_{x+\beta} - p'\ \Sigma_{\beta\geq k}\ \pi'_\beta\ D_{x+\beta}$$

and then
$$(B/pp')\ D_{x+k}[{}_{\bullet k|}V'_x - {}_{\bullet k|}V_x]$$
$$= \Sigma_{\alpha\geq 0}\ \pi'_\alpha\ D_{x+\alpha}\ \Sigma_{\beta\geq k}\ \pi_\beta\ D_{x+\beta} - \Sigma_{\alpha\geq 0}\ \pi_\alpha\ D_{x+\alpha}\ \Sigma_{\beta\geq k}\ \pi'_\beta\ D_{x+\beta}$$
$$= (\Sigma_{\alpha<k}+\Sigma_{\alpha\geq k})\ \pi'_\alpha\ D_{x+\alpha}\ \Sigma_{\beta\geq k}\ \pi_\beta\ D_{x+\beta} - (\Sigma_{\alpha<k}+\Sigma_{\alpha\geq k})\ \pi_\alpha\ D_{x+\alpha}\ \Sigma_{\beta\geq k}\ \pi'_\beta\ D_{x+\beta}$$
$$= (\Sigma_{\alpha<k}+\Sigma_{\alpha\geq k})\ \pi'_\alpha\ D_{x+\alpha}\ \Sigma_{\beta\geq k}\ \pi_\beta\ D_{x+\beta} - (\Sigma_{\beta<k}+\Sigma_{\beta\geq k})\ \pi_\beta\ D_{x+\beta}\ \Sigma_{\alpha\geq k}\ \pi'_\alpha\ D_{x+\alpha}$$
$$= \Sigma_{\alpha<k}\ \pi'_\alpha\ D_{x+\alpha}\ \Sigma_{\beta\geq k}\ \pi_\beta\ D_{x+\beta} - \Sigma_{\beta<k}\ \pi_\beta\ D_{x+\beta}\ \Sigma_{\alpha\geq k}\ \pi'_\alpha\ D_{x+\alpha}$$
$$= \Sigma_{\alpha<k}\ \pi'_\alpha\ D_{x+\alpha}\ \Sigma_{\beta\geq k}\ \pi_\beta\ D_{x+\beta} - \Sigma_{\alpha<k}\ \pi_\alpha\ D_{x+\alpha}\ \Sigma_{\beta\geq k}\ \pi'_\beta\ D_{x+\beta}$$
$$= \Sigma_{\alpha<k}\ \Sigma_{\beta\geq k}\ (\pi'_\alpha\ \pi_\beta - \pi_\alpha\ \pi'_\beta)\ D_{x+\alpha}\ D_{x+\beta}$$
$$= \Sigma_{\alpha<k}\ \Sigma_{\beta\geq k}\ (\pi'_\alpha/\pi_\alpha - \pi'_\beta/\pi_\beta)\ \pi_\alpha\ \pi_\beta\ D_{x+\alpha}\ D_{x+\beta} \geq 0,$$

because $\alpha<\beta$ in the double sum •

Corollary

If the reserves $_{\bullet k|}V_x$ of contract ($C^{\circ\circ}$, p $_n\ddot{a}_x$) are positive, then the reserves $_{\bullet k|}V'_x$ of contract ($C^{\circ\circ}$, p′ $_m\ddot{a}_x$) ($0<m\leq n$) are positive.

Proof
Here the sequence of inequalities (26) is $1 \geq 1 \geq \ldots \geq 1 \geq 0 \geq 0 \geq \ldots$ •

Theorem 3

Let the survival probability p_ξ be a decreasing function of ξ. The reserves $_{\bullet k|}V_x$ of contracts

$$(\alpha\ {}_n\hat{A}_x^{\circ\circ} + \beta\ {}_nE_x^{\circ\circ},\ p\ {}_m\ddot{a}_x^{\circ\circ})\quad (\alpha\geq 0,\ \beta\geq 0,\ 0<m\leq n\leq\infty) \qquad (27)$$

and
$$(\alpha\ {}_nA_x^{\circ\circ} + \beta\ {}_nE_x^{\circ\circ},\ p\ {}_m\ddot{a}_x^{\circ\circ})\quad (\alpha\geq 0,\ \beta\geq 0,\ 0<m\leq n\leq\infty) \qquad (28)$$

are positive.

Proof

By the foregoing Corollary of Theorem 2, it is enough to consider the case m=n. By (21) and (23), it is enough to verify that

$$Q := {}_n\ddot{a}_x - {}_{n-k}\ddot{a}_{x+k} - {}_{n-k}E_{x+k}\ {}_k\ddot{a}_x \geq 0 \quad (k\leq n).$$

where $Q = \sum_{0\leq\beta\leq n-1} {}_\beta E_x - \sum_{0\leq\beta\leq n-k-1} {}_\beta E_{x+k} - {}_{n-k}E_{x+k} \sum_{0\leq\beta\leq k-1} {}_\beta E_x$

$$= \sum_{0\leq\beta\leq n-1} {}_\beta E_x - \sum_{k\leq\beta\leq n-1} {}_{\beta-k}E_{x+k} - {}_{n-k}E_{x+k} \sum_{0\leq\beta\leq k-1} {}_\beta E_x$$

$$= \sum_{0\leq\beta\leq n-1} D_{x+\beta}/D_x - \sum_{k\leq\beta\leq n-1} D_{x+\beta}/D_{x+k} - (D_{x+n}/D_{x+k}) \sum_{0\leq\beta\leq k-1} D_{x+\beta}/D_x.$$

Multiplying by $D_x\, D_{x+k}$, it is enough to prove that

$$Q_k := D_{x+k} \sum_{0\leq\beta\leq n-1} D_{x+\beta} - D_x \sum_{k\leq\beta\leq n-1} D_{x+\beta} - D_{x+n} \sum_{0\leq\beta\leq k-1} D_{x+\beta} \geq 0.$$

Let $$D'_\xi := D_\xi - D_{\xi+1}.$$

Then $$\sum_{k\leq\beta\leq n-1} D'_{x+\beta} = -[D_{x+\beta}]_k^n = D_{x+k} - D_{x+n}\,,$$

$$\sum_{0\leq\alpha\leq k-1} D'_{x+\alpha} = -[D_{x+\alpha}]_0^k = D_x - D_{x+k}$$

and $$Q_k := D_{x+k} \sum_{0\leq\beta\leq n-1} D_{x+\beta} - [(D_x - D_{x+k}) + D_{x+k}] \sum_{k\leq\beta\leq n-1} D_{x+\beta}$$
$$- [D_{x+k} - (D_{x+k} - D_{x+n})] \sum_{0\leq\beta\leq k-1} D_{x+\beta}$$

$$= -(D_x - D_{x+k}) \sum_{k\leq\beta\leq n-1} D_{x+\beta} + (D_{x+k} - D_{x+n}) \sum_{0\leq\beta\leq k-1} D_{x+\beta}$$

$$= -(D_x - D_{x+k}) \sum_{k\leq\beta\leq n-1} D_{x+\beta} + (D_{x+k} - D_{x+n}) \sum_{0\leq\alpha\leq k-1} D_{x+\alpha}$$

$$= -\sum_{0\leq\alpha\leq k-1} D'_{x+\alpha} \sum_{k\leq\beta\leq n-1} D_{x+\beta} + \sum_{k\leq\beta\leq n-1} D'_{x+\beta} \sum_{0\leq\alpha\leq k-1} D_{x+\alpha}$$

$$= \sum_{0\leq\alpha\leq k-1} \sum_{k\leq\beta\leq n-1} (D_{x+\alpha}\, D'_{x+\beta} - D'_{x+\alpha}\, D_{x+\beta})$$

where

$$(D_{x+\alpha}\, D'_{x+\beta} - D'_{x+\alpha}\, D_{x+\beta}) = D_{x+\alpha}(D_{x+\beta} - D_{x+\beta+1}) - (D_{x+\alpha} - D_{x+\alpha+1})D_{x+\beta}$$

$$= D_{x+\alpha+1}\, D_{x+\beta} - D_{x+\alpha}\, D_{x+\beta+1} = v^{2x+\alpha+\beta}(l_{x+\alpha+1}\, l_{x+\beta} - l_{x+\alpha}\, l_{x+\beta+1})$$

$$= v^{2x+\alpha+\beta}\, l_{x+\alpha}\, l_{x+\beta}\, (p_{x+\alpha} - p_{x+\beta}) \geq 0$$

because $\alpha<\beta$ •

9.8. Variation of prices with interest rate i

The price Q of any time-capital (with positive amounts) **on the life x is a decreasing function of interest rate i.** Indeed, the price is a sum $\sum_\tau c_\tau v^\tau$ with $c_\tau \geq 0$ (continuous components $\int c_\tau v^\tau d\tau$ are not excluded; we recall that $d_\tau q_x$ equals ${}_\tau p_x\, \mu_{x+\tau}\, d\tau$).

Let accents represent prices calculated at interest rate i′ instead of i. Then

$$({}_n a_x)' = \Sigma_{1\le k\le n}\, v'^k\, {}_k p_x = \Sigma_{1\le k\le n}\, [v + (v'-v)]^k\, {}_k p_x$$

$$\Sigma_{1\le k\le n}\, [v + (v'-v)]^k\, {}_k p_x = \Sigma_{1\le k\le n}\, [v^k + k\, v^{k-1}\, (v'-v) + \dots]\, {}_k p_x$$

$$\Sigma_{1\le k\le n}\, v^k\, {}_k p_x + [(v'-v)/v]\, \Sigma_{1\le k\le n}\, k\, v^k\, {}_k p_x + \dots,$$

where the dots represent terms with factor $(v'-v)^k$ $(k\ge 2)$. Hence,

$$({}_n a_x)' \approx {}_n a_x - {}_n(Ia)_x\, (v-v')/v \quad (i' \text{ close to } i). \tag{29}$$

Similarly,

$$({}_n A_x)' = \Sigma_{0\le k\le n-1}\, v'^k\, \Delta\, {}_k q_x = \Sigma_{0\le k\le n-1}\, [v^k + k\, v^{k-1}\, (v'-v) + \dots]\, \Delta\, {}_k q_x$$

$$= \Sigma_{0\le k\le n-1}\, v^k\, \Delta\, {}_k q_x + [(v'-v)/v]\, \Sigma_{0\le k\le n-1}\, k\, v^k\, \Delta\, {}_k q_x + \dots$$

$$({}_n A_x)' \approx {}_n A_x - {}_n(IA)_x\, (v-v')/v \quad (i' \text{ close to } i). \tag{30}$$

9.9. Variation of reserves with interest rate i

a. The reserves of any single premium contract on the life x are decreasing functions of interest rate i. Indeed, reserves of single-premium contracts are prices of time-capitals with positive amounts.

The following is a practical, not a theoretical fact.

b. The reserves of practical contracts on the life x are decreasing functions of interest rate i. An explanation (which is not a proof) is that such reserves are differences

$$\Sigma_\tau\, c_\tau\, v^\tau - \Sigma_\tau\, c'_\tau\, v^\tau$$

(perhaps with continuous components) with positive c_τ and c'_τ, where the decreasing part $\Sigma_\tau\, c_\tau v^\tau$ dominates the increasing part $-\Sigma_\tau\, c'_\tau v^\tau$ because reserves are positive.

Here follows an example of a theoretical contract with strictly positive reserve which increases strictly with i. It is the contract

$$({}_4A_x^{\circ\circ},\ \pi\ {}_4\ddot{a}_x^{\circ\circ})$$

in case of survival probabilities

$$p_x = 1-\varepsilon^2,\ p_{x+1} = p_{x+2} = p_{x+3} = 1-\varepsilon$$

with $\varepsilon > 0$, ε near zero. Indeed, then

$${}_1p_x = p_x = 1-\varepsilon^2,\quad {}_2p_x = p_x\, p_{x+1} = (1-\varepsilon^2)(1-\varepsilon),$$

$$_3p_x = p_x\, p_{x+1}\, p_{x+2} = (1-\varepsilon^2)(1-\varepsilon)^2$$

$$_3\ddot{a}_x = 1 + v\, _1p_x + v^2\, _2p_x = 1 + v(1-\varepsilon^2) + v^2(1-\varepsilon^2)(1-\varepsilon),$$

$$_4\ddot{a}_x = 1 + v\, _1p_x + v^2\, _2p_x = 1 + v(1-\varepsilon^2) + v^2(1-\varepsilon^2)(1-\varepsilon) + v^3(1-\varepsilon^2)(1-\varepsilon)^2,$$

$$_1E_{x+3} = v\, p_{x+3} = v(1-\varepsilon).$$

By (23), $$_{\bullet 3|}V_x = (_4\ddot{a}_x - \, _1\ddot{a}_{x+3} - \, _1E_{x+3}\, _3\ddot{a}_x)/\, _4\ddot{a}_x$$
$$= (_4\ddot{a}_x - 1 - \, _1E_{x+3}\, _3\ddot{a}_x)/_4\ddot{a}_x = v\varepsilon(1-\varepsilon)/_4\ddot{a}_x$$

Let accents represent derivatives with respect to v. Then

$$(_{\bullet 3|}V_x)'(_4\ddot{a}_x)^2 = \, _4\ddot{a}_x\, \varepsilon(1-\varepsilon) - (_4\ddot{a}_x)'\, v\varepsilon(1-\varepsilon)$$
$$= [1 + v(1-\varepsilon^2) + v^2(1-\varepsilon^2)(1-\varepsilon) + v^3(1-\varepsilon^2)(1-\varepsilon)^2]\varepsilon(1-\varepsilon) -$$
$$[(1-\varepsilon^2) + 2v(1-\varepsilon^2)(1-\varepsilon) + 3v^2(1-\varepsilon^2)(1-\varepsilon)^2]v\varepsilon(1-\varepsilon)$$
$$= \varepsilon(1-\varepsilon)[1 - v^2(1-\varepsilon^2)(1-\varepsilon) - 2v^3(1-\varepsilon^2)(1-\varepsilon)^2]. \tag{31}$$

Let $\varepsilon>0$ be fixed such that

$$1 - (1-\varepsilon^2)(1-\varepsilon) - 2(1-\varepsilon^2)(1-\varepsilon)^2] < 0,$$

say $\varepsilon:=0.1$. Then (31) is strictly negative for $i=0$. For continuity reasons, (31) remains strictly negative for $i\in[0,i_0]$, where i_0 is some fixed strictly positive interest rate. Then $_{\bullet 3|}V_x$ is a strictly decreasing function of v, hence a strictly increasing function of $i\in[0,i_0]$.

This example emphasizes the fact that b. is true in practice, but certainly not in theory. In some cases, it can be proved that reserves decrease when i increases. The following Theorem 4 is a non-trivial illustration.

Lemma

We consider the rational function

$$\mathbf{f(x) := (\textstyle\sum_{0\le\alpha\le n} a_\alpha x^\alpha)/(\sum_{0\le\alpha\le n} b_\alpha x^\alpha) \quad (x\ge 0),} \tag{32}$$

where $a_\alpha\ge 0$ and $b_\alpha>0$. If the sequence

$$\mathbf{a_0/b_0\ ,\ a_1/b_1\ ,\ a_2/b_2\ ,\ \dots\ ,\ a_n/b_n} \tag{33}$$

is increasing (decreasing), f is an increasing (decreasing) function of $x\ge 0$.

Proof $$f'(x).(\textstyle\sum_{0\le\alpha\le n} b_\alpha x^\alpha)^2$$

$$= \textstyle\sum_{0\le\alpha\le n} b_\alpha x^\alpha \sum_{0\le\alpha\le n} \alpha\, a_\alpha x^{\alpha-1} - \sum_{0\le\alpha\le n} \alpha\, b_\alpha x^{\alpha-1} \sum_{0\le\alpha\le n} a_\alpha x^\alpha$$

$$= \sum_{0\le\beta\le n} b_\beta x^\beta \sum_{0\le\alpha\le n} \alpha\, a_\alpha x^{\alpha-1} - \sum_{0\le\alpha\le n} \alpha\, b_\alpha x^{\alpha-1} \sum_{0\le\beta\le n} a_\beta x^\beta$$

$$= \sum_{0\le\alpha\le n} \sum_{0\le\beta\le n} \alpha\, x^{\alpha+\beta-1} (a_\alpha b_\beta - a_\beta b_\alpha)$$

$$= \sum_{0\le\alpha\le n} \sum_{0\le\beta\le n} \alpha\, x^{\alpha+\beta-1} (a_\alpha b_\beta - a_\beta b_\alpha)$$

and permuting the dummy summation variables α and β,

$$f'(x).(\sum_{0\le\alpha\le n} b_\alpha x^\alpha)^2 = \sum_{0\le\alpha\le n} \sum_{0\le\beta\le n} \beta\, x^{\alpha+\beta-1} (a_\beta b_\alpha - a_\alpha b_\beta)$$

$$= - \sum_{0\le\alpha\le n} \sum_{0\le\beta\le n} \beta\, x^{\alpha+\beta-1} (a_\alpha b_\beta - a_\beta b_\alpha).$$

Then,

$$2 f'(x).(\sum_{0\le\alpha\le n} b_\alpha x^\alpha)^2 = \sum_{0\le\alpha\le n} \sum_{0\le\beta\le n} (\alpha-\beta)\, x^{\alpha+\beta-1} (a_\alpha b_\beta - a_\beta b_\alpha)$$

$$= \sum_{0\le\alpha\le n} \sum_{0\le\beta\le n} x^{\alpha+\beta-1} b_\alpha b_\beta [(\alpha-\beta)(a_\alpha/b_\alpha - a_\beta/b_\beta)].$$

The product in square brackets is positive if sequence (33) is increasing because then

$$\alpha \le \beta \Rightarrow a_\alpha/b_\alpha \le a_\beta/b_\beta \quad \text{and} \quad \alpha \ge \beta \Rightarrow a_\alpha/b_\alpha \ge a_\beta/b_\beta.$$

It is negative if sequence (32) is decreasing •

Theorem 4

Let the survival probability p_ξ be a decreasing function of ξ. The reserves ${}_{\bullet k|}V_x$ of contract

$$(\alpha\, {}_nA_x^{oo} + \beta\, {}_nE_x^{oo}, p\, {}_m\ddot{a}_x^{oo}) \quad (0\le\alpha\le\beta, 0<m\le n\le\infty) \qquad (34)$$

are decreasing functions of interest rate i.

Proof

By (23), ${}_{\bullet k|}V_x = \alpha - \alpha\, {}_{n-k}\ddot{a}_{x+k} / {}_n\ddot{a}_x + (\beta-\alpha)\, {}_{n-k}E_{x+k}\, {}_k\ddot{a}_x / {}_n\ddot{a}_x$ $(k\le n)$

Hence, it is enough to verify that

a. $f(v) := {}_{n-k}\ddot{a}_{x+k} / {}_n\ddot{a}_x$ is a decreasing function of v,

b. $g(v) := {}_{n-k}E_{x+k}\, {}_k\ddot{a}_x / {}_n\ddot{a}_x$ is an increasing function of v.

For the proof of a, we observe that

$$f(v) = (\sum_{0\le\alpha\le n-k-1} {}_\alpha p_{x+k} v^\alpha)/(\sum_{0\le\alpha\le n-1} {}_\alpha p_x v^\alpha)$$

and that the corresponding sequence (33) is

$${}_0p_{x+k}/{}_0p_x\, ,\ {}_1p_{x+k}/{}_1p_x\, ,\ {}_2p_{x+k}/{}_2p_x\, ,\ \dots\, ,\ {}_{n-k-1}p_{x+k}/{}_{n-k-1}p_x\, ,\ 0\, ,\ 0\, ,\ \dots\, ,\ 0.$$

Hence, it is enough to verify that

$$ {}_{\alpha}p_{x+k}/{}_{\alpha}p_x \geq {}_{\alpha+1}p_{x+k}/{}_{\alpha+1}p_x. \tag{35}$$

But $\quad {}_{\alpha+1}p_{x+k} = {}_{\alpha}p_{x+k}\ {}_1p_{x+k+\alpha}\ ,\ {}_{\alpha+1}p_x = {}_{\alpha}p_x\ {}_1p_{x+\alpha}$

and then (35) becomes the relation $p_{x+\alpha} \geq p_{x+\alpha+1}$.

For the proof of b, we observe that

$$ {}_{n-k}E_{x+k}\ {}_k\ddot{a}_x = \sum_{0\leq\alpha\leq k-1} {}_{\alpha}p_x\, v^{\alpha}\ {}_{n-k}p_{x+k}\, v^{n-k} = {}_{n-k}p_{x+k} \sum_{0\leq\alpha\leq k-1} {}_{\alpha}p_x\, v^{\alpha+n-k}$$

$$= {}_{n-k}p_{x+k} \sum_{n-k\leq\alpha\leq n-1} {}_{\alpha-n+k}p_x\, v^{\alpha}$$

and $\quad {}_n\ddot{a}_x = \sum_{0\leq\alpha\leq n-1} {}_{\alpha}p_x\, v^{\alpha}.$

Neglecting the constant factor ${}_{n-k}p_x$, the sequence (33) in case of g(v)

is $\quad 0, 0, \ldots, 0\ ,\ {}_0p_x/{}_{n-k}p_x\ ,\ {}_1p_x/{}_{n-k+1}p_x\ ,\ {}_2p_x/{}_{n-k+2}p_x\ ,\ \ldots\ ,\ {}_{k-1}p_x/{}_{n-1}p_x.$

It is an increasing sequence because

$$ {}_{\alpha}p_x/{}_{\beta}p_x \leq {}_{\alpha+1}p_x/{}_{\beta+1}p_x \quad (\alpha\leq\beta) \tag{36}$$

$$ {}_{\alpha+1}p_x = {}_{\alpha}p_x\ {}_1p_{x+\alpha}\ ,\ {}_{\beta+1}p_x = {}_{\beta}p_x\ {}_1p_{x+\beta}$$

and then (36) becomes $p_{x+\beta} \leq p_{x+\alpha}$ $(\alpha\leq\beta)$ •

9.10. Variation of reserves with time t

The variation of ${}_{\bullet t|}V_x$ with t is illustrated by the three typical examples of Figure 9.1, corresponding to contract ($C^{\circ\circ}$, p ${}_n\ddot{a}_x^{\circ\circ}$).

The reserve ${}_{\bullet t|}V_x$ is discontinuous at point k=0,1,...,n−1. Indeed

$$ {}_{\bullet k+|}V_x = p + {}_{\bullet k-|}V_x$$

because the insurer collects the premium p at k. Hence, the (small) discontinuities are not shown in the approximative representations.

9.11. Transformation of a contract

The basic theoretical principle is that **the reserve ${}_{\bullet t|}V_x$ belongs to the insured x** (supposed to be alive at instant t). Hence,

- he can recover it at t,
- he can use it as single premium of a new contract at t,
- he can use it as amount paid at t of a new contract at t with more future premiums.

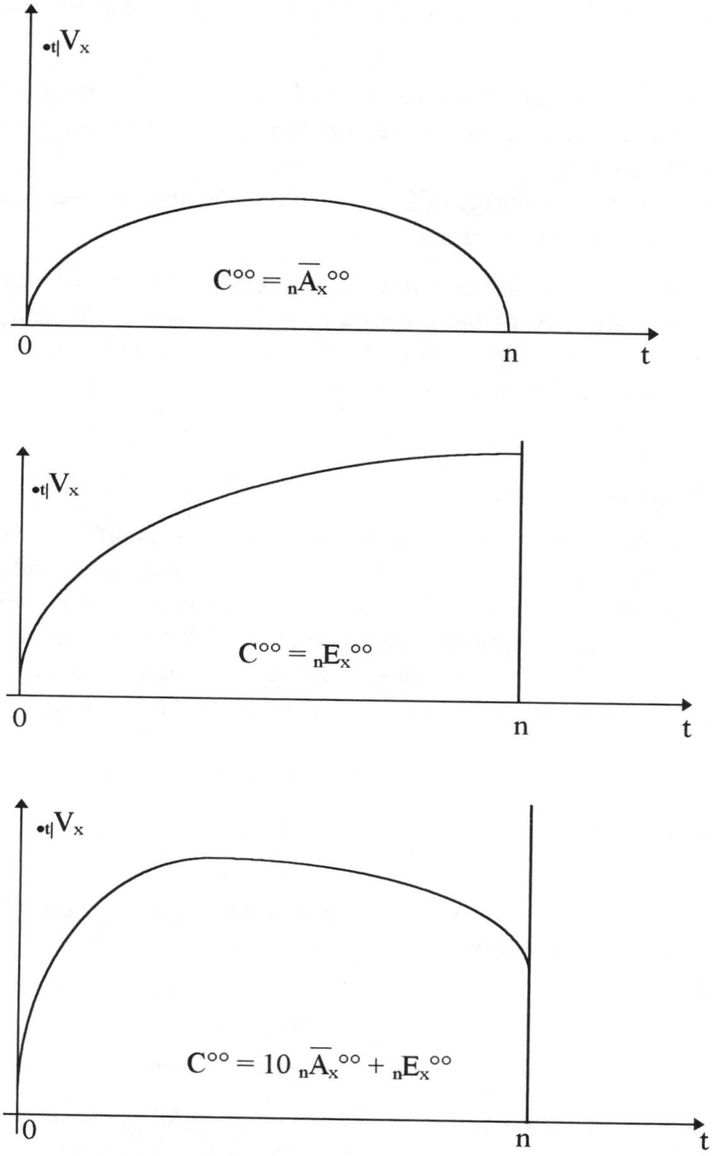

Figure 9.1. Variation of reserves with time t

Of course, the theoretical principle has several practical restrictions. For instance,

- the insurer can require some indemnity for contract interruption,
- the insurance can recover some expenses (e.g. acquisition expenses; see following section),
- the reserve of components of $C^{\circ\circ}$ such as $\overline{A}_x^{\circ\circ}$ cannot be recovered for obvious antiselection reasons.

The so-called **flexible life** or **universal life** insurance is based on (11). ${}_{\bullet k|}V_x$ is fixed, but any two of the quantities π_k, ${}_{\bullet k|1}C_x$ and ${}_{\bullet k+1|}V_x$ can be determined more or less arbitraryly by the insured (all parameters must remain positive; more conditions may be imposed in order to prevent an anti-selection risk).

9.12. Expense loadings

The allocation of expenses is somewhat arbitrary. It is different from country to country. It is not the same in case of group insurances and in case of individual contracts. As an illustration, we develop the most widespread system in case of a particular net contract ($C^{\circ\circ}$,$P^{\circ\circ}$). We assume that the duration of $C^{\circ\circ}$ is n (this means that all reserves of $C^{\circ\circ}$ vanish at $t>n$ but that some do not vanish at $t\leq n$). For instance $C^{\circ\circ}$ may be the endowment insurance

$$C^{\circ\circ} := {}_n\overline{A}_x^{\circ\circ} + {}_nE_x^{\circ\circ}.$$

We suppose that

$$P^{\circ\circ} := p\ {}_m\ddot{a}_x^{\circ\circ},$$

where $m\leq n$.

The insured will pay the **loaded time-capital** $p''{}_m\ddot{a}_x^{\circ\circ}$ where $p''>p$ is the **expense-loaded premium**. Hence, the net time capital $P^{\circ\circ}$ is augmented by the loading

$$L^{\circ\circ} = (p''-p)\ {}_m\ddot{a}_x^{\circ\circ}.$$

The expenses of the insurer are partitioned as follows:

a. **Acquisition expenses** $(\alpha,0)$. These comprise all expenses related to a new policy issue (commissions, advertising, medical examination, ...).

b. **Administration expenses** $\gamma\ {}_n\ddot{a}_x^{\circ\circ}$. The duration n of the life annuity is the same as the duration n of the insurer's engagement $C^{\circ\circ}$. These expenses cover the daily administration costs which last as long as the contract exists.

c. **Collection expenses** $\beta\, p''\ {}_{m}\ddot{a}_x^{\circ\circ}$. From each premium p″ paid by the insured, the proportion β p″ disappears in collection expenses.

Hence, the **expense time-capital of the insurer** is

$$E^{\circ\circ} = (\alpha,0) + \gamma\ {}_{n}\ddot{a}_x^{\circ\circ} + \beta\, p''\ {}_{m}\ddot{a}_x^{\circ\circ}.$$

Then p″ is fixed by the condition that the price C+E of $C^{\circ\circ}+E^{\circ\circ}$ must be equal to the price P+L of $P^{\circ\circ}+L^{\circ\circ} = p''\ {}_{m}\ddot{a}_x^{\circ\circ}$.

$$C + \alpha + \gamma\ {}_{n}\ddot{a}_x + \beta\, p''\ {}_{m}\ddot{a}_x = p''\ {}_{m}\ddot{a}_x\,,$$

$$p'' = (C + \alpha + \gamma\ {}_{n}\ddot{a}_x)/[(1-\beta)\ {}_{m}\ddot{a}_x].$$

An **expense-loaded reserve of a contract** is the net reserve (studied previously) completed by the reserve of the annuity $\gamma\ {}_{n}\ddot{a}_x^{\circ\circ}$ covering the administration expenses. In some countries, the expense-loaded reserves take the acquisition costs into account.

Chapter 10

RUIN PROBABILITY OF A LIFE INSURANCE COMPANY

10.1. True interest rate and true mortality

Let us call **technical interest rate i** and **technical life table** l_ξ, those used by the insurer in the evaluation of present values, prices, premiums and reserves. The technical interest rate i is different from the **true interest rate** i* produced by reserves and the technical mortality is not necessarily the same as the **true mortality**.

Insurance companies can survive because differences between technical and true interest rates and mortalities imply the existence of an implicit security loading allowing to make profits. Indeed, we will see in section 10.4 that the probability of ruin in a closed portfolio is 1/2 if the premiums are evaluated with true interest rate and mortality.

We assume that the true interest rate and the true life table remain constant. This is not a realistic assumption, but it can hardly be avoided because long term forecasts are not safe and because mathematical models with variable (stochastic) interest rates and mortalities are too complicated. Hence, the practical evaluation of insurance profits and probability of ruin should analyse different interest and mortality scenarios. Then the following theory allows to make practical statements such as "If the true interest rate is at least i* and if the true mortalility is the same as the technical one, then the probability of ruin is less than p".

In this Chapter, the notation $(\ )_{techn}$ indicates that the evaluations are made with technical interest rate and mortality table. The notation $(\ )_{true}$ is used for evaluations with true interest rate and mortality table.

Only contracts on one life x, vanishing with x, are considered for the moment. Extensions to more general contracts on several lives are obvious (Ch.15.1)

The following analysis is developed in case of net reserves. It is easy to incorporate administration expenses and to work with expense-loaded reserves. Another easy extension is the inclusion of a supplementary initial risk reserve in the ruin evaluations.

10.2. Profit of a contract

The **expected profit of contract** $(C^{\circ\circ},P^{\circ\circ})$ at subscription is $(P)_{true}-(C)_{true}$. We recall that $(P)_{tech}-(C)_{tech}=0$ in fair contracts, but $(P)_{true}-(C)_{true}$ should be strictly positive in practical contracts.

At instant t, the **expected profit of the contract** is

$$({}_{\bullet t|}V_x)_{tech} + ({}_{\bullet t|}P_x)_{true} - ({}_{\bullet t|}C_x)_{true} = ({}_{\bullet t|}V_x)_{tech} - ({}_{\bullet t|}V_x)_{true} ,$$

where it is of course assumed that x is still alive at t.

At t, the **present value of the profit of the contract** is the random variable

$$({}_{\bullet t|}V_x)_{tech} + ({}_{\bullet t|}P_x{}^{\circ})_{true} - ({}_{\bullet t|}C_x{}^{\circ})_{true} = ({}_{\bullet t|}V_x)_{tech} - ({}_{\bullet t|}V_x{}^{\circ})_{true} .$$

In the following sections 10.12–10.16, we will learn how to calculate its variance

$$\mathrm{Var}[({}_{\bullet t|}V_x)_{tech} - ({}_{\bullet t|}V_x{}^{\circ})_{true}] = \mathrm{Var}({}_{\bullet t|}V_x{}^{\circ})_{true} . \quad (1)$$

10.3. Profit of a closed portfolio

A **life insurance portfolio** is a collection of life insurance contracts. In particular, all contracts of some life insurance company constitute a portfolio. We consider a fixed portfolio now, at instant 0. Each policy of the portfolio is a contract on a life x subscribed t years ago. All values of t and x may occur in the contracts. For the moment, we suppose that the **portfolio** is **closed**, i.e. that no new contracts will join the portfolio in the future.

The **profit of the portfolio**, estimated now, is the sum

$$S^{\circ} := \sum [({}_{\bullet t|}V_x)_{tech} - ({}_{\bullet t|}V_x{}^{\circ})_{true}] \quad (2)$$

over all contracts of the portfolio. S° is the **basic random variable of the portfolio**. Its expectation

$$S := E(S^{\circ}) = \sum[({}_{\bullet t|}V_x)_{tech} - ({}_{\bullet t|}V_x)_{true}] \quad (3)$$

is the **expected profit of the portfolio**.

The lives x occurring in the contracts of the portfolio are supposed to be independent. Then, by (2),

$$\mathrm{Var}(S^\circ) := \sum \mathrm{Var}[({}_{\bullet t|}V_x)_{tech} - ({}_{\bullet t|}V_x{}^\circ)_{true}] \;\; = \sum \mathrm{Var}({}_{\bullet t|}V_x{}^\circ)_{true} \;. \qquad (4)$$

The **structure parameter** σ of the portfolio is

$$\sigma := \mathrm{Var}\, S^\circ/E(S^\circ) = S^{-1}\, \mathrm{Var}(S^\circ). \qquad (5)$$

It does not depend on the number of contracts if all random variables

$$({}_{\bullet t|}V_x)_{tech} - ({}_{\bullet t|}V_x{}^\circ)_{true} \qquad (6)$$

have the same distribution (this is of course a theoretical case).

10.4. Probability of ruin in a closed portfolio

The **probability of ruin in the portfolio** is the probability

$$\Psi := P(S^\circ < 0). \qquad (7)$$

We suppose that the portfolio is large enough and that **the standardized random variable**

$$(S^\circ - S)/\mathrm{Var}^{1/2}(S^\circ) \qquad (8)$$

can be treated as a standardized normal random variable Norm. (i.e. a normal random variable with expectation equal to 0 and variance equal to 1). Then the probability of ruin equals

$$\Psi = P(S^\circ < 0) = P[(S^\circ - S)/\mathrm{Var}^{1/2}(S^\circ) < -S/\mathrm{Var}^{1/2}(S^\circ)]$$

$$= P\{\mathrm{Norm} < -S/\mathrm{Var}^{1/2}(S^\circ)\} = P[-\mathrm{Norm} < -S/\mathrm{Var}^{1/2}(S^\circ)]$$

because Norm is symmetrically distributed. Hence,

$$\Psi = P(S^\circ < 0) = P\{\mathrm{Norm} > S/\mathrm{Var}^{1/2}(S^\circ)]. \qquad (9)$$

Let us assume, for a moment, that technical interest rate and mortality coincide with true interest and mortality. Then by (2),

$$S := \sum [({}_{\bullet t|}V_x)_{tech} - ({}_{\bullet t|}V_x)_{true}] = \sum [({}_{\bullet t|}V_x)_{tech} - ({}_{\bullet t|}V_x)_{tech}] = 0$$

and by (9) $\Psi = P(\mathrm{Norm} > 0) = 1/2.$

The probability of ruin in a closed portfolio is 1/2 if the insurer makes no interest or mortality profits.

10.5. Solvency parameter of a portfolio

If the probability of ruin in some portfolio can be displayed as Ψ= P(Norm>ρ), then ρ is called the **solvency parameter of the portfolio**. The ruin probability is small (large) if the solvency parameter is large (small). The evaluation of ρ may help to decide whether reinsurance should be considered or not.

Relation (9) is general. **In any portfolio with basic variable S°,**

$$\rho = S/Var^{1/2}(S°), \tag{10}$$

under normal assumptions. By (5), $\rho=(S/\sigma)^{1/2}$ in case of a closed portfolio.

10.6. Merger of closed portfolios considered at the same moment

We consider at instant 0 two independent closed portfolios with basic random variables $S_1°$ and $S_2°$ and their merger with basic random variable $S°=S_1°+S_2°$. The solvency parameter of the merger portfolio equals

$$\rho = S\ Var^{-1/2}(S°) = S\ [Var(S_1°) + Var(S_2°)]^{-1/2}$$

$$= S(\sigma_1 S_1 + \sigma_2 S_2)^{-1/2}. \tag{11}$$

Let us assume that the two initial portfolios have the same structure parameter $\sigma_1=\sigma_2=:\sigma$. Then the structure parameter of the merger portfolio is σ. Indeed, it equals

$$Var(S°)/S = [Var(S_1°) + Var(S_2°)]/S = \sigma(S_1 + S_2)/S = \sigma.$$

Then the solvency parameter of the merger portfolio equals

$$\rho = (S/\sigma)^{1/2} = \sigma^{-1/2}(S_1+S_2)^{1/2}. \tag{12}$$

It exceeds the solvency parameters $\rho_1=(S_1/\sigma)^{1/2}$ and $\rho_2=(S_2/\sigma)^{1/2}$ of the initial portfolios. Hence, **the probability of ruin is smaller in the merger portfolio than in each of the initial portfolios**.

10.7. Merger of closed portfolios considered at different moments

We consider now, at 0, a first closed portfolio with basic random variable $S_1°$ and at $\tau>0$ a second closed portfolio with basic random variable $S_2°$. Then the basic random variable, evaluated now, of the merger at τ of the two portfolios is $S°=S_1°+v^{*\tau}S_2°$, where $v^*:=1/(1+i^*)$.

The solvency parameter of the merger portfolio equals

$$\rho = S\ Var^{-1/2}(S°) = S\ [Var(S_1°) + v^{*2\tau}\ Var(S_2°)]^{-1/2}$$
$$= S(\sigma_1 S_1 + v^{*2\tau}\ \sigma_2 S_2)^{-1/2}. \qquad (13)$$

10.8. Probability of ruin in an open portfolio

We consider a portfolio at moment 0 with basic random variable $S_0°$ and we suppose that new contracts join the portfolio at instants $k-1/2$ ($k=1,2,...$). The collection of new contracts at $k-1/2$ is regarded as a new portfolio at that instant, with basic random variable $S_k°$. Let σ_0 be the structure parameter of the initial portfolio at 0 at σ_k the structure variable of the new portfolio at instant $k-1/2$ ($k=1,2,...$). Then the **open portfolio** is the merger of the portfolios at 0, 1/2, 3/2, ... By an extension of (13), the solvency parameter of the open portfolio is

$$\rho = (S_0 + \textstyle\sum_{k\geq 1} v^{*k-1/2}\ S_k)(\sigma_0 S_0 + \sum_{k\geq 1} v^{*2k-1}\ \sigma_k S_k)^{-1/2}. \qquad (14)$$

Let n_k ($k=1,2,...$) be the number of contracts of the new portfolio at $k-1/2$ and let $\gamma_k := n_k/n_1$ (hence $\gamma_1=1$). We assume that the new portfolios at $k-1/2$ have the same structure. Explicitly, we assume that

$$\sigma_1 = \sigma_2 = ... , \qquad (15)$$

and that

$$S_k = \gamma_k S_1. \qquad (16)$$

Then the solvency parameter (14) of the open portfolio becomes

$$\rho = (S_0 + S_1 \textstyle\sum_{k\geq 1} v^{*k-1/2}\ \gamma_k)(\sigma_0 S_0 + \sigma_1 S_1 \sum_{k\geq 1} v^{*2k-1}\ \gamma_k)^{-1/2}. \qquad (17)$$

Several assumptions can be made on the proportions γ_k. A first conclusion resulting from (17) is the following: **if the size of an open portfolio is multiplied by α, then its solvency parameter is multiplied by $\alpha^{1/2}$**. Indeed, if the size is multiplied by α, then both S_0 and S_1 are multiplied by α (the other parameters are supposed to be invariable).

10.9. Open portfolio with constant entries

Let $1=\gamma_1=\gamma_2=...$ Then

$$\textstyle\sum_{k\geq 1} v^{*k-1/2}\ \gamma_k = v^{*1/2}(1 + v^* + v^{*2} + ...) = v^{*1/2}/(1-v^*),$$
$$\textstyle\sum_{k\geq 1} v^{*2k-1}\ \gamma_k = \sum_{k\geq 1} v^{*2k-1} = v^*(1+v^{*2} + v^{*4} + ...) = v^*/(1-v^{*2})$$

and by (17),

$$\rho = [S_0 + S_1\, v^{*1/2}/(1-v^*)][\sigma_0\, S_0 + \sigma_1\, S_1\, v^*/(1-v^{*2})]^{-1/2}. \qquad (18)$$

We recall that $S_0=E(S_0^\circ)$ and $S_1=E(S_1^\circ)$, where S_0° is the basic random variable of the portfolio at 0 and S_1° the basic random variable of the collection of new contracts of the first year. The parameter σ_0 is the structure parameter of the initial portfolio at 0 and σ_1 is the structure variable corresponding to S_1°.

In order to calculate σ_1, the distribution of the set of new contracts of the first year must be known. Of course, that distribution is estimated from past observations over any number of years. Then the variance $\mathrm{Var}({}_{\bullet t|}V_x^\circ)_{true}$ with t=0, corresponding to each new contract must be calculated. The evaluation of σ_0 is based on variances $\mathrm{Var}({}_{\bullet t|}V_x^\circ)_{true}$ with $t\geq 0$. Hereafter, we learn how to calculate these variances. Then ρ results from (18) and then the probability of ruin in the open portfolio equals $\Psi=P(\mathrm{Norm}>\rho)$.

10.10. Open portfolio with exponential growth

We now consider an open portfolio with exponential growth of new contracts defined by $\gamma_k=(1+\gamma)^{k-1}$ (k=1,2,...) in (17). Then

$$\Sigma_{k\geq 1}\, v^{*k-1/2}\, \gamma_k = \Sigma_{k\geq 1}\, v^{*k-1/2}\, (1+\gamma)^{k-1} = \Sigma_{k\geq 0}\, v^{*k+1/2}\, (1+\gamma)^k$$

$$= v^{*1/2}\, \Sigma_{k\geq 0}\, v^{*k}\, (1+\gamma)^k = v^{*1/2}/[1-v^*(1+\gamma)], \qquad (19)$$

$$\Sigma_{k\geq 1}\, v^{*2k-1}\, \gamma_k = \Sigma_{k\geq 1}\, v^{*2k-1}\, (1+\gamma)^{k-1} = \Sigma_{k\geq 0}\, v^{*2k+1}\, (1+\gamma)^k$$

$$= v^*\, \Sigma_{k\geq 0}\, v^{*2k}\, (1+\gamma)^k = v^*/[1-v^{*2}(1+\gamma)], \qquad (20)$$

and then substitution in (17) furnishes the solvency parameter ρ. Of course, it is assumed in (19) that $v^*(1+\gamma)<1$, i.e. $\gamma<i^*$. If $\gamma\geq i^*$, then $\rho=\infty$ and $\Psi=0$.

10.11. Open portfolio with linear growth

We here consider an open portfolio with linear growth of new contracts defined by $\gamma_k=[1+\gamma(k-1)]$ (k=1,2,...) in (17). We observe that for $|c|<1$,

$$\Sigma_{k\geq 0}\, c^k(1+\gamma k) = -(1-c)^{-1}\, \Sigma_{k\geq 0}\, (1+\gamma k)\, \Delta c^k$$

$$= -(1-c)^{-1}\, [(1+\gamma k)c^k]_0^\infty + (1-c)^{-1}\, \Sigma_{k\geq 0}\, c^{k+1} = (1-c)^{-1} + c\gamma(1-c)^{-1}$$

$$= (1-c+\gamma c)(1-c)^{-2}$$

by a summation by parts. Then

$$\Sigma_{k\geq 1}\, v^{*k-1/2}\, \gamma_k = \Sigma_{k\geq 1}\, v^{*k-1/2}[1+\gamma(k-1)] = \Sigma_{k\geq 0}\, v^{*k+1/2}(1+\gamma k)$$

$= v^{*1/2} \sum_{k\geq 0} v^{*k}(1+\gamma k) = v^{*1/2}(1-v^*+\gamma v^*)(1-v^*)^{-2}$

and $\sum_{k\geq 1} v^{*2k-1}\gamma_k = \sum_{k\geq 1} v^{*2k-1}[1+\gamma(k-1)] = \sum_{k\geq 0} v^{*2k+1}(1+\gamma k)$

$= v^* \sum_{k\geq 0} v^{*k}(1+\gamma k) = v^{*2}(1-v^{*2}+\gamma v^{*2})(1-v^{*2})^{-2}$.

Substitution in (17) furnishes the solvency parameter ρ.

10.12. Evaluation of variances. General methodology

Interest rates

Hereafter, i is an interest rate and we define a related interest rate i' by the relation $v^2=v'$, i.e.

$$1/(1+i)^2 = 1/(1+i'), \quad 1+i' = (1+i)^2.$$

Hence, $i'=i^2+2i$. The indication (i') is used for present values and prices evaluated at interest rate i'. Nothing is mentioned if the interest rate is i. For instance, $\overline{A}_x{}^\circ(i') = v'^X$, $\overline{A}_x{}^\circ = v^X$.

(We recall that the variances needed in the evaluation of ruin probabilities must be calculated with the true interest rate i*, not the technical rate i.)

Elimination of discrete life annuities

It is not necessary to evaluate variances with the same precision as prices. Practical discrete life annuities are replaced by corresponding continuous annuities. This approximation simplifies the theoretical formulas for variances considerably and it has no practical impact on the ruin probabilities.

Hence, discrete life annuities are approximated by annuities ${}_{m|n}\overline{a}_x(c_\tau)^{\circ\circ}$ with a continuous capital-function c_τ. The latter is fixed in such a way that the amount paid by the insurer during any year [k,k+1] (neglecting actualizations and supposing x alive at k+1) is the same in case of the initial discrete annuity and in case of its continuous approximation. For instance, $a_x{}^{\circ\circ}$ and $\ddot{a}_x{}^{\circ\circ}$ are both replaced by $\overline{a}_x{}^{\circ\circ}$ when variances are considered, but $(Ia)_x{}^{\circ\circ}$ and $(I\ddot{a})_x{}^{\circ\circ}$ are approximated by

$$\overline{a}_x(\tau+1/2)^{\circ\circ} = (\overline{I}\overline{a})_x{}^{\circ\circ} + (1/2)\,\overline{a}_x{}^{\circ\circ}.$$

These approximations can be improved a bit by taking

$$a_x{}^{\circ\circ} \approx v^{1/2}\,\overline{a}_x{}^{\circ\circ}, \quad \ddot{a}_x{}^{\circ\circ} \approx u^{1/2}\,\overline{a}_x{}^{\circ\circ}, \tag{21}$$

$$(Ia)_x{}^{\circ\circ} \approx v^{1/2}\,\overline{a}_x(\tau+1/2)^{\circ\circ}, \quad (I\ddot{a})_x{}^{\circ\circ} \approx u^{1/2}\,\overline{a}_x(\tau+1/2)^{\circ\circ}. \tag{22}$$

However we recall that the evaluation of ruin probabilities is based on long term estimates which can only be very approximative (such as the future true interest rate, treated as being constant, and the future evolution of the portfolio). Then it is not very coherent to handle particular points with exaggerated precision.

Elimination of deferred or temporary life annuities and life insurances

It is convenient to avoid deferred and temporary life insurances and life annuities by the consideration of general capital-functions C_τ and c_τ.

For instance, $${}_{s|t}\overline{A}_x{}^{\circ\circ} \equiv \overline{A}_x(C_\tau)^{\circ\circ}$$

if C_τ is defined by the conditions: $C_\tau \equiv 0$ on $[0,s[$, $C_\tau \equiv 1$ on $[s,s+t[$ and $C_\tau \equiv 0$ on $[s+t,\infty[$.

Replacement of life annuities by life insurances

Expressions of variances of life insurances are very simple. It is convenient to eliminate the annuities by formulas of Ch.7. Formula Ch.7.(20), with s=0 and t=∞ will be most useful:

$$\overline{a}_x(c_\tau)^\circ = C_0 - \overline{A}_x(C_\tau)^\circ \quad (C_\tau \text{ and } c_\tau \text{ associated capital functions}). \qquad (23)$$

Discretizations by ^-approximations

Variances are expectations $E\varphi(X)$. In numerical evaluations, they are approximated by $E\varphi(\hat{X})$.

Estimation of squared present values

The variance of any time-capital $Q^{\circ\circ}$ is the variance of its present value Q° and the latter equals

$$\mathrm{Var}(Q^\circ) = E(Q^\circ)^2 - E^2(Q^\circ) = E(Q^\circ)^2 - Q^2,$$

where Q is the price $E(Q^\circ)$ of $Q^{\circ\circ}$. By the foregoing Chapters, we know how to calculate prices. The new problem is the evaluation of the expected value of squared present values $(Q^\circ)^2$.

10.13. Deferred life capital

$${}_tE_x{}^\circ = 1_{X>t}\, v^t\,,\ ({}_tE_x{}^\circ)^2 = 1_{X>t}\, v^{2t} = 1_{X>t}\, v'^t = {}_tE_x(i')^\circ.$$

Hence $$\mathrm{Var}({}_tE_x{}^\circ) = {}_tE_x(i') - ({}_tE_x)^2. \qquad (24)$$

10.14. General life insurance

$$\bar{A}_x(C_\tau)^\circ = C_X v^X,\quad [\bar{A}_x(C_\tau)^\circ]^2 = (C_X)^2 v^{2X} = (C_X)^2 v'^X = \bar{A}_x(C_\tau^2, i')^\circ.$$

Hence, $$\mathrm{Var}[\bar{A}_x(C_\tau)^\circ] = \bar{A}_x(C_\tau^2, i') - [\bar{A}_x(C_\tau)]^2. \qquad (25)$$

We observe that $C^2_\tau = C_\tau$ if C_τ takes only values 0 and 1. Hence

$$\mathrm{Var}({}_{s|t}\bar{A}_x^\circ) = {}_{s|t}\bar{A}_x(i') - ({}_{s|t}\bar{A}_x)^2. \qquad (26)$$

10.15. Life annuities

We consider the general anuuity $\bar{a}_x(c_\tau)^{\circ\circ}$. Let C_τ be an associated capital-function (defined up to an additive constant) of c_τ. By (23),

$$\bar{a}_x(c_\tau)^\circ = C_0 - \bar{A}_x(C_\tau)^\circ,\ \mathrm{Var}[\bar{a}_x(c_\tau)^\circ] = \mathrm{Var}[\bar{A}_x(C_\tau)^\circ], \qquad (27)$$

where the latter variance results from (25). We recall that $\bar{A}_x(C_\tau)^\circ = C_X v^X$.

Constant life annuity

We consider the annuity ${}_{s|t}\bar{a}_x^{\circ\circ}$. This is $\bar{a}_x(c_\tau)^{\circ\circ}$ with c_τ defined as follows:

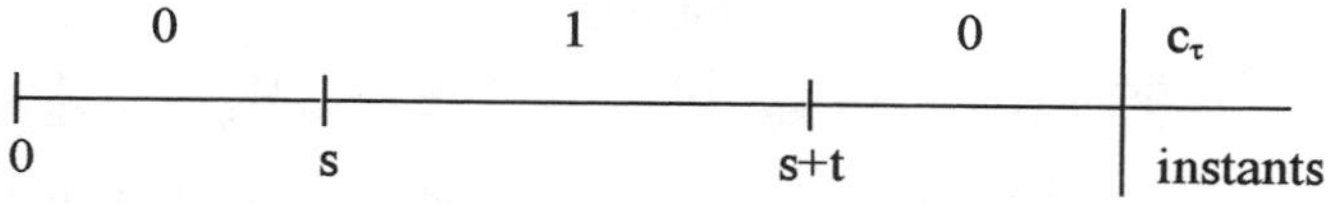

(28)

Then $C_\tau v^\tau$ is any **continuous function** such that

$$\partial/\partial\tau (C_\tau v^\tau) = -\, c_\tau v^\tau$$

(at isolated points excepted). Hence, we can adopt for $C_\tau v^\tau$ the following function:

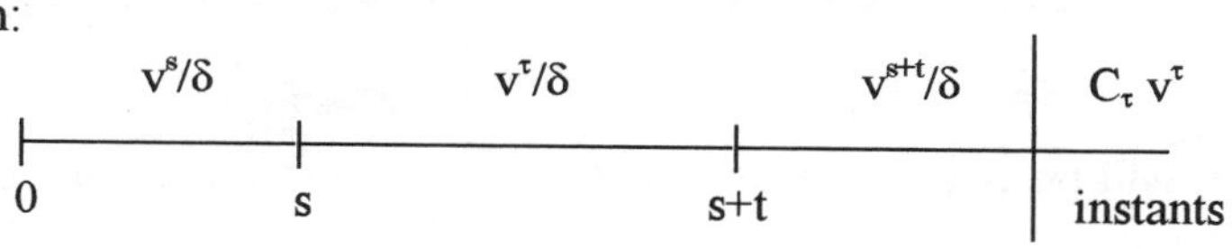

(29)

and then C_τ is the function

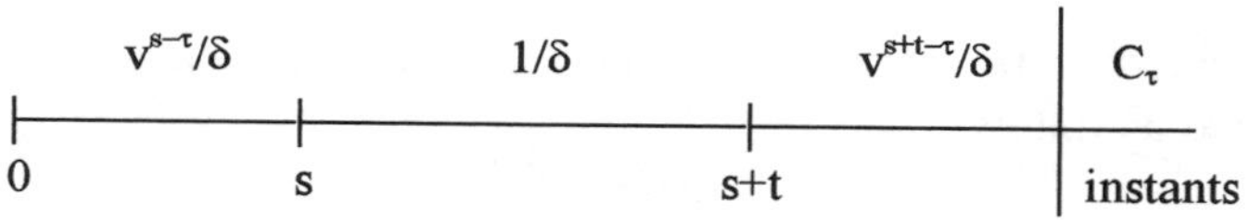

(30)

Then

$${}_{s|t}\bar{a}_x^\circ = C_0 - \bar{A}_x(C_\tau)^\circ,\quad \mathrm{Var}({}_{s|t}\bar{a}_x^\circ) = \bar{A}_x(C_\tau^2, i')^\circ - [\bar{A}_x(C_\tau)^\circ]^2. \qquad (31)$$

The function C_τ can be eliminated in the last member of (31). Indeed,

$$\bar{A}_x(C_\tau) = {}_s\bar{A}_x(C_\tau) + {}_{s|t}\bar{A}_x(C_\tau) + {}_{t|}\bar{A}_x(C_\tau)$$

and
$$\bar{A}_x(C_\tau^2,i') = {}_s\bar{A}_x(C_\tau^2,i') + {}_{s|t}\bar{A}_x(C_\tau^2,i') + {}_{s+t|}\bar{A}_x(C_\tau^2,i'),$$

where

$${}_s\bar{A}_x(C_\tau) = (1/\delta)\int_{(0,s)} v^{s-\tau}\, v^\tau\, d\, {}_\tau q_x = (v^s/\delta)\int_{(0,s)} d\, {}_\tau q_x = v^s\, {}_s q_x/\delta = (v^s - {}_sE_x)/\delta,$$

$${}_{s|t}\bar{A}_x(C_\tau) = {}_{s|t}\bar{A}_x/\delta,$$

$${}_{s+t|}\bar{A}_x(C_\tau) = (1/\delta)\int_{(s+t,\infty)} v^{s+t-\tau}\, v^\tau\, d\, {}_\tau q_x = (v^{s+t}/\delta)\int_{(s+t,\infty)} d\, {}_\tau q_x$$

$$= v^{s+t}\, {}_{s+t}p_x/\delta = {}_{s+t}E_x/\delta,$$

$${}_s\bar{A}_x(C_\tau^2,i') = (1/\delta^2)\int_{(0,s)} v^{2(s-\tau)}\, v'^\tau\, d\, {}_\tau q_x = (v'^s/\delta^2)\int_{(0,s)} d\, {}_\tau q_x$$

$$= v'^s\, {}_s q_x/\delta^2 = [v'^s - {}_sE_x(i')]/\delta^2,$$

$${}_{s|t}\bar{A}_x(C_\tau^2,i') = {}_{s|t}\bar{A}_x(i')/\delta^2,$$

$${}_{s+t|}\bar{A}_x(C^2_\tau,i') = (1/\delta^2)\int_{(s+t,\infty)} v^{2(s+t-\tau)}\, v'^\tau\, d\, {}_\tau q_x = (v'^{s+t}/\delta^2)\int_{(s+t,\infty)} d\, {}_\tau q_x$$

$$= v'^{s+t}\, {}_{s+t}p_x/\delta^2 = {}_{s+t}E_x(i')/\delta^2.$$

Then by (31),
$$\delta^2\, \mathrm{Var}({}_{s|t}\bar{a}_x{}^\circ)$$
$$= v'^s - {}_sE_x(i') + {}_{s+t}E_x(i') + {}_{s|t}\bar{A}_x(i') - [v^s - {}_sE_x + {}_{s+t}E_x + {}_{s|t}\bar{A}_x]^2. \qquad (32)$$

${}_{s|t}A_x$ and ${}_{s|t}A_x(i')$ can be eliminated by the relation Ch.7.(1) and by the corresponding relation for interest rate i′ (with δ'=2i). Then

$$\delta^2\, \mathrm{Var}({}_{s|t}\bar{a}_x{}^\circ) = 2\delta[v^s\, {}_{s|t}\bar{a}_x - {}_{s|t}\bar{a}_x(i')] - \delta^2\, ({}_{s|t}\bar{a}_x)^2. \qquad (33)$$

It is not necessary to introduce the function C_τ in order to obtain (32) or (33). Indeed, one can start directly from the relation Ch.7.(6), displayed as

$${}_{s|t}\bar{A}_x{}^\circ = 1_{s<X}\, v^s - 1_{s+t<X}\, v^{s+t} - \delta\, 1_{s<X\le s+t}\, v^X.$$

However, it will be clear in section 10.16 why it is preferable to work with functions c_τ and C_τ.

Particular case: deferred life capital

When variances are considered, the deferred life capital can be approximated as follows

$${}_sE_x{}^{\circ\circ} = {}_{s|1}\ddot{a}_x{}^{\circ\circ} \approx u^{1/2}\, {}_{s|1}\bar{a}_x{}^{\circ\circ}.$$

Then
$${}_{s|1}\bar{a}_x{}^\circ = C_0 - \bar{A}_x(C_\tau)^\circ,\quad \mathrm{Var}({}_{s|1}\bar{a}_x{}^\circ) = \mathrm{Var}[\bar{A}_x(C_\tau)^\circ], \qquad (34)$$

where C_τ is defined as

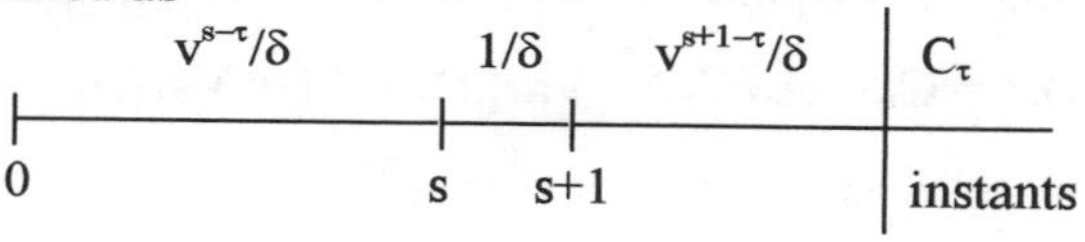

$$\begin{array}{cccc} v^{s-\tau}/\delta & 1/\delta & v^{s+1-\tau}/\delta & C_\tau \\ \vdash\!\!\!-\!\!\!-\!\!\!-\!\!\!-\!\!\!-\!\!\!+\!\!\!-\!\!\!-\!\!\!-\!\!\!+\!\!\!-\!\!\!-\!\!\!-\!\!\!-\!\!\!-\!\!\!| & & \\ 0 & s \quad s+1 & & \text{instants} \end{array} \qquad (35)$$

Classical variable life annuities

We consider the variable annuities with continuous capital-function defined by Ch.7.(24), (25) and (26).

a. In case of $_{s|t}(\bar{I}\,\bar{a})_x^{\circ\circ}$, c_τ equals $\tau-s$ on the interval $[s,s+t]$. The derivative of function $-C_\tau v^\tau$ must be $c_\tau v^\tau = (\tau-s)v^\tau$ on that interval. Hence, we can take

$$C_\tau v^\tau = (1-\delta s+\delta\tau)v^\tau/\delta^2 \quad (s\leq\tau\leq s+t). \qquad (36)$$

The function $C_\tau v^\tau$ must be continuous on $[0,\infty[$ and its derivative must be equal to 0 on $[0,s[$ and on $]s+t,\infty[$. Hence, the function equals $C_\tau v^\tau \equiv C_s v^s$ on $[0,s]$ and $C_\tau v^\tau \equiv C_{s+t}v^{s+t}$ on $[s+t,\infty]$, where C_s and C_{s+t} result from (36). Finally, C_τ is defined as follows:

$$\begin{array}{cccc} v^{s-\tau}/\delta^2 & (1-\delta s+\delta\tau)/\delta^2 & (1+\delta t)v^{s+t-\tau}/\delta^2 & C_\tau \\ \vdash\!\!\!-\!\!\!-\!\!\!-\!\!\!-\!\!\!+\!\!\!-\!\!\!-\!\!\!-\!\!\!-\!\!\!-\!\!\!-\!\!\!+\!\!\!-\!\!\!-\!\!\!-\!\!\!-\!\!\!-\!\!\!-\!\!\!| & & \\ 0 & s & s+t & \text{instants} \end{array} \qquad (37)$$

Then

$$_{s|t}(\bar{I}\,\bar{a})_x^\circ = C_0 - \bar{A}_x(C_\tau)^\circ, \quad \mathrm{Var}[_{s|t}(\bar{I}\,\bar{a})_x^\circ] = \mathrm{Var}[\bar{A}_x(C_\tau)^\circ]. \qquad (38)$$

b. In case of $(\bar{I}_{\overline{t}|}\bar{a})_x^{\circ\circ}$, c_τ equals τ on interval $[0,t]$ and t on $[t,\infty[$. The derivative of $-C_\tau v^\tau$ must be τv^τ on $[0,t[$ and tv^τ on $]t,\infty[$. Moreover, $C_\tau v^\tau$ must be continuous on $[0,\infty[$. Hence, we can take

$$C_\tau v^\tau = (1+\delta\tau)v^\tau/\delta^2 \quad (0\leq\tau\leq t) \qquad (39)$$

and we must have

$$C_\tau v^\tau = \mathrm{const.} + tv^\tau/\delta \quad (t\leq\tau). \qquad (40)$$

Then for $\tau=t$,

$$(1+\delta t)v^t/\delta^2 = \mathrm{const.} + tv^t/\delta.$$

Hence, const.$=v^t/\delta^2$ and C_τ is defined as follows:

$$\begin{array}{ccc} (1+\delta\tau)/\delta^2 & (v^{t-\tau}+\delta t)/\delta^2 & C_\tau \\ \vdash\!\!\!-\!\!\!-\!\!\!-\!\!\!-\!\!\!-\!\!\!+\!\!\!-\!\!\!-\!\!\!-\!\!\!-\!\!\!-\!\!\!-\!\!\!| & & \\ 0 & t & \text{instants} \end{array} \qquad (41)$$

Then

$$(\bar{I}_{\overline{t}|}\bar{a})_x^\circ = C_0 - \bar{A}_x(C_\tau)^\circ, \quad \mathrm{Var}[(\bar{I}_{\overline{t}|}\bar{a})_x^\circ] = \mathrm{Var}[\bar{A}_x(C_\tau)^\circ]. \qquad (42)$$

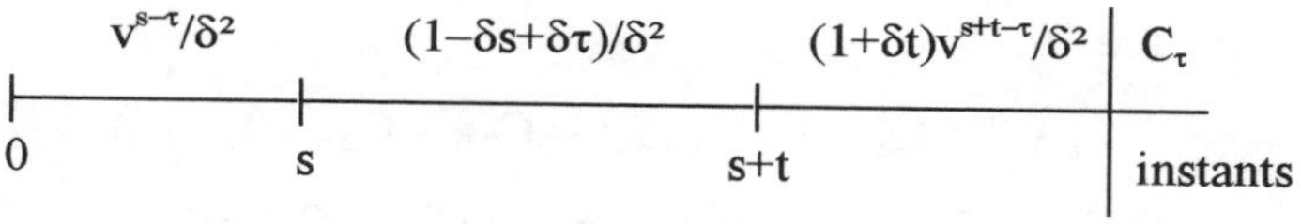

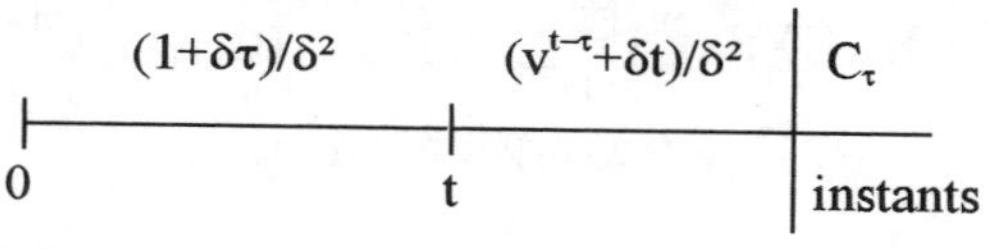

c. In case of ${}_s(\bar{D}\bar{a})_x^{\circ\circ}$, c_τ equals $s-\tau$ on $[0,s]$ and 0 on $[s,\infty[$. Then

$$ {}_s(\bar{D}\bar{a})_x^{\circ} = C_0 - \bar{A}_x(C_\tau)^{\circ}, \quad \mathrm{Var}[{}_s(\bar{D}\bar{a})_x^{\circ}] = \mathrm{Var}[\bar{A}_x(C_\tau)^{\circ}] \tag{43} $$

if C_τ is defined as follows:

0 ———	——— s ———	
$(\delta s-\delta\tau-1)/\delta^2$	$-v^{s-\tau}/\delta^2$	C_τ
0	s	instants

(44)

10.16. Variance of reserves

As an illustration we show how to calculate the variance $\mathrm{Var}({}_{\bullet 0|}V_x^{\circ})$ of contract

$$ (\alpha\, {}_n\bar{A}_x^{\circ\circ} + \beta\, {}_nE_x^{\circ\circ} + \gamma\, {}_{n|}a_x^{\circ\circ},\ p\, {}_m\ddot{a}_x^{\circ\circ}) \quad (m \le n). \tag{45} $$

The first step is to replace the contract by the theoretical continuous contract

$$ (\alpha\, {}_n\bar{A}_x^{\circ\circ} + \beta\, u^{1/2}\, {}_{n|1}\bar{a}_x^{\circ\circ} + \gamma\, v^{1/2}\, {}_{n|}\bar{a}_x^{\circ\circ},\ \bar{p}\, u^{1/2}\, {}_m\bar{a}_x^{\circ\circ}). \tag{46} $$

The second step is the introduction of capital-functions $C_{1,\tau}$, $C_{2,\tau}$, $C_{3,\tau}$ and $C_{4,\tau}$ such that (see 10.15)

$$ {}_n\bar{A}_x^{\circ} = C_{1,X}\, v^X, \quad {}_{n|1}\bar{a}_x^{\circ} = C_{2,0} - C_{2,X}\, v^X, $$

$$ {}_{n|}\bar{a}_x^{\circ} = C_{3,0} - C_{3,X}\, v^X, \quad {}_m\bar{a}_x^{\circ} = C_{4,0} - C_{4,X}\, v^X. $$

Then

$$ {}_{\bullet 0|}V_x^{\circ} = \alpha\, {}_n\bar{A}_x^{\circ} + \beta\, u^{1/2}\, {}_{n|1}\bar{a}_x^{\circ} + \gamma\, v^{1/2}\, {}_{n|}\bar{a}_x^{\circ} - \bar{p}\, u^{1/2}\, {}_m\bar{a}_x^{\circ} = \text{const.} + C_X\, v^X, $$

with

$$ C_\tau := \alpha\, C_{1,\tau} - \beta\, u^{1/2}\, C_{2,\tau} - \gamma\, v^{1/2}\, C_{3,\tau} + \bar{p}\, u^{1/2}\, C_{4,\tau}\,. $$

Then

$$ \mathrm{Var}({}_{\bullet 0|}V_x^{\circ}) = E(C_X\, v^X)^2 - E^2(C_X\, v^X) $$

and then the last step is the numerical evaluation of the expectations in the last member by ^-approximations:

$$ E(C_X\, v^X) \approx E(C_{\hat{X}}\, v^{\hat{X}}) = \sum_{k\ge 0} \int_{(k,k+1)} C_{k+1/2}\, v^{k+1/2}\, d_\tau q_x $$

$$ = \sum_{k\ge 0} C_{k+1/2}\, v^{k+1/2}\, \Delta_k q_x\,, $$

$$ E(C_X\, v^X)^2 \approx E[(C_{\hat{X}})^2\, v^{2\hat{X}}] = \sum_{k\ge 0} \int_{(k,k+1)} (C_{k+1/2})^2\, v^{2k+1}\, d_\tau q_x $$

$$ = \sum_{k\ge 0} (C_{k+1/2})^2\, v^{2k+1}\, \Delta_k q_x\,. $$

Chapter 11

INSURANCES ON A STATUS (SEVERAL LIVES)

11.1. Definition of a status

We consider several lives x, y, ..., z with future lifetimes X, Y, ..., Z resp. A **status on the lives x, y, ..., z** is a fictitious life ρ, such that the event $\rho\uparrow t$ ($:\Leftrightarrow$ ρ is alive at t), depending on X, Y, ..., Z, is defined for all t≥0. Then the event $\rho\downarrow t$ ($:\Leftrightarrow$ ρ is dead at t) is the negation of event $\rho\uparrow t$:

$$\rho\downarrow t \;:\Leftrightarrow \text{not}(\rho\uparrow t) \Leftrightarrow: (\rho\uparrow t)| ,$$

where the notation of App.B (*Multiple events*) is used. Hence, the status ρ can equally well be defined by the events $\rho\downarrow t$ (t≥0) as by the events $\rho\uparrow t$ (t≥0).

The statuses on one life are x and x|. They are defined by the equivalences

$$x\uparrow t :\Leftrightarrow X > t \quad \text{and} \quad x|\uparrow t :\Leftrightarrow x\downarrow t.$$

The following are statuses on two lives x and y.

$$xy\ ,\ \overline{xy}\ ,\ x|y\ ,\ x|y|\ ,\ \overline{xy}^{[1]},\ \overset{1}{x}y\ ,\ x\overset{1}{y}\ ,\ \overset{2}{x}y\ ,\ x\overset{2}{y}.$$

They are defined by the equivalences (the notation of App.B is used).

$$xy\uparrow t :\Leftrightarrow x\uparrow t \text{ and } y\uparrow t \Leftrightarrow: x\uparrow t,\ y\uparrow t,$$

$$\overline{xy}\uparrow t :\Leftrightarrow x\uparrow t \text{ or } y\uparrow t \Leftrightarrow: \overline{x\uparrow t,\ y\uparrow t},$$

$$x|y\uparrow t :\Leftrightarrow x|\uparrow t \text{ and } y\uparrow t \Leftrightarrow x\downarrow t \text{ and } y\uparrow t \Leftrightarrow: x\downarrow t,\ y\uparrow t,$$

$$x|y|\uparrow t :\Leftrightarrow x|\uparrow t \text{ and } y|\uparrow t \Leftrightarrow x\downarrow t \text{ and } y\downarrow t \Leftrightarrow: x\downarrow t,\ y\downarrow t,$$

$$\overline{xy}^{[1]}\uparrow t :\Leftrightarrow \text{exactly one life is alive at t} \Leftrightarrow: \overline{x\uparrow t,\ y\uparrow t}^{[1]}$$

$$\overset{1}{x}y\downarrow t :\Leftrightarrow x\downarrow t \text{ and } X<Y,$$

$$\overset{2}{x}y\downarrow t :\Leftrightarrow x\downarrow t \text{ and } Y<X,$$

The following equivalences define statusses on three lives x, y and z.

$$xyz\uparrow t :\Leftrightarrow x\uparrow t \text{ and } y\uparrow t \text{ and } z\uparrow t \Leftrightarrow: x\uparrow t, y\uparrow t, z\uparrow t,$$

$$\overline{xyz}\uparrow t :\Leftrightarrow x\uparrow t \text{ or } y\uparrow t \text{ or } z\uparrow t \Leftrightarrow: \overline{x\uparrow t, y\uparrow t, z\uparrow t},$$

$$\overline{xyz}^{k}\uparrow t :\Leftrightarrow \text{at least k lives are alive} \Leftrightarrow: \overline{x\uparrow t, y\uparrow t, z\uparrow t}^{k} \quad \text{where } k=0,1,2 \text{ or } 3.$$

$$\overline{xyz}^{[k]}\uparrow t :\Leftrightarrow \text{exactly k lives are alive} \Leftrightarrow: \overline{x\uparrow t, y\uparrow t, z\uparrow t}^{[k]} \quad \text{where } k=0,1,2 \text{ or } 3.$$

Simple statusses σ

A status σ is **simple** if it is alive on some interval $[0,T[$ and dead on $[T,\infty[$, where T may take the value $+\infty$. Then $T\equiv T_\sigma$ is the **instant of death** of σ. The status does not die if $T=\infty$. Any positive function $T=f(X,Y,\ldots,Z)$ defines a simple status σ on the lives x, y, ..., z. Then $\sigma\downarrow t:\Leftrightarrow T\leq t$. Hence, any simple status is a status according to the initial definition.

The following statuses xy, $\overline{xy}$, $\overset{1}{x}y$, $\overset{2}{x}y$, xyz, $\overline{xyz}$ are simple with instant of death

$$T_{xy} := X\wedge Y, \quad T_{\overline{xy}} := X\vee Y,$$

$$T_{\overset{1}{x}y} := 1_{X<Y}\,X + 1_{(X<Y)|}.\infty, \quad T_{\overset{2}{x}y} := 1_{Y<X}\,X + 1_{(Y<X)|}.\infty,$$

$$T_{xyz} := X\wedge Y\wedge Z, \quad T_{\overline{xyz}} := X\vee Y\vee Z.$$

The simple statuses

$$\overset{1}{x}y \ , \ \overset{2}{x}y \ , \ \overset{1}{x}\underset{2}{y}z \ , \ \overset{2}{x}\underset{1}{y}z \ , \ \overset{3}{x}yz \ , \ \ldots$$

are defined by the following general rule. The death of the status coincides with the death of the life with superior index if the lives die in the order indicated by all indices, otherwise the status does not die. For instance,

$$T_{\overset{2}{x}\underset{1}{y}z} := 1_{Z<X<Y}\,X + 1_{(Z<X<Y)|}.\infty.$$

The theoretical status $\overset{1}{x}y\underset{2}{z}$ cannot be considered in practice, because it is not necessarily known at the moment of death of x whether the status dies or not at that moment.

The status xy...z is alive at t iff all lives x, y, ..., z are alive at t. The statuses x, xy, xyz, ... are **joint-life statuses** or **statuses dying at first decease**. The status $\overline{xy...z}$ is alive at t if at least one life x, y, ..., z is alive at t. The statuses x, $\overline{xy}$, $\overline{xyz}$, ... are **last-survivor statuses** or **statuses dying at last decease**.

Deterministic lives

$\overline{t|}$ denotes the simple status with instant of death $T_{\overline{t|}} := t$. It can be used in the construction of other statuses. Hence, $\overset{1}{x}\overline{t|}$ dies with x if x dies before t, $\overset{2}{x}\overline{t|}$ dies with x if x dies after t, $x\overset{1}{\overline{t|}}$ dies at t if x is still alive at t and $x\overset{2}{\overline{t|}}$ dies at t if x is already dead at t.

11.2. Probabilities on a status

We represent by ρ any status and by σ a simple status.

$$ {}_tp_\rho := P(\rho\uparrow t), \tag{1}$$

$$ {}_tq_\rho := P(\rho\downarrow t) = 1 - {}_tp_\rho . \tag{2}$$

$$ {}_tp_\sigma := P(\sigma\uparrow t) = P(\, T_\sigma > t\,), \tag{3}$$

$$ {}_tq_\sigma := P(\sigma\downarrow t) = P(T_\sigma \le t), \tag{4}$$

$$ \Delta\, {}_{s+k}q_\sigma = P(s+k < T_\sigma \le s+k+1), \tag{5}$$

$$ d\, {}_\tau q_\sigma = P(T_\sigma \in d\tau). \tag{6}$$

Reducible statuses

For A:=x↑t, B:=y↑t and C:=z↑t in the formulas App.C.(10)–(18):

$$ 1_{x|\uparrow t} = 1 - 1_{x\uparrow t}, \tag{7}$$

$$ 1_{x|y\uparrow t} = 1_{y\uparrow t} - 1_{xy\uparrow t}, \tag{8}$$

$$ 1_{\overline{xy}\uparrow t} = 1_{x\uparrow t} + 1_{y\uparrow t} - 1_{xy\uparrow t}, \tag{9}$$

$$ 1_{\overline{xy}^{[1]}\uparrow t} = 1_{x\uparrow t} + 1_{y\uparrow t} - 2.1_{xy\uparrow t}, \tag{10}$$

$$ 1(\overline{xyz}^{\,1}\uparrow t) = (1_{x\uparrow t} + 1_{y\uparrow t} + 1_{z\uparrow t}) - (1_{xy\uparrow t} + 1_{yz\uparrow t} + 1_{zx\uparrow t}) + 1_{xyz\uparrow t} \tag{11}$$

$$ 1(\overline{xyz}^{\,2}\uparrow t) = (1_{xy\uparrow t} + 1_{yz\uparrow t} + 1_{zx\uparrow t}) - 2.1_{xyz\uparrow t} \tag{12}$$

$$ 1(\overline{xyz}^{\,[1]}\uparrow t) = (1_{x\uparrow t} + 1_{y\uparrow t} + 1_{z\uparrow t}) - 2(1_{xy\uparrow t} + 1_{yz\uparrow t} + 1_{zx\uparrow t}) + 3.1_{xyz\uparrow t} \tag{13}$$

$$ 1(\overline{xyz}^{\,[2]}\uparrow t) = (1_{xy\uparrow t} + 1_{yz\uparrow t} + 1_{zx\uparrow t}) - 3.1_{xyz\uparrow t} \tag{14}$$

In these formulas, x, y and z may be replaced by statuses ρ, ρ′, ρ″. For instance, by (8),

$$ 1_{\rho|\rho'\uparrow t} = 1_{\rho'\uparrow t} - 1_{\rho\rho'\uparrow t}. \tag{15}$$

Of course $\quad 1_{xy\uparrow t} = 1_{x\uparrow t}.1_{y\uparrow t}, \quad 1_{xyz\uparrow t} = 1_{x\uparrow t}.1_{y\uparrow t}.1_{z\uparrow t},$ (16)

and more generally, $\quad 1_{\rho\rho'\ldots\rho''\uparrow t} = 1_{\rho\uparrow t}.1_{\rho'\uparrow t}\ldots 1_{\rho''\uparrow t}.$ (17)

Theorem 1

Let ρ, ρ_1, ..., ρ_v be statuses and α_1, ..., α_v real numbers, such that

$$1_{\rho\uparrow t} = \alpha_1\, 1_{\rho_1\uparrow t} + ... + \alpha_v\, 1_{\rho_v\uparrow t} \quad (t \geq 0). \tag{18}$$

Then $$ {}_t p_\rho = \alpha_1\, {}_t p_{\rho_1} + ... + \alpha_v\, {}_t p_{\rho_v} . \tag{19}$$

If σ, σ_1, ..., σ_v are simple statuses such that

$$1_{\sigma\uparrow t} = \alpha_1\, 1_{\sigma_1\uparrow t} + ... + \alpha_v\, 1_{\sigma_v\uparrow t} \quad (t \geq 0), \tag{20}$$

then $$\Delta\, {}_{s+k} q_\sigma = \alpha_1\, \Delta\, {}_{s+k} q_{\sigma_1} + ... + \alpha_v\, \Delta\, {}_{s+k} q_{\sigma_v} \tag{21}$$

and $$d\, {}_\tau q_\sigma = \alpha_1\, d\, {}_\tau q_{\sigma_1} + ... + \alpha_v\, d\, {}_\tau q_{\sigma_v} \tag{22}$$

Proof

(19) results from the application of E to (18). In the same way, by (20)

$$ {}_t p_\sigma = \alpha_1\, {}_t p_{\sigma_1} + \ldots + \alpha_v\, {}_t p_{\sigma_v} \ , \ {}_\tau p_\sigma = \alpha_1\, {}_\tau p_{\sigma_1} + \ldots + \alpha_v\, {}_\tau p_{\sigma_v} ,$$

and by difference,

$$({}_t p_\sigma - {}_\tau p_\sigma) = \alpha_1 ({}_t p_{\sigma_1} - {}_\tau p_{\sigma_1}) + \alpha_v ({}_t p_{\sigma_v} - {}_\tau p_{\sigma_v})$$

i.e. $$({}_\tau q_\sigma - {}_t q_\sigma) = \alpha_1 ({}_\tau q_{\sigma_1} - {}_t q_{\sigma_1}) + \alpha_v ({}_\tau q_{\sigma_v} - {}_t q_{\sigma_v})$$

We obtain (22) by differentiation with respect to τ. For $\tau := s+k+1$ and $t = s+k$, we obtain (21) •

We say that ρ is a **reducible status** if joint-life statuses ρ_1, ..., ρ_v exist such that (18) is satisfied for all $t \geq 0$. Hence, the statuses occurring in the first member of relations (8)–(14) are reducible.

For reducible statuses, the evaluation of basic probabilities (1)–(6) amounts to the evaluation of corresponding probabilities on joint-life statuses. We consider the status xy (any other joint-life status can be treated similarly). **We assume that the lives x and y are independent**, i.e. that X and Y are independent random variables (none of the foregoing relations is based on independence assumptions). The basic probabilities on status xy are

$$ {}_t p_{xy} = P(x\uparrow t, y\uparrow t) = P(x\uparrow t) P(y\uparrow t) = {}_t p_x\, {}_t p_y = (l_{x+t}\, l_{y+t})/(l_x\, l_y), \tag{23}$$

$$ {}_t q_{xy} = 1 - {}_t p_{xy} = (l_x\, l_y - l_{x+y}\, l_{y+t})/(l_x\, l_y), \tag{24}$$

$$\Delta\, {}_{s+k} q_{xy} = -\Delta\, {}_{s+k} p_{xy} = {}_{s+k} p_{xy} - {}_{s+k+1} p_{xy} \tag{25}$$

$$= (l_{x+s+k}\, l_{y+s+k} - l_{x+s+k+1}\, l_{y+s+k+1})/(l_x\, l_y) =: d_{x+s+k,y+s+k}/(l_x\, l_y), \tag{26}$$

$$({}_\tau q_{xy})' = -({}_\tau p_{xy})' = -(l_{x+\tau} l_{y+\tau})'/(l_x\, l_y) = -(l'_{x+\tau}\, l_{y+\tau} + l_{x+\tau}\, l'_{y+\tau})/(l_x\, l_y)$$

$$= (\mu_{x+\tau}\, l_{x+\tau}\, l_{y+\tau} + l_{x+\tau}\, \mu_{y+\tau}\, l_{y+\tau})/(l_x\, l_y) = {}_\tau p_x\, {}_t p_y\, (\mu_{x+\tau} + \mu_{y+\tau}), \qquad (27)$$

where accents represent derivatives with respect to τ. Hence,

$$d\, {}_\tau q_{xy} = {}_\tau p_x\, {}_t p_y\, (\mu_{x+\tau} + \mu_{y+\tau}) d\tau. \qquad (28)$$

Non-reducible statuses

In case of non-reducible statusses such as $\overset{1}{x}y$, $\overset{2}{x}y$ or $\overset{2}{x}\underset{1}{y}z$, the following obvious relations are useful (supposing the lives independent)

$$d\, {}_\tau q_{\overset{1}{x}y} = {}_\tau p_y\, d\, {}_\tau q_x \qquad (29)$$

($\overset{1}{x}y$ dies in $d\tau$ if x dies in $d\tau$ and if y is till alive at τ),

$$d\, {}_\tau q_{\overset{2}{x}y} = {}_\tau q_y\, d\, {}_\tau q_x \qquad (30)$$

($\overset{2}{x}y$ dies in $d\tau$ if x dies in $d\tau$ and if y is already dead at τ),

$$d\, {}_\tau q_{\overset{2}{x}\underset{1}{y}z} = {}_\tau q_y\, {}_\tau p_z\, d\, {}_\tau q_x \qquad (31)$$

($\overset{2}{x}\underset{1}{y}z$ dies in $d\tau$ if x dies in $d\tau$ and if y is already dead and z still alive at τ).

No such simple expression exists in case of status $\underset{1}{x}y\overset{3}{z}$. Here the general method must be used. The distribution function of the triplet (X,Y,Z) is the product of the distribution functions of X, Y, Z. It is the function ${}_\xi q_x\, {}_\eta q_y\, {}_\zeta q_z$ of ξ, η, ζ. Hence

$${}_\tau q_{\underset{1}{x}y\overset{3}{z}} = P(X<Y<Z<\tau) = \iiint_{\xi<\eta<\zeta<\tau} d\, {}_\xi q_x\, d\, {}_\eta q_y\, d\, {}_\zeta q_z. \qquad (32)$$

The latter integral can be transformed in various ways.

Reduction to a twin status

We consider the status xy and we assume that the distribution of the independent random variables X and Y result from the same Makeham life table with parameters a, s, g and c (Ch.2.6). We will see that xy can often be replaced by a joint life status ww on two lives of the same age w. Indeed, it is direct that

$$[{}_t p_{xy} = {}_t p_{ww}\ (t \geq 0)] \Leftrightarrow [c^x + c^y = 2c^w] \Leftrightarrow [\mu_w = (\mu_x + \mu_y)/2].$$

Hence, if $w = w(x,y)$ results from the equation $c^x + c^y = 2c^w$, then ${}_t p_{xy} = {}_t p_{ww}$ for all $t \geq 0$. In order to find w, we can proceed as follows.

Let $x \le y$. Then relation $c^x + c^y = 2c^w$ is equivalent to relation $c^0 + c^{y-x} = c^{w-x}$.

Hence, $w(0,y-x) = w(x,y) - x, \quad w(x,y) = x + w(0,y-x)$

and the problem is reduced to the case in which one age equals 0. Hence, when numerical tables are constructed, it is sufficient to consider $w(0,x)$ for all ages x instead of $w(x,y)$ for all ages x and y.

The solution w of the equation $c^x + c^y = 2c^w$ is such that $(x+y)/2 \le w \le x \vee y$. Indeed, if the last inequality is not satisfied, then $w>x$, $w>y$ and then $2c^w > c^x + c^y$ because $c>1$. For the proof of the inequality $(x+y)/2 \le w$, we notice that

$$0 \le (c^{(x-y)/2} - 1)^2 = c^{-y}[c^x + c^y - 2c^{(x+y)/2}] = c^{-y}[2c^w - 2c^{(x+y)/2}],$$

hence, $c^w \ge c^{(x+y)/2}$.

We say that ρ and ρ' are **equivalent statuses** if ${}_tp_\rho = {}_tp_{\rho'}$ $(t \ge 0)$. Hence, xy and ww are equivalent statusses. If ρ and ρ' are equivalent, then ρ can be replaced by ρ' in relations among prices. The equivalence of xy and ww does not imply that x and y can separately be replaced by w and w. For instance, it does not imply the equivalence of $\overline{xy}$ and $\overline{ww}$.

11.3. Deferred capitals on a status

In the definitions of Ch.5.1, x can be replaced everywhere by any status ρ.

For instance, $\quad {}_sE_\rho{}^{\circ\circ} := (1_{\rho \uparrow s}, s)$

and then $\quad {}_sE_\rho = {}_sp_\rho\, v^s.$

The iterative relation Ch.5.(1) holds in case of a joint-life status,

$${}_{s+t}E_{xy} = {}_sE_{xy}\, {}_tE_{x+s,y+s}\,,$$

but not necessarily in case of other statusses. By the following Theorem, deferred capitals on reducible statusses can be reduced to deferred life capitals on joint-life statusses.

Theorem 2

Let $\rho, \rho_1, \ldots, \rho_\nu$ be statuses and $\alpha_1, \ldots, \alpha_\nu$ real numbers, such that

$$\mathbf{1_{\rho \uparrow t} = \alpha_1\, 1_{\rho_1 \uparrow t} + \ldots + \alpha_\nu\, 1_{\rho_\nu \uparrow t} \quad (t \ge 0).} \tag{33}$$

Then

$$\mathbf{{}_tE_\rho = \alpha_1\, {}_tE_{\rho_1} + \ldots + \alpha_\nu\, {}_tE_{\rho_\nu} \quad [^\circ, ^{\circ\circ}, c_\tau].} \tag{34}$$

Proof

$$ {}_tE_\rho(c_\tau)^{\circ\circ} = c_t\,(1_\rho\!\uparrow_t, t) = c_t\,(\alpha_1\, 1_{\rho_1}\!\uparrow_t + \ldots + \alpha_v\, 1_{\rho_v}\!\uparrow_t\, , t) $$
$$ = c_t\,(\alpha_1\, 1_{\rho_1}\!\uparrow_t\, , t) + \ldots + c_t\,(\alpha_v\, 1_{\rho_v}\!\uparrow_t, t) = \alpha_1\, {}_tE_{\rho_1}(c_\tau)^{\circ\circ} + \ldots + \alpha_v\, {}_tE_{\rho_n}(c_\tau)^{\circ\circ} + \ldots $$

•

The following particular cases of (34) result from (8), (9) and (10).

$$ {}_tE_{x|y} = {}_tE_y - {}_tE_{xy} \quad [{}^\circ, {}^{\circ\circ}, c_\tau], \tag{35} $$

$$ {}_tE_{\overline{xy}} = {}_tE_x + {}_tE_y - {}_tE_{xy} \quad [{}^\circ, {}^{\circ\circ}, c_\tau], \tag{36} $$

$$ {}_tE_{\overline{xy}}{}^{[1]} = {}_tE_x + {}_tE_y - 2\, {}_tE_{xy} \quad [{}^\circ, {}^{\circ\circ}, c_\tau]. \tag{37} $$

11.4. Life annuities on a status

In the definitions and general relations of Ch.5.2, Ch.5.3, Ch.5.4 and Ch.5.5, x may be replaced everywhere by any status ρ. Exceptions to this rule are the iterative relations Ch.5.(9) and Ch.5.(24) and the relations in which commutation functions are involved. One must be careful with the particularization of relations such as Ch.5.(15), (16) and (17). For instance, in case of status x|y, the relation Ch.5.(15) becomes

$$ a_{x|y}{}^{(r)} \approx a_{x|y} $$

for s=0 and n=∞. Indeed, status x|y is dead at 0, hence ${}_0E_{x|y}$=0.

By the following Theorem, resulting from (34), annuities on reducible statusses can be reduced to annuities on joint-life statusses.

Theorem 3

Let $\rho, \rho_1, \ldots, \rho_v$ be statuses and $\alpha_1, \ldots, \alpha_v$ real numbers, such that

$$ \mathbf{1_\rho\!\uparrow_t = \alpha_1\, 1_{\rho_1}\!\uparrow_t + \ldots + \alpha_v\, 1_{\rho_v}\!\uparrow_t \quad (t \geq 0).} \tag{38} $$

Then $$ \mathbf{a_\rho = \alpha_1\, a_{\rho_1} + \ldots + \alpha_v\, a_{\rho_v} \quad [{}^\circ, {}^{\circ\circ}, {}_{s|n}, \bar{}, \ddot{}, {}^{(r)}, c_\tau, \delta_\tau]} \bullet \tag{39} $$

By (8), (9) and (10), particular cases of (39) are

$$ a_{x|y} = a_y - a_{xy} \quad [{}^\circ, {}^{\circ\circ}, {}_{s|n}, \bar{}, \ddot{}, {}^{(r)}, c_\tau, \delta_\tau], \tag{40} $$

$$ a_{\overline{xy}} = a_x + a_y - a_{xy} \quad [{}^\circ, {}^{\circ\circ}, {}_{s|n}, \bar{}, \ddot{}, {}^{(r)}, c_\tau, \delta_\tau], \tag{41} $$

$$ a_{\overline{xy}}{}^{[1]} = a_x + a_y - 2\, a_{xy} \quad [{}^\circ, {}^{\circ\circ}, {}_{s|n}, \bar{}, \ddot{}, {}^{(r)}, c_\tau, \delta_\tau]. \tag{42} $$

11.5. Life insurances on a status

In the definitions and general relations of Ch.6, x may be replaced everywhere by a simple status σ. Exceptions to this rule are the iterative relations Ch.6.(11) and Ch.6.(21) and the relations in which commutation functions are involved.

By the following Theorem, insurances on reducible statusses can be reduced to insurances on joint-life statusses.

Theorem 4

Let $\sigma, \sigma_1, ..., \sigma_\nu$ be simple statuses and $\alpha_1, ..., \alpha_\nu$ real numbers, such that

$$\mathbf{1}_{\sigma\uparrow t} = \alpha_1 \mathbf{1}_{\sigma_1\uparrow t} + ... + \alpha_\nu \mathbf{1}_{\sigma_\nu\uparrow t} \ (t\geq 0). \tag{43}$$

Then

$$\bar{A}_\sigma = \alpha_1 \bar{A}_{\sigma_1} + ... + \alpha_\nu \bar{A}_{\sigma_\nu} \ [^\circ,^{\circ\circ}, {}_{s|t}, c_\tau, \delta_\tau] \tag{44}$$

and

$$\hat{A}_\sigma = \alpha_1 \hat{A}_{\sigma_1} + ... + \alpha_\nu \hat{A}_{\sigma_\nu} \ [^\circ,^{\circ\circ}, {}_{s|n}, c_\tau, \delta_\tau]. \tag{45}$$

Proof

Let T, $T_1, ..., T_\nu$ be the instant of death of $\sigma, \sigma_1, ..., \sigma_\nu$ resp. The relations

$$1_{s<T\leq s+t} = 1_{s<T} - 1_{s+t<T} = 1_{\sigma\uparrow s} - 1_{\sigma\uparrow s+t},$$

similar relations for $T_1, ..., T_\nu$ and (43) imply that

$$1_{s<T\leq s+t} = \alpha_1 1_{s<T_1\leq s+t} + ... + \alpha_\nu 1_{s<T_\nu\leq s+t}. \tag{46}$$

Then (44) and (45) result from Ch.6. (1), (2), (3), (15), (16), (17) (for a simple status instead of a life x) •

Particular cases of (44) and (45) are

$$\bar{A}_{\overline{xy}} = \bar{A}_x + \bar{A}_y - \bar{A}_{xy} \quad [^\circ,^{\circ\circ}, {}_{s|t}, c_\tau, \delta_\tau], \tag{47}$$

$$\hat{A}_{\overline{xy}} = \hat{A}_x + \hat{A}_y - \hat{A}_{xy} \quad [^\circ,^{\circ\circ}, {}_{s|t}, c_\tau, \delta_\tau]. \tag{48}$$

As an illustration, let us show how the price $\bar{A}^{\ 1}_{xy}$ is evaluated numerically. By (29),

$$
\begin{aligned}
{}_n\bar{A}^{\ 1}_{xy} &= \int_{(0,n)} v^\tau \, d\, {}_\tau q_{xy} = \int_{(0,n)} v^\tau \, {}_\tau p_y \, d\, {}_\tau q_x = \textstyle\sum_{0\leq k\leq n-1} \int_{(k,k+1)} v^\tau \, {}_\tau p_y \, d\, {}_\tau q_x \\
&\approx \textstyle\sum_{0\leq k\leq n-1} \int_{(k,k+1)} (v^k \, {}_k p_y + v^{k+1} \, {}_{k+1} p_y)/2 \ d\, {}_\tau q_x \\
&= (1/2) \textstyle\sum_{0\leq k\leq n-1} (v^k \, {}_k p_y + v^{k+1} \, {}_{k+1} p_y) \, \Delta \, {}_k q_x.
\end{aligned} \tag{49}
$$

Other linear relations than those resulting from Th.4 can exist between insurances on statusses. For instance

$$\bar{A}^{\,1}_{xy}{}^{oo} + \bar{A}^{\,2}_{xy}{}^{oo} = (1_{X<Y}\,,X) + (1_{Y<X}\,,X) = (1_{X<Y} + 1_{Y<X}\,,X) = \bar{A}_x{}^{oo}. \qquad (50)$$

Similarly

$$\bar{A}^{\,1}_{xy}(c_\tau)^{oo} + \bar{A}^{\,2}_{xy}(c_\tau)^{oo} = \bar{A}_x(c_\tau)^{oo}. \qquad (51)$$

For the systematic verification of relations such as (51), we can proceed as in the following table. We consider the two cases X<Y and Y<X and in each case we examine the amounts paid at X and at Y.

Table 11.1. Systematic verification of relations between insurances on statuses.

Cases	Instants	$\bar{A}^{\,1}_{xy}(c_\tau)^{oo}$	+	$\bar{A}^{\,2}_{xy}(c_\tau)^{oo}$	=	$\bar{A}_x(c_\tau)^{oo}$.
X<Y	X	c_X	+	0	=	c_X
X<Y	Y	0	+	0	=	0
Y<X	X	0	+	c_X	=	c_X
Y<X	Y	0	+	0	=	0

When 3 lives x, y, z are involved, the 6 cases

X<Y<Z, Y<Z<X, Z<X<Y, Y<X<Z, X<Z<Y, Z<Y<X

and in each case, the 3 instants X, Y and Z, must be examined. That makes 18 verifications.

11.6. Alternative notations

By the meaning of the statusses on usual and deterministic lives, it is clear now that

$$\bar{A}^{\,1}_{x\overline{t|}}\,,\ \bar{A}^{\,2}_{x\overline{t|}}\,,\ \bar{A}_{x\,\overset{1}{\overline{t|}}}\,,\ \bar{A}_{x\,\overset{2}{\overline{t|}}}\,,\ \bar{a}_{x\overline{t|}}\,,\ \bar{a}_{\overline{x|\overline{t|}}}\,,\ a_{x\overline{n|}}\,,\ \ddot{a}_{\overline{x|\overline{n|}}}\,,\ \ldots$$

are identical to

$${}_t\bar{A}_x\,,\ {}_{t|}\bar{A}_x\,,\ {}_tE_x\,,\ {}_tE_{\overline{x|}}\,,\ {}_t\bar{a}_x\,,\ {}_t\bar{a}_{\overline{x|}}\,,\ {}_na_x\,,\ {}_n\ddot{a}_{\overline{x|}}\,,\ \ldots$$

resp. at any level.

Chapter 12

DECOMPOSITIONS OF TIME-CAPITALS (SEVERAL LIVES)

12.1. Reserves of a time-capital on two lives

For simplicity, only time-capitals on two lives x and y are treated in this Chapter. All definitions and proofs are easily adapted to the case of more lives.

Let $Q^{\circ\circ}$ be a time-capital on x and y (life insurance components are supposed to be payable at death; however see Ch.8.6).

We denote by ${}_{s|t}Q^{\circ\circ}$ the **restriction of $Q^{\circ\circ}$ to the interval [s,s+t[**. The usual abbreviations are adopted: ${}_{0|t} \equiv {}_{t}$, ${}_{s|\infty} \equiv {}_{s|}$.

We denote by ${}_{\bullet s|t}Q^{\circ\circ}$ the restricted time-capital ${}_{s|t}Q^{\circ\circ}$ with s as a new origin of times.

We denote resp. by

$${}_{\bullet s|t}Q_{xy}{}^{\circ\circ},\quad {}_{\bullet s|t}Q_{x|y}{}^{\circ\circ},\quad {}_{\bullet s|t}Q_{y|x}{}^{\circ\circ},\quad {}_{\bullet s|t}Q_{x|y|}{}^{\circ\circ}$$

the time-capital ${}_{\bullet s|t}Q^{\circ\circ}$ evaluated under the assumption

– that x and y are alive at s,
– that x is dead at s and y alive at s,
– that y is dead at s and x alive at s,
– that x and y are dead at s

(the last case must be partitioned in two sub-cases if the order of deaths is relevant; we do not consider it).

The prices ${}_{\bullet t|}Q_{xy}$, ${}_{\bullet t|}Q_{x|y}$, ${}_{\bullet t|}Q_{y|x}$, ${}_{\bullet t|}Q_{x|y|}$ are called (mathematical) **reserves at t** under the assumptions clarified by the subscripts ${}_{xy,\ x|y,\ y|x,\ x|y|}$.

12.2. Time-capitals vanishing at first decease

The time-capital $Q^{\circ\circ}$ **vanishes at first decease** if

$${}_{\bullet t|}Q_{x|y} = {}_{\bullet t|}Q_{y|x} = {}_{\bullet t|}Q_{x|y|} = 0 \quad (t>0).$$

Examples

a. $Q^{\circ\circ} := \bar{a}_{xy}{}^{\circ\circ}$. Then

$${}_{\bullet t|}Q_{xy} = \bar{a}_{x+t,y+t}\,, \quad {}_{\bullet t}Q_{x|y} = {}_{\bullet t|}Q_{y|x} = {}_{\bullet t|}Q_{x|y|} = 0.$$

$Q^{\circ\circ}$ vanishes at first decease.

b. $Q^{\circ\circ} := \bar{A}_{xy}{}^{\circ\circ}$. Then

$${}_{\bullet t|}Q_{xy} = \bar{A}_{x+t,y+t}\,, \quad {}_{\bullet t}Q_{x|y} = {}_{\bullet t|}Q_{y|x} = {}_{\bullet t|}Q_{x|y|} = 0.$$

$Q^{\circ\circ}$ vanishes at first decease.

c. $Q^{\circ\circ} := \bar{A}^{1}_{xy}{}^{\circ\circ}$. Then

$${}_{\bullet t|}Q_{xy} = \bar{A}^{1}_{x+t,y+t}\,, \quad {}_{\bullet t}Q_{x|y} = {}_{\bullet t|}Q_{y|x} = {}_{\bullet t|}Q_{x|y|} = 0.$$

$Q^{\circ\circ}$ vanishes at first decease.

d. $Q^{\circ\circ} := \bar{a}_{\overline{xy}}{}^{\circ\circ}$. Then

$${}_{\bullet t|}Q_{xy} = \bar{a}_{\overline{x+t,y+t}}\,, \quad {}_{\bullet t|}Q_{x|y} = \bar{a}_{y+t}\,, \quad {}_{\bullet t|}Q_{y|x} = \bar{a}_{x+t}\,, \quad {}_{\bullet t|}Q_{x|y|} = 0.$$

$Q^{\circ\circ}$ does not vanish at first decease.

e. $Q^{\circ\circ} := \bar{A}^{2}_{xy}{}^{\circ\circ}$. Then

$${}_{\bullet t|}Q_{xy} = \bar{A}^{2}_{x+t,y+t}\,, \quad {}_{\bullet t|}Q_{x|y} = 0, \quad {}_{\bullet t|}Q_{y|x} = \bar{A}_{x+t}\,, \quad {}_{\bullet t|}Q_{x|y|} = 0.$$

$Q^{\circ\circ}$ does not vanish at first decease.

f. $Q^{\circ\circ} := \bar{a}_{x|y}{}^{\circ\circ}$. Then

$${}_{\bullet t|}Q_{xy} = \bar{a}_{x+t|y+t}\,, \quad {}_{\bullet t|}Q_{x|y} = \bar{a}_{y+t}\,, \quad {}_{\bullet t|}Q_{y|x} = {}_{\bullet t|}Q_{x|y|} = 0.$$

$Q^{\circ\circ}$ does not vanish at first decease.

g. $Q^{\circ\circ} := \bar{A}_{x}{}^{\circ\circ}$, regarded as a time-capital on x and y.

$${}_{\bullet t|}Q_{xy} = \bar{A}_{x+t}\,, \quad {}_{\bullet t|}Q_{x|y} = 0, \quad {}_{\bullet t|}Q_{y|x} = \bar{A}_{x+t}\,, \quad {}_{\bullet t|}Q_{x|y|} = 0.$$

$Q^{\circ\circ}$ does not vanish at first decease.

12.3. The decomposition formula

Theorem 1

Let Q be a time-capital on the lives x and y. Then

$$\mathbf{Q} = {}_{0|t}\mathbf{Q}_{xy} + {}_{t}\mathbf{E}_{xy}\ {}_{\bullet t|}\mathbf{Q}_{xy} + {}_{t}\mathbf{E}_{x|y}\ {}_{\bullet|t}\mathbf{Q}_{x|y} + {}_{t}\mathbf{E}_{y|x}\ {}_{\bullet t|}\mathbf{Q}_{y|x} + {}_{t}\mathbf{E}_{x|y|}\ {}_{\bullet|t}\mathbf{Q}_{x|y|}\,. \tag{1}$$

If $\mathbf{Q}^{\circ\circ}$ vanishes at first decease, then

$$\mathbf{Q} = {}_{0|t}\mathbf{Q}_{xy} + {}_{t}\mathbf{E}_{xy}\ {}_{\bullet t|}\mathbf{Q}_{xy}\,. \tag{2}$$

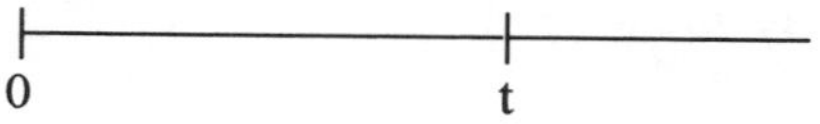

Proof

$$Q^{\circ} = {}_{t}Q^{\circ} + {}_{t|}Q^{\circ} = {}_{t}Q^{\circ} + v^{t}\ {}_{\bullet t|}Q^{\circ}$$

and then
$$E(Q^{\circ}) = E({}_{t}Q^{\circ}) + v^{t}\ E({}_{\bullet t|}Q^{\circ})$$

$$= {}_{t}Q + v^{t}\ P(x\uparrow t,\ y\uparrow t)\ E({}_{\bullet t|}Q^{\circ} / x\uparrow t,\ y\uparrow t) + v^{t}\ P(x\downarrow t,\ y\uparrow t)\ E({}_{\bullet t|}Q^{\circ} / x\downarrow t,\ y\uparrow t)$$

$$+ v^{t}\ P(x\uparrow t,\ y\downarrow t)\ E({}_{\bullet t|}Q^{\circ} / x\uparrow t,\ y\downarrow t) + v^{t}\ P(x\downarrow t,\ y\downarrow t)\ E({}_{\bullet t|}Q^{\circ} / x\downarrow t,\ y\downarrow t)$$

$$= {}_{0|t}Q_{xy} + {}_{t}E_{xy}\ {}_{\bullet t|}Q_{xy} + {}_{t}E_{x|y}\ {}_{\bullet|t}Q_{x|y} + {}_{t}E_{y|x}\ {}_{\bullet t|}Q_{y|x} + {}_{t}E_{x|y|}\ {}_{\bullet|t}Q_{x|y|} \quad \bullet$$

Corollary

Let $\mathbf{Q}^{\circ\circ}$ be a time capital on the lives x and y and let 0<s<t. Then

$$\begin{aligned} {}_{\bullet s|}\mathbf{Q} = {}_{\bullet s|t-s}\mathbf{Q}_{xy} &+ {}_{t-s}\mathbf{E}_{x+s,y+s}\ {}_{\bullet t|}\mathbf{Q}_{xy} + {}_{t-s}\mathbf{E}_{x+s|y+s}\ {}_{\bullet|t}\mathbf{Q}_{x|y} \\ &+ {}_{t-s}\mathbf{E}_{y+s|x+s}\ {}_{\bullet t|}\mathbf{Q}_{y|x} + {}_{t-s}\mathbf{E}_{x+s|y+s|}\ {}_{\bullet|t}\mathbf{Q}_{x|y|}\,. \end{aligned} \tag{3}$$

If $\mathbf{Q}^{\circ\circ}$ vanishes at first decease, then

$${}_{\bullet s|}\mathbf{Q} = {}_{\bullet s|t-s}\mathbf{Q}_{xy} + {}_{t-s}\mathbf{E}_{x+s,y+s}\ {}_{\bullet t|}\mathbf{Q}_{xy} \quad \bullet \tag{4}$$

12.4. Iterative formulas

All iterative formulas result from general decomposition formulas. For instance,

$${}_{s+t}E_{xy} = {}_{s}E_{xy}\ {}_{t}E_{x+s,y+s}\,,$$

$${}_{s|t}\bar{A}_{xy} = {}_{s}E_{xy}\ {}_{t}\bar{A}_{x+s,y+s}\,,$$

$$ {}_{s|n}a_{xy} = {}_sE_{xy}\; {}_na_{x+s,y+s}\,, $$

$$ {}_{s+t}E_{\overline{xy}} = {}_sE_{xy}\; {}_tE_{\overline{x+s,y+s}} + {}_sE_{x|y}\; {}_tE_{y+s} + {}_sE_{y|x}\; {}_tE_{x+s}\,, $$

$$ {}_{s|t}\bar{A}_{\overline{xy}} = {}_sE_{xy}\; {}_t\bar{A}_{\overline{x+s,y+s}} + {}_sE_{x|y}\; {}_t\bar{A}_{y+s} + {}_sE_{y|x}\; {}_t\bar{A}_{x+s}\,, $$

$$ {}_{s|n}a_{\overline{xy}} = {}_sE_{xy}\; {}_na_{\overline{x+s,y+s}} + {}_sE_{x|y}\; {}_na_{y+s} + {}_sE_{y|x}\; {}_na_{x+s}\,, $$

$$ {}_{s|t}\bar{A}^{\,1}_{xy} = {}_sE_{xy}\; {}_t\bar{A}^{\,1}_{x+s,y+s}\,, $$

$$ {}_{s|t}\bar{A}^{\,2}_{xy} = {}_sE_{xy}\; {}_t\bar{A}^{\,2}_{x+s,y+s} + {}_sE_{y|x}\; {}_t\bar{A}_{x+s}\,, $$

by the decomposition formula 0—s— .

12.5. Evaluation of a reserve at a non-integer instant

As in the case of one life x, it is convenient to reduce the evaluation of ${}_{\bullet k+\theta|}Q_\rho$ (ρ = xy, x|y, y|x, x|y|) to the evaluations of ${}_{\bullet k|}Q_\rho$ and ${}_{\bullet k+1|}Q_\rho$. The general version of formulas Ch.8.(6) and (7) is

$$ {}_{\bullet k+\theta|}\mathbf{Q}_\rho \approx (1-\theta)\; {}_{\bullet k|}\mathbf{Q}_\rho + \theta\; {}_{\bullet k+1|}\mathbf{Q}_\rho - [(1-\theta)\; {}_{\bullet k|1}\mathbf{Q}_\rho - {}_{\bullet k+\theta|1-\theta}\mathbf{Q}_\rho] \qquad (5) $$

$$ [\rho = \mathbf{xy},\ \mathbf{x|y},\ \mathbf{y|x},\ \mathbf{x|y|}]. $$

The justification of (5) is based on the same arguments as in Ch.8.3. As an example, we treat the case ρ=xy. By the decomposition formula k+θ—k+1— combined with linear interpolations,

$$ {}_{\bullet k+\theta|}Q_{xy} = {}_{\bullet k+\theta|1-\theta}Q_{xy} + {}_{1-\theta}E_{x+k+\theta,y+k+\theta}\; {}_{\bullet k+1|}Q_{xy} $$

$$ + {}_{1-\theta}E_{x+k+\theta|y+k+\theta}\; {}_{\bullet k+1|}Q_{x|y} + {}_{1-\theta}E_{y+k+\theta|x+k+\theta}\; {}_{\bullet k+1|}Q_{y|x} + {}_{1-\theta}E_{x+k+\theta|y+k+\theta|}\; {}_{\bullet k+1|}Q_{x|y|} $$

$$ \approx {}_{\bullet k+\theta|1-\theta}Q_{xy} + [(1-\theta)\; {}_1E_{x+k,y+k} + \theta.1]\; {}_{\bullet k+1|}Q_{xy} $$

$$ + (1-\theta)[{}_1E_{x+k|y+k}\; {}_{\bullet k+1|}Q_{x|y} + {}_1E_{y+k|x+k}\; {}_{\bullet k+1|}Q_{y|x} + {}_1E_{x+k|y+k|}\; {}_{\bullet k+1|}Q_{x|y|}] $$

Hence,

$$ {}_{\bullet k+\theta|}Q_{xy} \approx {}_{\bullet k+\theta|1-\theta}Q_{xy} + \theta\; {}_{\bullet k+1|}Q_{xy} + (1-\theta)\,R, \qquad (6) $$

where

$$ R := [{}_1E_{x+k,y+k}\; {}_{\bullet k+1|}Q_{xy}\; {}_1E_{x+k|y+k}\; {}_{\bullet k+1|}Q_{x|y} + {}_1E_{y+k|x+k}\; {}_{\bullet k+1|}Q_{y|x} + {}_1E_{x+k|y+k|}\; {}_{\bullet k+1|}Q_{x|y|}]. $$

For θ=0,

$$ {}_{\bullet k|}Q_{xy} \approx {}_{\bullet k|1}Q_{xy} + R. $$

This relation furnishes R. Then substitution in (6) furnishes (5) for ρ=xy.

12.6. Fouret's formula

Theorem 2

Let Q^{oo} be a time-capital on the lives x and y vanishing at first decease.

Then $${}_{\bullet k+1|}Q_{xy} = ({}_{\bullet k|}Q_{xy} - {}_{\bullet k|1}Q_{xy})/{}_1E_{x+k,y+k} \quad (k=0,1,2,\dots) \tag{7}$$

Proof

By the decomposition formula k—k+1—,

$${}_{\bullet k|}Q_{xy} = {}_{\bullet k|1}Q_{xy} + {}_1E_{x+k,y+k}\ {}_{\bullet k+1|}Q_x \quad \bullet$$

12.7. Thiele's formula

Theorem 3

Let Q^{oo} be a time-capital on the lives x and y vanishing at first decease.

Then $$\partial/\partial t\ {}_{\bullet t|}Q_{xy} = {}_{\bullet t|}Q_{xy}\,(\delta + \mu_{x+t} + \mu_{y+t}) - \lim_{\varepsilon\downarrow 0}\ {}_{\bullet t|\varepsilon}Q_{xy}/\varepsilon. \tag{8}$$

if the derivative exists.

Proof

By an obvious adaptaton of the proof of Ch.8.5 •

Chapter 13

LIFE INSURANCE CONTRACTS (SEVERAL LIVES)

13.1. Life insurance contract on several lives

A **life insurance contract** on the lifes x, y, ..., z is a couple $(C^{\circ\circ},P^{\circ\circ})$ of time-capitals $C^{\circ\circ}$ and $P^{\circ\circ}$ depending on x, y, ..., z. The time-capital $C^{\circ\circ}$ is the **engagement of the insurer** to be paid to the insureds x, y, ..., z and $P^{\circ\circ}$ is the **engagement of the insureds**. All definitions of Ch.9 and most results of that Chapter extend to the case of several lives. Here we recall and adapt some considerations in case of two lives x and y only.

In a case of a **single premium contract** the insureds pay a single premium P at the subscription time 0. Hence, then $P^{\circ\circ}:=(1,P)$. We use the notation $(C^{\circ\circ},P)$, instead of $(C^{\circ\circ},(0,P))$ for single premium contracts. Very often

$$P^{\circ\circ} := p\ {}_n\ddot{a}_{xy}{}^{\circ\circ} \ \text{ or } \ P^{\circ\circ} := p\ {}_n\ddot{a}_{xy}{}^{(r)\circ\circ}.$$

A **fair contract** is a contract satisfying the **equivalence principle** C=P. This principle allows to fix the premiums. All contracts are supposed to be fair.

As an example, we consider the contract

$$(\bar{A}^{\,1}_{xy}{}^{\circ\circ},\ p\ {}_n\ddot{a}_{xy}{}^{\circ\circ}).$$

Then

$$p = \bar{A}^{\,1}_{xy}/{}_n\ddot{a}_{xy}$$

by the equivalence principle.

13.2. Reserves of a contract

Let $(C^{\circ\circ},P^{\circ\circ})$ be a contract on lives x and y. The **reserve time-capital** is $V^{\circ\circ}:=C^{\circ\circ}-P^{\circ\circ}$. We notice that V=0, because the contract is supposed to be fair: C=P.

At moment t, the following reserves can be considered:

$$_{\bullet t|}V_{xy}\,(x\uparrow t,\ y\uparrow t),\quad _{\bullet t|}V_{x|y}\,(x\downarrow t,\ y\uparrow t),\quad _{\bullet t|}V_{y|x}\,(x\uparrow t,\ y\downarrow t),\quad _{\bullet t|}V_{x|y|}\,(x\downarrow t,\ y\downarrow t).$$

(in the latter case it is assumed that the order of decease is irrelevant).

The contract vanishes at first decease if both $C^{\circ\circ}$ and $P^{\circ\circ}$ vanish at first decease.

Theorem 1

Let ($C^{\circ\circ}$,$P^{\circ\circ}$) be a contract on the lives x and y.

a. (Prospective expression of reserves)

$$_{\bullet t|}\mathbf{V}_\rho = {}_{\bullet t|}\mathbf{C}_\rho - {}_{\bullet t|}\mathbf{P}_\rho \quad (\rho = \mathbf{xy},\ \mathbf{x|y},\ \mathbf{y|x},\ \mathbf{x|y|}). \tag{1}$$

b. (Retrospective expression of reserve)

If the contract vanishes at first decease,

$$_{\bullet t|}\mathbf{V}_{xy} = ({}_{\bullet 0|t}\mathbf{P}_{xy} - {}_{\bullet 0|t}\mathbf{C}_{xy})/{}_t\mathbf{E}_{xy}\,. \tag{2}$$

c. (Recurrent expression of reserve or Fouret's formula)

If the contract vanishes at first decease,

$$_{\bullet k+1|}\mathbf{V}_{xy} = ({}_{\bullet k|}\mathbf{V}_{xy} + {}_{\bullet k|1}\mathbf{P}_{xy} - {}_{\bullet k|1}\mathbf{C}_{xy})/{}_1\mathbf{E}_{x+k,y+k} \quad (\mathbf{k=0,1,2,\ldots}), \tag{3}$$

with $_{\bullet 0|}V_x$=V=0.

d. (Mixed expression of reserve)

If the contract vanishes at first decease,

$$_{\bullet t|}\mathbf{V}_{xy} = ({}_{\bullet 0|t}\mathbf{P}_{xy}\ {}_{\bullet t|}\mathbf{C}_{xy} - {}_{\bullet 0|t}\mathbf{C}_{xy}\ {}_{\bullet t|}\mathbf{P}_{xy})/\mathbf{P}. \tag{4}$$

Proof

Same proof as in Ch.9.2 •

13.3. Practical constraints on contracts

Contracts with strictly negative reserves at some instant t are never considered in practice. For the same reason as in the case of contracts on one life.

The reserves of single premium contracts ($C^{\circ\circ}$, P) are always positive. Indeed, then

$$_{\bullet t|}V_\rho = {}_{\bullet t|}C_\rho - {}_{\bullet t|}P_\rho = {}_{\bullet t|}C_\rho \geq 0 \quad (t>0;\ \rho = xy,\ x|y,\ y|x,\ x|y|).$$

The reserves of contract ($C^{\circ\circ}$, p $_n\ddot{a}_{xy}$) are positive if n is small enough. Indeed, in the extreme case n=1, the contract becomes a single premium contract.

13.4. Contracts with partitioned premiums

In practice, contract

$$(C^{\circ\circ},\ p^{(r)}\ {}_m\ddot{a}_{xy}^{(r)\circ\circ}) \tag{5}$$

is reduced to contract

$$(C^{\circ\circ},\ p\ {}_m\ddot{a}_{xy}^{\circ\circ}) \tag{6}$$

by the same approximations as in the case of one life (Ch.9.4).

At integer instants k, the reserves of contract (5) are approximated by those of contract (6):

$$_{\bullet k|}V_\rho^{(r)} \approx {}_{\bullet k|}V_\rho \quad (\rho = xy,\ x|y,\ y|x,\ x|y|).$$

Chapter 14

MULTIPLE DECREMENT MODELS

14.1. Extinction graphs of a group of lives

A **graph** is a finite number of **states** 0, 1, 2, ... connected by arrows. At each moment $\tau \geq 0$, exactly one state is **active**. We denote by S_τ the state which is active at τ. An arrow from state α to state β indicates that a **transition** from state α to state β can occur at some moment. Such an arrow can exist if $\alpha<\beta$ only (the latter condition is dropped in case of **graphs with returns**; see last part of section 14.3).

In **extinction graphs of a group of lives** x, y, ..., z, the **initial state** 0 is the joint-life status xy...z and the other states 1, 2, ... are statuses resulting from xy...z by decease of the involved lives.

We denote by $x_1|^\circ x_2|^\circ ... ^\circ x_m|y_1y_2...y_n$ the status which is alive at t if $x_1, x_2, ..., x_m$ are deceased at t, in the indicated order, and if $y_1, y_2, ..., y_n$ are still alive at t. Here the symbol ° connecting the deceased lives must be regarded as the first letter of "order". Hence,

$$x_1|^\circ x_2|^\circ ... ^\circ x_m|y_1y_2...y_n \uparrow t \;:\Leftrightarrow$$

$$x_1{\downarrow}t,\ x_2{\downarrow}t,\ ...,\ x_m{\downarrow}t,\ y_1{\uparrow}t,\ y_2{\uparrow}t,\ ...,\ y_n{\uparrow}t \text{ and } X_1<X_2<...<X_m,$$

where $X_1, X_2, ..., X_m$ is the future lifetime of $x_1, x_2, ..., x_m$ resp.

We recall that the order of decease is irrelevant in case of lives not connected by the symbol ° :

$$x|y|{\uparrow}t \Leftrightarrow y|x|{\uparrow}t \Leftrightarrow x{\downarrow}t \text{ and } y{\downarrow}t.$$

In a **complete** extinction graph of a group of lives x, y, ..., z, all possible states resulting from the joint-life status xy...z are considered. Some of these states may be merged in an extinction graph of a group of lives **with amalgamated states**. The notation $Gr_n(x,y,...z)$ is used for extinction graphs. Then n is the number of states of the graph.

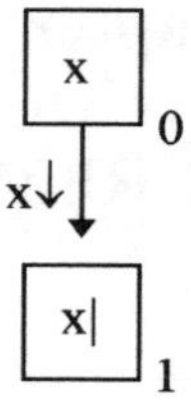

Figure 14.1. Extinction graph $Gr_2(x)$

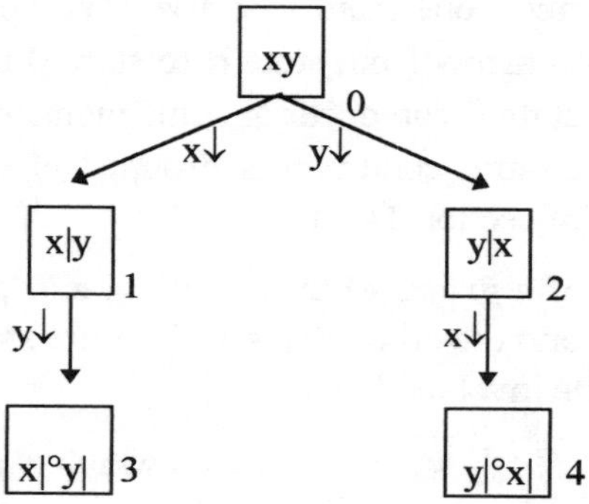

Figure 14.2. Complete extinction graph $Gr_5(x,y)$

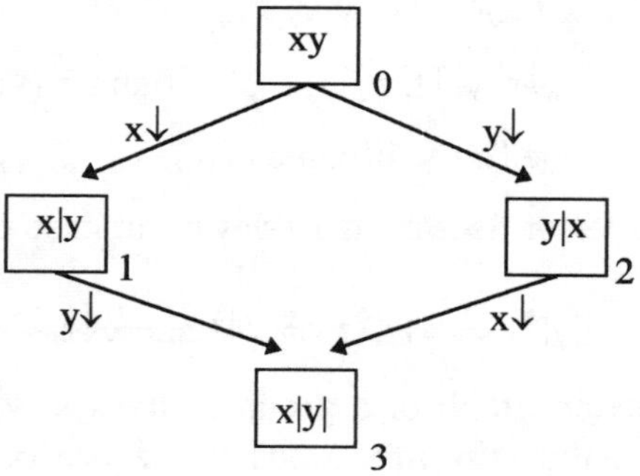

Figure 14.3. Extinction graph $Gr_4(x,y)$ with amalgamated states

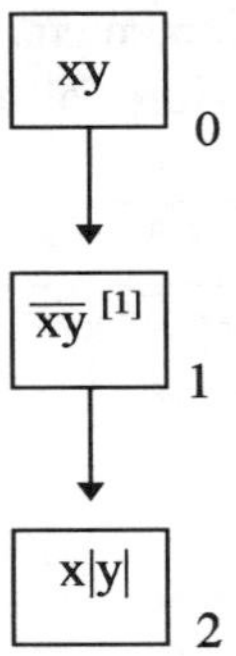

Figure 14.4. Extinction graph $Gr_3(x,y)$ with amalgamated states

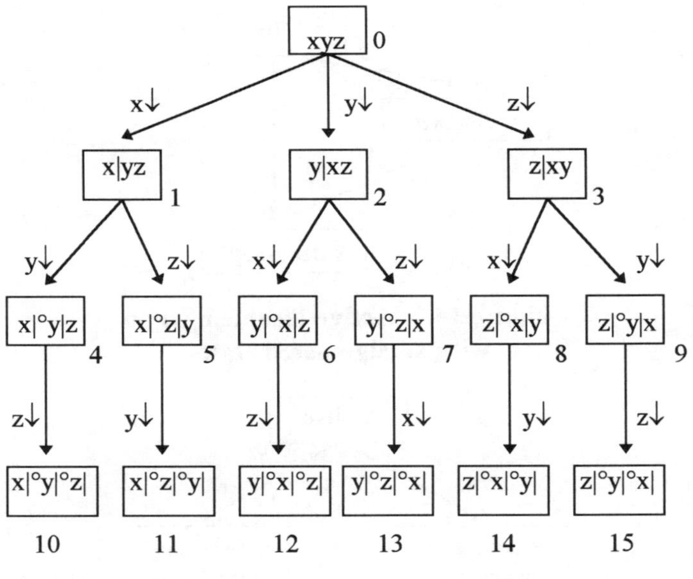

Figure 14.5. Complete extinction graph $Gr_{16}(x,y,z)$

14.2. Other graphs

Insurance models in which persons can leave some state due to one of mutually exclusive causes of decrement, i.e. **multiple decrement models** can best be pictured by graphs. Here follow some examples.

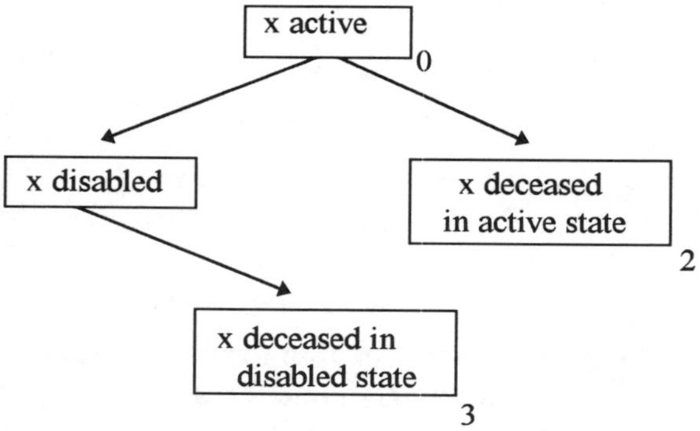

Figure 14.6. Complete active-disabled graph

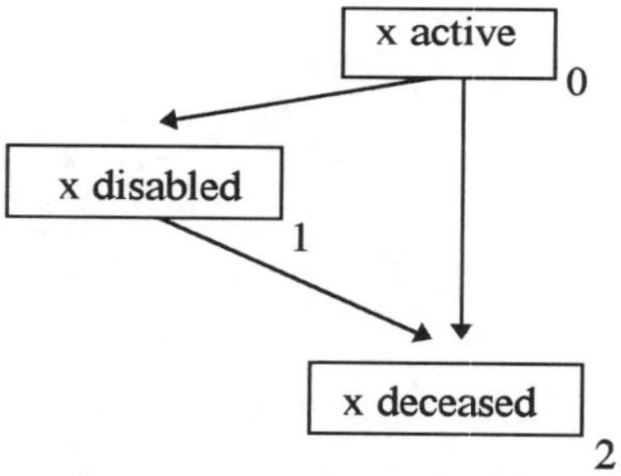

Figure 14.7. Active-disabled graph with amalgamated states

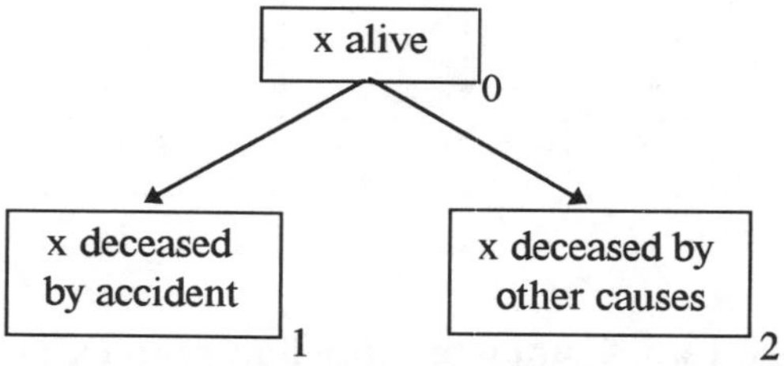

Figureure 14.8. Accidental death graph

This model is appropriate in connection with assurances which provide double indemnity on accidental death.

14.3. Events and probabilities on a graph

We consider a graph and corresponding stochastic process S_τ ($\tau \geq 0$). The states α and β are **direct successive states** if an arrow from α to β exists. Then α is a **direct predecessor** of β and β is a **direct successor** of α. For fixed β, we denote by $'\beta$ the set of direct predecessors of β. For fixed α, we denote by α' the set of direct successors of α. A **predecessor** of β is a direct predecessor of a direct predecessor ... of a direct predecessor of β. A **successor** of α is a direct successor of a direct successor ... of a direct successor of α. For fixed β, we denote by $''\beta$ the set of predecessors of β. Then $''\beta - '\beta$ is the set of predecessors of β which are not direct predecessors of β. For fixed α, we denote by α'' the set of successors of α. Then $\alpha'' - \alpha'$ is the set of successors of α which are not direct successors of α. An **initial state** is a state with no predecessors. In all our graphs, 0 is the unique initial state. A **final state** is a state with no successors.

The following are examples in $Gr_{16}(x,y,z)$.

$$'6 = \{2\}, \quad ''6 = \{0, 2\}, \quad 2' = \{6, 7\}, \quad 2'' = \{6, 7, 12, 13\}.$$

The final states of the graph are 10, 11, 12, 13, 14 and 15.

We now return to a general graph. The event $\alpha \to \beta$ is defined as follows:

$\alpha \to \beta$ occurs $:\Leftrightarrow$ A transition from α to β occurs at some moment τ

$\Leftrightarrow$ τ exists such that $S_{\tau-} = \alpha$ and $S_{\tau+} = \beta$.

α and β are any states, but it is assumed that the event $\alpha \to \beta$ can only occur if α and β are direct successive states. We denote by $T_{\alpha\to\beta} \equiv T(\alpha \to \beta)$ the **transition moment from α to β**. If no transition from α to β occurs, then $T_{a\to\beta} := \infty$. Hence, $T_{\alpha\to\beta} < \infty$ iff the event $\alpha \to \beta$ occurs. The indicator function of that event is $1_{\alpha\to\beta} \equiv 1(\alpha \to \beta)$. The random variable $T_{\alpha\to\beta}$ appears mostly in products $1_{\alpha\to\beta}\, \varphi(T_{\alpha\to\beta})$ (which are equal to 0 if no transition from α to β occurs, independently of the definition of $T_{\alpha\to\beta}$ in that case).

The event $\alpha]$ is defined as follows.

$\alpha]$ occurs $:\Leftrightarrow$

state α becomes active at some moment τ and it remains active on $]\tau,\infty[$.

The indicator function of $\alpha]$ is $1_{\alpha]} \equiv 1(\alpha])$.

Probabilities

$$ {}_t p_\alpha := P(S_t = \alpha), \quad {}_t q_{\alpha\to\beta} := P(T_{\alpha\to\beta} \le t). \tag{1}$$

Hence, the function ${}_t q_{\alpha\to\beta}$ of t is the distribution function of $T_{\alpha\to\beta}$.

$$ {}_\infty q_{\alpha\to\beta} := \lim_{t\uparrow\infty} {}_t q_{\alpha\to\beta} = P(T_{\alpha\to\beta} < \infty) = P(\alpha\to\beta) \le 1. \tag{2}$$

Random variables such as $T_{\alpha\to\beta}$ with values ∞ not excluded, and with distribution function not necessarily equal to 1 at infinity, are called **defective random variables**.

The **instantaneous transition rate from α to β at t** is the limit (supposed to exist whenever it is used)

$$ {}_t\mu_{\alpha\to\beta} := \lim_{\varepsilon\downarrow 0} (1/\varepsilon)\, P(S_{t+\varepsilon}=\beta \,/\, S_t=\alpha). \tag{3}$$

We recall that conditional probabilities can be defined arbitrarily (e.g. by 0) if the probability of the condition equals 0. Of course, ${}_t\mu_{\alpha\to\beta} = 0$ if α and β are not direct successive states. By (3),

$$ {}_t\mu_{\alpha\to\beta}\, \varepsilon \approx P(S_{t+\varepsilon}=\beta \,/\, S_t=\alpha) \tag{4}$$

for small strictly positive ε. Hence,

$$ {}_t\mu_{\alpha\to\beta}\, dt = P(S_{t+dt}=\beta \,/\, S_t=\alpha). \tag{5}$$

We observe that

$$ \mathbf{d\, {}_t q_{\alpha\to\beta} = {}_t p_\alpha\, {}_t\mu_{\alpha\to\beta}\, dt} \tag{6}$$

because a transition from α to β at t can occur only if state α is active at t and if then the transition occurs in time interval dt. More explicitly,

$$ d\, {}_t q_{\alpha\to\beta} = P(T_{\alpha\to\beta} \in dt) = P(S_t=\alpha, S_{t+dt}=\beta)$$

$$ = P(S_t=\alpha)P(S_{t+dt}=\beta \,/\, S_t=\alpha) = {}_t p_\alpha\, {}_t\mu_{\alpha\to\beta}\, dt.$$

Theorem 1 (Transition Theorem for probabilities in a graph)

For any state β of a graph,

$$ \partial/\partial t\, {}_t p_\beta = \sum_{\alpha\in'\beta} {}_t p_\alpha\, {}_t\mu_{\alpha\to\beta} - {}_t p_\beta \sum_{\gamma\in\beta'} {}_t\mu_{\beta\to\gamma} \tag{7}$$

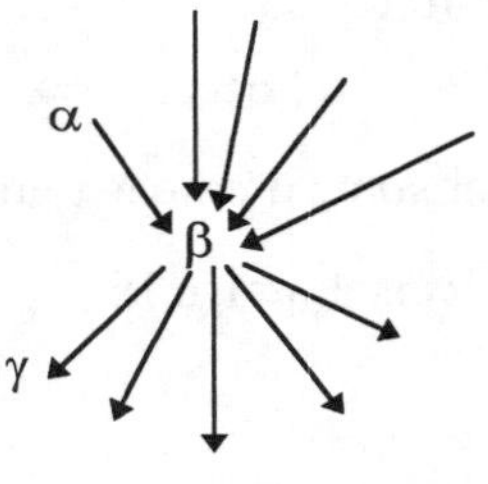

Proof

If $S_{t+\varepsilon}=\beta$, then $S_t=\beta$ or $S_t=\alpha$, where $\alpha\in''\beta$. Hence,

$$_{t+\varepsilon}p_\beta = P(S_{t+\varepsilon}=\beta) = P(S_t=\beta,\ S_{t+\varepsilon}=\beta) + \textstyle\sum_{\alpha\in''\beta} P(S_t=\alpha,\ S_{t+\varepsilon}=\beta).$$

If $S_t=\beta$, then $S_{t+\varepsilon}=\beta$ or $S_{t+\varepsilon}\gamma$, where $\gamma\in\beta''$. Hence,

$$_tp_\beta = P(S_t=\beta) = P(S_t=\beta,\ S_{t+\varepsilon}=\beta) + \textstyle\sum_{\gamma\in\beta''} P(S_t=\beta,\ S_{t+\varepsilon}=\gamma).$$

By difference,

$$_{t+\varepsilon}p_\beta - {}_tp_\beta = \textstyle\sum_{\alpha\in''\beta} P(S_t=\alpha,\ S_{t+\varepsilon}=\beta) - \sum_{\gamma\in\beta''} P(S_t=\beta,\ S_{t+\varepsilon}=\gamma)$$

$$= \textstyle\sum_{\alpha\in'\beta} P(S_t=\alpha,\ S_{t+\varepsilon}=\beta) + \sum_{\alpha\in''\beta-'\beta} P(S_t=\alpha,\ S_{t+\varepsilon}=\beta)$$
$$- \textstyle\sum_{\gamma\in\beta} P(S_t=\beta,\ S_{t+\varepsilon}=\gamma) - \sum_{\gamma\in\beta''-\beta'} P(S_t=\beta,\ S_{t+\varepsilon}=\gamma).$$

We divide by $\varepsilon>0$ and we let $\varepsilon\downarrow 0$. The conclusion is (7) because

$$(1/\varepsilon)\ P(S_t=\alpha,\ S_{t+\varepsilon}=\beta) = P(S_t=\alpha).\ P(S_{t+\varepsilon}=\beta/S_t=\alpha)/\varepsilon$$
$$\to {}_tp_\alpha\ {}_t\mu_{\alpha\to\beta} \quad (\alpha\in'\beta),$$

$$(1/\varepsilon)\ P(S_t=\alpha,\ S_{t+\varepsilon}=\beta) = P(S_t=\alpha).\ P(S_{t+\varepsilon}=\beta/S_t=\alpha)/\varepsilon \to 0 \quad (\alpha\in''\beta-'\beta),$$

$$(1/\varepsilon)\ P(S_t=\beta,\ S_{t+\varepsilon}=\gamma) = P(S_t=\beta).\ P(S_{t+\varepsilon}=\gamma/S_t=\beta)/\varepsilon$$
$$\to {}_tp_\beta\ {}_t\mu_{\beta\to\gamma} \quad (\gamma\in\beta'),$$

$$(1/\varepsilon)\ P(S_t=\beta,\ S_{t+\varepsilon}=\gamma) = P(S_t=\beta).\ P(S_{t+\varepsilon}=\gamma/S_t=\beta)/\varepsilon \to 0 \quad (\gamma\in\beta''-\beta') \bullet$$

Corollary

The probabilities $_tp_\alpha$ and $_tq_{\alpha\to\beta}$ ($t\geq 0$; $\alpha,\beta=0,1,2,...$) are determined by the instantaneous transition rates $_t\mu_{\alpha\to\beta}$ ($t\geq 0$; α and β are direct successive states).

Proof

Relation (7) is a differential equation of type App.D.(1) for $_tp_\beta$. Then $_tp_0$, $_tp_1$, $_tp_2$, ... result successively from App.D.(5) and from the initial conditions

$$_0p_0 = 1,\ \ {}_0p_1 = 0,\ \ {}_0p_2 = 0,\ \ ...$$

Then $_tq_{\alpha\to\beta}$ results from (6) and then $_tq_{\alpha\to\beta}$ is obtained by integration:

$$_tq_{\alpha\to\beta} = \int_{(0,t)} d\ {}_\tau q_{\alpha\to\beta} \quad \bullet$$

Extinction graphs

We now consider an extinction graph on the lives x, y, ..., z with future lifetimes X, Y, ..., Z resp. Then ${}_tp_\alpha$, ${}_tq_{\alpha\to\beta}$, d ${}_tq_{\alpha\to\beta}$ and ${}_t\mu_{\alpha\to\beta}$ are determined by the distribution function of (X,Y,...,Z). Explicit expressions result from the usual assumptions: X, Y, ..., Z are independent and the survival probabilities can be expressed from life tables by formulas Ch.2.(3), (but Theorem 1 is not based on such assumptions).

In the case of extinction graph $Gr_4(x,y)$,

$$ {}_tp_0 = {}_tp_{xy} = {}_tp_x\, {}_tp_y, \quad {}_tp_1 = {}_tp_{x|y} = {}_tq_x\, {}_tp_y, $$

$$ {}_tp_2 = {}_tp_{y|x} = {}_tq_y\, {}_tp_x, \quad {}_tp_3 = {}_tp_{x|y|} = {}_tq_x\, {}_tq_y, $$

$$ {}_t\mu_{0\to1} = \mu_{x+t}, \; {}_t\mu_{0\to2} = \mu_{y+t}, \; {}_t\mu_{1\to3} = \mu_{y+t}, \; {}_t\mu_{2\to3} = \mu_{x+t}, $$

$$ d\, {}_tq_{0\to1} = {}_tp_0\, {}_t\mu_{0\to1} = {}_tp_y\, {}_tp_x\, \mu_{x+t}\, dt = {}_tp_y\, d\, {}_tq_x, $$

$$ d\, {}_tq_{0\to2} = {}_tp_0\, {}_t\mu_{0\to2} = {}_tp_x\, {}_tp_y\, \mu_{y+t}\, dt = {}_tp_x\, d\, {}_tq_y, $$

$$ d\, {}_tq_{1\to3} = {}_tp_1\, {}_t\mu_{1\to3} = {}_tq_x\, {}_tp_y\, \mu_{y+t}\, dt = {}_tq_x\, d\, {}_tq_y, $$

$$ d\, {}_tq_{2\to3} = {}_tp_2\, {}_t\mu_{2\to3} = {}_tq_y\, {}_tp_x\, \mu_{x+t}\, dt = {}_tq_y\, d\, {}_tq_x $$

and by Theorem 1 at states β=0,1,2 and 3 resp.,

$$ \partial/\partial t\; {}_tp_{xy} = -\, {}_tp_{xy}(\mu_{x+t} + \mu_{y+t}), $$

$$ \partial/\partial t\; {}_tp_{x|y} = {}_tp_{xy}\, \mu_{x+t} - {}_tp_{x|y}\, \mu_{y+t}, $$

$$ \partial/\partial t\; {}_tp_{y|x} = {}_tp_{xy}\, \mu_{y+t} - {}_tp_{y|x}\, \mu_{x+t}, $$

$$ \partial/\partial t\; {}_tp_{x|y|} = {}_tp_{x|y}\, \mu_{y+t} + {}_tp_{y|x}\, \mu_{x+t}. $$

Extension: graphs with returns

In a **graph with returns** (not considered hitherto), state α can be a successor and a predecessor of state β simultaneously. In a graph with returns, arrows from any state α to any other state β are allowed. The following **healthy-sick graph** is an example of a graph with returns.

The foregoing Theorem 1 and its Corollary are true in case of graphs with returns. The proof of Theorem 1 remains valid. For the Corollary, in the case of a graph with returns, let us assume that the number of states is n. Then (7) is a system of n differential equations with n unknown functions ${}_tp_0$, ${}_tp_1$, ..., ${}_tp_{n-1}$. It has a unique solution (under classical assumptions).

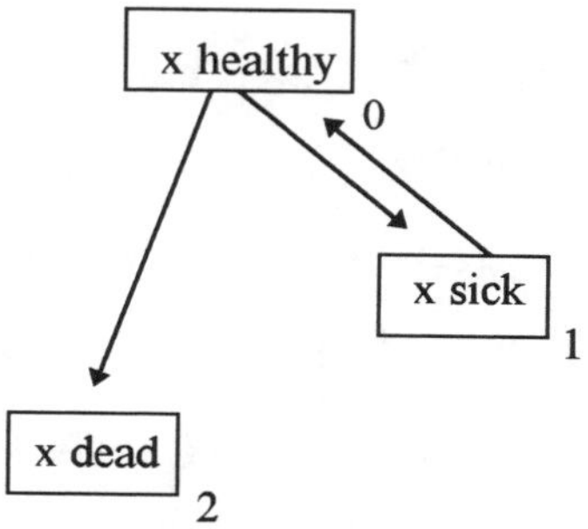

Figure 14.9. Healthy-sick graph with returns

For the sake of simplicity, we exclude returns in graphs considered hereafter (but some direct extensions are nevertheless indicated). Proofs at present value level become more complicated when returns are allowed because then several random variables $T_{k,\alpha\to\beta}$ (k=1, 2,...) corresponding to several transitions from state α to state β must be considered. Hence, $T_{\alpha\to\beta}$ and ${}_tq_{\alpha\to\beta}$ are not defined in general graphs with returns.

14.4. Annuities on states of a graph

We consider a general graph and a general capital-function c_τ. As usual α, β, ... denote states. We recall that $S_\tau \equiv S(\tau)$ is the state which is active at τ.

Deferred capitals on a state

$$ {}_tE_\alpha{}^{oo} := (1_{S(t)=\alpha}, t), \tag{8}$$

$$ {}_tE_\alpha(c_\tau)^{oo} := (c_t\, 1_{S(t)=\alpha}, t) = c_t\, {}_tE_\alpha{}^{oo}. \tag{9}$$

The corresponding prices are

$$ {}_tE_\alpha = {}_tp_\alpha\, v^t, \tag{10}$$

$$ {}_tE_\alpha(c_\tau) := c_t\, {}_tp_\alpha\, v^t. \tag{11}$$

Annuities on a state

$$ {}_{s|n}a_\alpha(c_\tau)^{oo} := \textstyle\sum_{1\le k\le n} (c_{s+k-}\, 1_{S(s+k)=\alpha}, s+k), \tag{12}$$

$$ {}_{s|n}\ddot{a}_\alpha(c_\tau)^{oo} := \textstyle\sum_{0\le k\le n-1} (c_{s+k+}\, 1_{S(s+k)=\alpha}, s+k), \tag{13}$$

$$ {}_{s|t}\overline{a}_\alpha(c_\tau)^{oo} := \textstyle\int_{(s,s+t)} (c_\tau\, 1_{S(\tau)=\alpha} d\tau, \tau), \tag{14}$$

$$ {}_{s|n}a_\alpha{}^{(r)}(c_\tau)^{oo} := (1/r) \textstyle\sum_{1\le \nu\le nr} (c_{s+\nu/r-}\, 1_{S(s+\nu/r)=\alpha}, s+\nu/r), \tag{15}$$

$$ {}_{s|n}\ddot{a}_\alpha{}^{(r)}(c_\tau)^{oo} := (1/r) \textstyle\sum_{0\le \nu\le nr-1} (c_{s+\nu/r+}\, 1_{S(s+\nu/r)=\alpha}, s+\nu/r). \tag{16}$$

Obviously,

$$ {}_{s|n}a_\alpha(c_\tau)^{oo} = \textstyle\sum_{1\le k\le n} c_{s+k-}\ {}_{s+k}E_\alpha{}^{oo}, \tag{17}$$

$$ {}_{s|n}\ddot{a}_\alpha(c_\tau)^{oo} = \textstyle\sum_{0\le k\le n-1} c_{s+k+}\ {}_{s+k}E_\alpha{}^{oo}, \tag{18}$$

$$ {}_{s|t}\bar{a}_\alpha(c_\tau)^{oo} = \textstyle\int_{(s,s+t)} c_\tau\ {}_\tau E_\alpha{}^{oo}\, d\tau, \tag{19}$$

$$ {}_{s|n}a_\alpha{}^{(r)}(c_\tau)^{oo} = (1/r) \textstyle\sum_{1\le v\le nr} c_{s+v/r-}\ {}_{s+v/r}E_\alpha{}^{oo}, \tag{20}$$

$$ {}_{s|n}\ddot{a}_\alpha{}^{(r)}(c_\tau)^{oo} = (1/r) \textstyle\sum_{0\le v\le nr-1} c_{s+v/r+}\ {}_{s+v/r}E_\alpha{}^{oo} \tag{21}$$

and then these relations are also valid at the present value and price levels.

Approximations for partitioned annuities

By App.B.Th.2 with $f_\tau := c_\tau\ {}_\tau E_\alpha$ $(s\le\tau\le s+n)$,

$$ {}_{s|n}a_\alpha{}^{(r)}(c_\tau) \approx {}_{s|n}a_\alpha(c_\tau) + [{}_{s|n}\ddot{a}_\alpha(c_\tau) - {}_{s|n}a_\alpha(c_\tau)].(r-1)/(2r), \tag{22}$$

$$ {}_{s|n}\ddot{a}_\alpha{}^{(r)}(c_\tau) \approx {}_{s|n}\ddot{a}_\alpha(c_\tau) - [{}_{s|n}\ddot{a}_\alpha(c_\tau) - {}_{s|n}a_\alpha(c_\tau)].(r-1)/(2r), \tag{23}$$

$$ {}_{s|n}\bar{a}_\alpha(c_\tau) \approx [{}_{s|n}\ddot{a}_\alpha(c_\tau) + {}_{s|n}a_\alpha(c_\tau)]/2. \tag{24}$$

These relations are best remembered in succint form:

$$ a_\alpha{}^{(r)} \approx a_\alpha + (\ddot{a}_\alpha - a_\alpha).(r-1)/(2r) \quad [{}_{s|n}, c_\tau], \tag{25}$$

$$ \ddot{a}_\alpha{}^{(r)} \approx \ddot{a}_\alpha - (\ddot{a}_\alpha - a_\alpha).(r-1)/(2r) \quad [{}_{s|n}, c_\tau], \tag{26}$$

$$ \bar{a}_\alpha \approx (\ddot{a}_\alpha + a_\alpha)/2 \quad [{}_{s|n}, c_\tau]. \tag{27}$$

If c_τ is a continuous function of τ, then $f_s := c_\tau\ {}_\tau E_x$ is a continuous function of τ. By App.B.Th.3,

$$ {}_{s|n}a_\alpha{}^{(r)}(c_\tau) \approx {}_{s|n}a_\alpha(c_\tau) + [{}_sE_\alpha(c_\tau) - {}_{s+n}E_\alpha(c_\tau)].(r-1)/(2r), \tag{28}$$

$$ {}_{s|n}\ddot{a}_\alpha{}^{(r)}(c_\tau) \approx {}_{s|n}\ddot{a}_\alpha(c_\tau) - [{}_sE_\alpha(c_\tau) - {}_{s+n}E_\alpha(c_\tau)].(r-1)/(2r), \tag{29}$$

$$ \begin{aligned} {}_{s|n}\bar{a}_\alpha(c_\tau) &\approx {}_{s|n}a_\alpha(c_\tau) + [{}_sE_\alpha(c_\tau) - {}_{s+n}E_\alpha(c_\tau)]/2 \\ &= {}_{s|n}\ddot{a}_\alpha(c_\tau) - [{}_sE_\alpha(c_\tau) - {}_{s+n}E_\alpha(c_\tau)]/2 = [{}_{s|n}\ddot{a}_\alpha(c_\tau) + {}_{s|n}a_\alpha(c_\tau)]/2. \end{aligned} \tag{30}$$

Extension: graphs with returns

The definitions (8), (9) and (12)–(16) are also adopted in case of a graph with returns. Then all formulas (10), (11) and (17)–(30) remain valid.

14.5. Transition capitals on a graph

We consider a general graph and a general capital-function c_τ. We assume that α and β are direct successive states. We recall that $T_{\alpha\to\beta}\equiv T(\alpha\to\beta)$ is the transition instant from state α to state β (or $+\infty$ if no such transition occurs).

$$_{s|t}\bar{A}_{\alpha\to\beta}(c_\tau)^{\circ\circ} := (c_{T(\alpha\to\beta)}\ 1_{s<T(\alpha\to\beta)\le s+t},\ T_{\alpha\to\beta}), \tag{31}$$

$$_{s|n}\hat{A}_{\alpha\to\beta}(c_\tau)^{\circ\circ} := \Sigma_{0\le k\le n-1}\ (c_{s+k+1/2}\ 1_{s+k<T(\alpha\to\beta)\le s+k+1},\ s+k+1/2). \tag{32}$$

If s is an integer m, then an equivalent definition is

$$_{m|n}\hat{A}_{\alpha\to\beta}(c_\tau)^{\circ\circ} := (c_{T(\alpha\to\beta)}\ 1_{m<T(\alpha\to\beta)\le m+n},\ \hat{T}_{\alpha\to\beta}). \tag{33}$$

The prices are

$$_{s|t}\bar{A}_{\alpha\to\beta}(c_\tau) = \int_{(s,s+t)} c_\tau\ v^\tau d\ _\tau q_{\alpha\to\beta}, \tag{34}$$

$$_{s|n}\hat{A}_{\alpha\to\beta}(c_\tau) = \Sigma_{0\le k\le n-1}\ c_{s+k+1/2}\ v^{s+k+1/2}\ \Delta\ _{s+k}q_{\alpha\to\beta}. \tag{35}$$

Extension: graph with returns

In the case of a graph with returns, $_{s|t}\bar{A}_{\alpha\to\beta}(c_\tau)^{\circ\circ}$ can still be defined as follows: the insurer pays the amount c_τ at each transition moment τ from state α to state β in the interval (s,s+t). Similarly for $_{s|n}\hat{A}_{\alpha\to\beta}(c_\tau)$: for each transition from state α to state β in the year (s+k,s+k+1) (k=0,1,...,n−1), the insurer pays $c_{s+k+1/2}$ in the middle of that year.

The probability of a transition from α to β in $d\tau$ equals $_\tau p_\alpha\ _\tau\mu_{\alpha\to\beta}\ d\tau$. Hence, in the continuous case, the insurer pays the amount c_τ at τ ($s<\tau<s+t$) with present values $c_\tau v^\tau$ and he pays it with a probability equal to $_\tau p_\alpha\ _\tau\mu_{\alpha\to\beta}\ d\tau$. Then the price is

$$_{s|t}\bar{A}_{\alpha\to\beta}(c_\tau) = \int_{(s,s+t)} c_\tau\ v^\tau\ _\tau p_\alpha\ _\tau\mu_{\alpha\to\beta}\ d\tau. \tag{36}$$

Similarly,

$$_{s|n}\hat{A}_{\alpha\to\beta}(c_\tau) = \Sigma_{0\le k\le n-1} \int_{(s+k,s+k+1)} c_{s+k+1/2}\ v^{s+k+1/2}\ _\tau p_\alpha\ _\tau\mu_{\alpha\to\beta}\ d\tau. \tag{37}$$

Of course, (36) and (37) are equivalent to (34) and (35) in the case of graphs without returns.

14.6. Transition Theorem for time-capitals (Price level)

Theorem 2 (Continuous case)

Let C_τ and c_τ be associated capital-functions on [s,s+t] (see Ch.7.4.). Then, for any state β of a graph,

$$\mathbf{{}_{s|t}\bar{a}_\beta(c_\tau) = \sum_{\alpha\in'\beta}\, {}_{s|t}\bar{A}_{\alpha\to\beta}(C_\tau) - \sum_{\gamma\in\beta'}\, {}_{s|t}\bar{A}_{\beta\to\gamma}(C_\tau) + [{}_sE_\beta(C_\tau) - {}_{s+t}E_\beta(C_\tau)].} \quad (38)$$

Proof

We consider the expression

$$- \int_{(s,s+t)} {}_\tau p_\beta \; d(C_\tau v^\tau). \quad (39)$$

It equals

$$\int_{(s,s+t)} {}_\tau p_\beta \; c_\tau \; v^\tau \, d\tau = \int_{(s,s+t)} c_\tau \; {}_\tau E_\alpha \; d\tau = {}_{s|t}a_\alpha(c_\tau) \quad (40)$$

by (19) at price level and by Ch.7.(18). By an integration by parts and by relation (7), (39) equals

$$- [{}_\tau p_\beta \; C_\tau v^\tau]_s^{s+t} + \int_{(s,s+t)} C_\tau v^\tau \, d\, {}_\tau p_\beta$$

$$= {}_sE_\beta(C_\tau) - {}_{s+t}E_\beta(C_\tau) + \int_{(s,s+t)} C_\tau v^\tau [\sum_{\alpha\in'\beta} {}_tp_\alpha \; {}_t\mu_{\alpha\to\beta} - {}_tp_\beta \sum_{\gamma\in\beta'} {}_t\mu_{\beta\to\gamma}] d\tau$$

$$= {}_sE_\beta(C_\tau) - {}_{s+t}E_\beta(C_\tau) + \sum_{\alpha\in'\beta} \int_{(s,s+t)} C_\tau v^\tau {}_tp_\alpha \; {}_t\mu_{\alpha\to\beta} - \sum_{\gamma\in\beta'} \int_{(s,s+t)} C_\tau v^\tau {}_t\mu_{\beta\to\gamma} \, d\tau$$

$$= {}_sE_\beta(C_\tau) - {}_{s+t}E_\beta(C_\tau) + \sum_{\alpha\in'\beta} {}_{s|t}\bar{A}_{\alpha\to\beta}(C_\tau) - \sum_{\gamma\in\beta'} {}_{s|t}\bar{A}_{\beta\to\gamma}(C_\tau) \quad (41)$$

by (36). Hence, (40) equals (41) •

Of course, the capital function C_τ or c_τ is omitted in the notations if it is the constant function 1. By (19), $c_\tau \equiv 1/\delta$ if $C_\tau \equiv 1$. This proves the following Corollary.

Corollary

$$\mathbf{\delta \; {}_{s|t}\bar{a}_\beta = \sum_{\alpha\in'\beta} {}_{s|t}\bar{A}_{\alpha\to\beta} - \sum_{\gamma\in\beta'} {}_{s|t}\bar{A}_{\beta\to\gamma} + ({}_sE_\beta - {}_{s+t}E_\beta)} \; \bullet \quad (42)$$

Theorem 3

For any state β of a graph,

$$\mathbf{\delta \; \bar{a}_\beta = \sum_{\alpha\in'\beta} \bar{A}_{\alpha\to\beta} - \sum_{\gamma\in\beta'} \bar{A}_{\beta\to\gamma} + (\ddot{a}_\beta - a_\beta) \quad [{}_{s|n}\text{, staircase } c_\tau]}. \quad (43)$$

Proof

By (42),

$$\delta \; {}_{s+k|1}\bar{a}_\beta = \sum_{\alpha\in'\beta} {}_{s+k|1}\bar{A}_{\alpha\to\beta} - \sum_{\gamma\in\beta'} {}_{s+k|1}\bar{A}_{\beta\to\gamma} + ({}_{s+k}E_\beta - {}_{s+k+1}E_\beta).$$

We multiply that relation by $c_{s+k+1/2} = c_{s+k+} = c_{s+k+1-}$ and we sum over k = 0, 1, ..., n−1. Then (43) (with $_{s|n}$ and c_τ) is obtained. See proof of Ch.7.Th.1.(10) •

Theorem 4 (Discrete case)

For any state β of a graph,

$$\mathbf{i\ a_\beta = u^{1/2}\textstyle\sum_{\alpha\in'\beta} \hat{A}_{\alpha\to\beta} - u^{1/2}\sum_{\gamma\in\beta'} \hat{A}_{\beta\to\gamma} + (\ddot{a}_\beta - a_\beta)\quad [_{s|n},\ staircase\ c_\tau]},\qquad(44)$$

$$\mathbf{iv\ \ddot{a}_\beta = v^{1/2}\textstyle\sum_{\alpha\in'\beta} \hat{A}_{\alpha\to\beta} - v^{1/2}\sum_{\gamma\in\beta'} \hat{A}_{\beta\to\gamma} + (\ddot{a}_\beta - a_\beta)\quad [_{s|n},\ staircase\ c_\tau]}.\qquad(45)$$

Proof

Multiplying (44) by v, it is obvious that the equivalence of (44) and (45) amounts to the exact relation

$$iv\ a_\beta - v(\ddot{a}_\beta - a_\beta) = iv\ \ddot{a}_\beta - (\ddot{a}_\beta - a_\beta)\quad [s|n,\ staircase\ c_\tau].$$

Hence, it is enough to prove (44). In fact, it is enough to prove that

$$i\ {}_{s+k|1}a_\beta = u^{1/2}\textstyle\sum_{\alpha\in'\beta}\ {}_{s+k|1}\hat{A}_{\alpha\to\beta} - u^{1/2}\sum_{\gamma\in\beta'}\ {}_{s+k|1}\hat{A}_{\beta\to\gamma} + ({}_{s+k}E_\beta - {}_{s+k+1}E_\beta)\qquad(46)$$

because then we can multiply by $c_{s+k+1/2} = c_{s+k+} = c_{s+k+1-}$ and we can sum over k=0, 1, ..., n−1. Relation

$${}_{s+k|1}\hat{A}_{\alpha\to\beta} = v^{s+k+1/2}\int_{(s+k,s+k+1)} {}_\tau p_\alpha\ {}_\tau\mu_{\alpha\to\beta}\, d\tau$$

is a particular case of (37). Using the similar relation for ${}_{s+k|1}\hat{A}_{\beta\to\gamma}$, (46) becomes

$$iv^{s+k+1}\ {}_{s+k+1}p_\beta = u^{1/2}\ v^{s+k+1/2}\int_{(s+k,s+k+1)} {}_\tau p_\alpha\ {}_\tau\mu_{\alpha\to\beta}\, d\tau$$
$$- u^{1/2}\ v^{s+k+1/2}\int_{(s+k,s+k+1)} {}_\tau p_\beta\ {}_\tau\mu_{\beta\to\gamma}\, d\tau + v^{s+k}\ {}_{s+k}p_\beta - v^{s+k+1}\ {}_{s+k+1}p_\beta.$$

The latter relation is equivalent to relation

$${}_{s+k+1}p_\beta - {}_{s+k}p_\beta = \int_{(s+k,s+k+1)} {}_\tau p_\alpha\ {}_\tau\mu_{\alpha\to\beta}\, d\tau - \int_{(s+k,s+k+1)} {}_\tau p_\beta\ {}_\tau\mu_{\beta\to\gamma}\, d\tau.\qquad(47)$$

Hence, it is enough to verify that (47) is correct. It is indeed because it results from (7) by integration over interval (s+k,s+k+1) •

Extension: graphs with returns

Theorems 2, 3 and 4 are valid in case of graphs with returns. Indeed, the proofs are only based on previous results which hold in the case of graphs with returns.

14.7. Illustration in the case of graph $Gr_4(x,y)$

In the case of $Gr_4(x,y)$, relation (42) becomes at states 0, 1, 2 and 3 resp.:

$$\delta\ {}_{s|t}\bar{a}_{xy} = -\ {}_{s|t}\bar{A}_{\overset{1}{x}y} -\ {}_{s|t}\bar{A}_{x\overset{1}{y}} +\ {}_{s}E_{xy} -\ {}_{s+t}E_{xy}, \tag{48}$$

$$\delta\ {}_{s|t}\bar{a}_{x|y} = +\ {}_{s|t}\bar{A}_{\overset{1}{x}y} -\ {}_{s|t}\bar{A}_{x\overset{2}{y}} +\ {}_{s}E_{x|y} -\ {}_{s+t}E_{x|y}, \tag{49}$$

$$\delta\ {}_{s|t}\bar{a}_{y|x} = +\ {}_{s|t}\bar{A}_{x\overset{1}{y}} -\ {}_{s|t}\bar{A}_{\overset{2}{x}y} +\ {}_{s}E_{y|x} -\ {}_{s+t}E_{y|x}, \tag{50}$$

$$\delta\ {}_{s|t}\bar{a}_{x|y|} = +\ {}_{s|t}\bar{A}_{x\overset{2}{y}} +\ {}_{s|t}\bar{A}_{\overset{2}{x}y} +\ {}_{s}E_{x|y|} -\ {}_{s+t}E_{x|y|}. \tag{51}$$

14.8. Transition Theorem for time-capitals (present value level)

General extension Theorem

The relations of Theorems 2, 3 and 4 are valid at present value level in any graph. The instantaneous transition rates from one state to another must not necessarily exist and no independence assumptions whatever (in case of extinction graphs of lives) must be made for their validity.

Proof of Theorem 2 at present value level

We assume that $\beta \neq 0$ (the proof is a bit simpler if β is the initial state 0).

$${}_{s|t}a_\beta(c_\tau)^\circ =$$

$$\textstyle\sum_{\alpha\in'\beta} \sum_{\gamma\in\beta'} 1_{\alpha\to\beta}\, 1_{\beta\to\gamma} \int_{[T(\alpha\to\beta),T(\beta\to\gamma)]\cap[s,s+t]} c_\tau\, v^\tau\, d\tau \tag{52}$$

$$+ \textstyle\sum_{\alpha\in'\beta} 1_{\alpha\to\beta}\, 1_{\beta]} \int_{[T(\alpha\to\beta),\infty[\cap[s,s+t]} c_\tau\, v^\tau\, d\tau. \tag{53}$$

The integral of (52) corresponds to a penetration into state β at moment $T(\alpha\to\beta)$ and an escape at moment $T(\beta\to\gamma)$. Then exactly one of the following cases occurs (null events are neglected):

C1:	$T_{\alpha\to\beta} < T_{\beta\to\gamma} < s$,	C4:	$s < T_{\alpha\to\beta} < T_{\beta\to\gamma} < s+t$,
C2:	$T_{\alpha\to\beta} < s < T_{\beta\to\gamma}$,	C5:	$s < T_{\alpha\to\beta} < s+t < T_{\beta\to\gamma}$,
C3:	$T_{\alpha\to\beta} < s < s+t < T_{\beta\to\gamma}$,	C6:	$s+t < T_{\alpha\to\beta} < T_{\beta\to\gamma}$.

Then(52) equals

$$\textstyle\sum_{\alpha\in'\beta} \sum_{\gamma\in\beta'} 1_{\alpha\to\beta}\, 1_{\beta\to\gamma}\, 1_{C2} \int_{[s,T(\beta\to\gamma)]} c_\tau\, v^\tau\, d\tau$$

$$+\textstyle\sum_{\alpha\in'\beta} \sum_{\gamma\in\beta'} 1_{\alpha\to\beta}\, 1_{\beta\to\gamma}\, 1_{C3} \int_{[s,s+t]} c_\tau\, v^\tau\, d\tau$$

$$+\textstyle\sum_{\alpha\in'\beta} \sum_{\gamma\in\beta'} 1_{\alpha\to\beta}\, 1_{\beta\to\gamma}\, 1_{C4} \int_{[T(\alpha\to\beta),T(\beta\to\gamma)]} c_\tau\, v^\tau\, d\tau$$

$$+\textstyle\sum_{\alpha\in'\beta} \sum_{\gamma\in\beta'} 1_{\alpha\to\beta}\, 1_{\beta\to\gamma}\, 1_{C5} \int_{[T(\alpha\to\beta),s+t]} c_\tau\, v^\tau\, d\tau$$

$$= \sum_{\alpha\in'\beta} \sum_{\gamma\in\beta'} 1_{\alpha\to\beta}\, 1_{\beta\to\gamma}\, 1_{C2}\, [C_s\, v^s - C_{T(\beta\to\gamma)} v^{T(\beta\to\gamma)}]$$

$$+ \sum_{\alpha\in'\beta} \sum_{\gamma\in\beta'} 1_{\alpha\to\beta}\, 1_{\beta\to\gamma}\, 1_{C3}\, [C_s\, v^s - C_{s+t}\, v^{s+t}]$$

$$+ \sum_{\alpha\in'\beta} \sum_{\gamma\in\beta'} 1_{\alpha\to\beta}\, 1_{\beta\to\gamma}\, 1_{C4}\, [C_{T(\alpha\to\beta)} v^{T(\alpha\to\beta)} - C_{T(\beta\to\gamma)} v^{T(\beta\to\gamma)}]$$

$$+ \sum_{\alpha\in'\beta} \sum_{\gamma\in\beta'} 1_{\alpha\to\beta}\, 1_{\beta\to\gamma}\, 1_{C5}\, [C_{T(\alpha\to\beta)} v^{T(\alpha\to\beta)} - C_{s+t} v^{s+t}]$$

$$= \sum_{\alpha\in'\beta} \sum_{\gamma\in\beta'} 1_{\alpha\to\beta}\, 1_{\beta\to\gamma}\, 1_{C2}\, C_s\, v^s \qquad (52_1)$$

$$- \sum_{\alpha\in'\beta} \sum_{\gamma\in\beta'} 1_{\alpha\to\beta}\, 1_{\beta\to\gamma}\, 1_{C2}\, C_{T(\beta\to\gamma)} v^{T(\beta\to\gamma)} \qquad (52_2)$$

$$+ \sum_{\alpha\in'\beta} \sum_{\gamma\in\beta'} 1_{\alpha\to\beta}\, 1_{\beta\to\gamma}\, 1_{C3}\, C_s\, v^s \qquad (52_3)$$

$$- \sum_{\alpha\in'\beta} \sum_{\gamma\in\beta'} 1_{\alpha\to\beta}\, 1_{\beta\to\gamma}\, 1_{C3}\, C_{s+t}\, v^{s+t} \qquad (52_4)$$

$$+ \sum_{\alpha\in'\beta} \sum_{\gamma\in\beta'} 1_{\alpha\to\beta}\, 1_{\beta\to\gamma}\, 1_{C4}\, C_{T(\alpha\to\beta)} v^{T(\alpha\to\beta)} \qquad (52_5)$$

$$- \sum_{\alpha\in'\beta} \sum_{\gamma\in\beta'} 1_{\alpha\to\beta}\, 1_{\beta\to\gamma}\, 1_{C4}\, C_{T(\beta\to\gamma)} v^{T(\beta\to\gamma)} \qquad (52_6)$$

$$+ \sum_{\alpha\in'\beta} \sum_{\gamma\in\beta'} 1_{\alpha\to\beta}\, 1_{\beta\to\gamma}\, 1_{C5}\, C_{T(\alpha\to\beta)} v^{T(\alpha\to\beta)} \qquad (52_7)$$

$$- \sum_{\alpha\in'\beta} \sum_{\gamma\in\beta'} 1_{\alpha\to\beta}\, 1_{\beta\to\gamma}\, 1_{C5}\, C_{s+t} v^{s+t}. \qquad (52_8)$$

The integral of (53) corresponds to a penetration into state β at moment $T(\alpha\to\beta)$ not followed by an escape. Then exactly one of the following cases occurs:

$$D1:\ T_{\alpha\to\beta} < s, \quad D2:\ s < T_{\alpha\to\beta} < s+t, \quad D3:\ s+t < T_{\alpha\to\beta}.$$

Hence, (53) equals

$$\sum_{\alpha\in'\beta} 1_{\alpha\to\beta}\, 1_{\beta]}\, 1_{D1} \int_{[s,s+t]} c_\tau\, v^\tau\, d\tau$$

$$+ \sum_{\alpha\in'\beta} 1_{\alpha\to\beta}\, 1_{\beta]}\, 1_{D2} \int_{[T(\alpha\to\beta),s+t]} c_\tau\, v^\tau\, d\tau$$

$$= \sum_{\alpha\in'\beta} 1_{\alpha\to\beta}\, 1_{\beta]}\, 1_{D1}\, [C_s\, v^s - C_{s+t}\, v^{s+t}]$$

$$+ \sum_{\alpha\in'\beta} 1_{\alpha\to\beta}\, 1_{\beta]}\, 1_{D2}\, [C_{T(\alpha\to b)}\, v^{T(\alpha\to\beta)} - C_{s+t}\, v^{s+t}]$$

$$= \sum_{\alpha\in'\beta} 1_{\alpha\to\beta}\, 1_{\beta]}\, 1_{D1}\, C_s\, v^s \qquad (53_1)$$

$$- \sum_{\alpha\in'\beta} 1_{\alpha\to\beta}\, 1_{\beta]}\, 1_{D1}\, C_{s+t}\, v^{s+t} \qquad (53_2)$$

$$+ \sum_{\alpha\in'\beta} 1_{\alpha\to\beta}\, 1_{\beta]}\, 1_{D2}\, C_{T(\alpha\to b)}\, v^{T(\alpha\to\beta)} \qquad (53_3)$$

$$- \sum_{\alpha\in'\beta} 1_{\alpha\to\beta}\, 1_{\beta]}\, 1_{D2}\, C_{s+t}\, v^{s+t}. \qquad (53_4)$$

We now consider (52_2) and (52_6). We observe that

$$1_{\alpha\to\beta}(1_{C2} + 1_{C4}) = 1_{\alpha\to\beta}\, 1_{s<T(\beta\to\gamma)<s+t}.$$

Hence,

$$(52_2) + (52_6) = -\sum_{\alpha\in'\beta}\sum_{\gamma\in\beta'} 1_{\alpha\to\beta}\, 1_{\beta\to\gamma}\ {}_{s|t}A_{\beta\to\gamma}(C_\tau)^\circ.$$

But

$$1_{\beta\to\gamma}\sum_{\alpha\in'\beta} 1_{\alpha\to\beta} = 1_{\beta\to\gamma}$$

because transition from β to γ implies previous transition from some state $\alpha\in'\beta$ to β. Hence,

$$(52_2) + (52_6) = -\sum_{\gamma\in\beta'} 1_{\beta\to\gamma}\ {}_{s|t}A_{\beta\to\gamma}(C_\tau)^\circ = -\sum_{\gamma\in\beta'} {}_{s|t}A_{\beta\to\gamma}(C_\tau)^\circ, \quad (52_{2,6})$$

where the indicator function $1_{\beta\to\gamma}$ could be dropped, because ${}_{s|t}A_{\beta\to\gamma}(C_\tau)^\circ=0$ if no transition from β to γ occurs.

We now consider (52_5) and (52_7) and we observe that

$$1_{\beta\to\gamma}(1_{C4} + 1_{C5}) = 1_{\beta\to\gamma}\ 1_{s<T(\alpha\to\beta)<s+t}.$$

Hence,

$$(52_5) + (52_7) = \sum_{\alpha\in'\beta}\sum_{\gamma\in\beta'} 1_{\alpha\to\beta}\, 1_{\beta\to\gamma}\ {}_{s|t}A_{\alpha\to\beta}(C_\tau)^\circ.$$

$(53)_3$ equals

$$(53_3) = \sum_{\alpha\in'\beta} 1_{\alpha\to\beta}\, 1_{\beta]}\ {}_{s|t}A_{\alpha\to\beta}(C_\tau)^\circ.$$

But

$$1_{\alpha\to\beta}\Big(\sum_{\gamma\in\beta'} 1_{\beta\to\gamma} + 1_{\beta]}\Big) = 1_{\alpha\to\beta}$$

because a transition from α to β implies a transition from β to some state $\gamma\in\beta'$ or that state β will remain active. Hence,

$$(52_5) + (52_7) + (53_3) = \sum_{\alpha\in'\beta} 1_{\alpha\to\beta}\ {}_{s|t}A_{\alpha\to\beta}(C_\tau)^\circ$$

$$= \sum_{\alpha\in'\beta} {}_{s|t}A_{\alpha\to\beta}(C_\tau)^\circ. \quad (52_{5,7}\,,\ 53_3)$$

We notice that

$${}_sE_\beta(C_\tau)^\circ = \sum_{\alpha\in'\beta}\sum_{\gamma\in\beta'} 1_{\alpha\to\beta}\, 1_{\beta\to\gamma}\, 1_{T(\alpha\to\beta)<s<T(\beta\to\gamma)}\, C_s\, v^s$$

$$+ \sum_{\alpha\in'\beta} 1_{\alpha\to\beta}\, 1_{\beta]}\, 1_{T(\alpha\to\beta)<s}\, C_s\, v^s. \quad (54)$$

Indeed, in the case of time-capital ${}_sE_\beta(C_\tau)^{\circ\circ}$ the insurer pays C_s at s if there is a penetration into state β before s, followed by an exit after s, or not followed by an exit. Hence,

$$(52_1) + (52_3) + (53_1) = {}_sE_\beta(C_\tau)^\circ \quad (52_{1,3}\,,\ 53_1)$$

because

$$1_{\alpha\to\beta}\, 1_{\beta\to\gamma}\,(1_{C2} + 1_{C3}) = 1_{\alpha\to\beta}\, 1_{\beta\to\gamma}\, 1_{T(\alpha\to\beta)<s<T(B\to\gamma)}.$$

Similarly

$$ {}_{s+t}E_\beta(C_\tau)^\circ = \sum_{\alpha\in'\beta} \sum_{\gamma\in\beta'} 1_{\alpha\to\beta}\, 1_{\beta\to\gamma}\, 1_{T(\alpha\to\beta)<s+t<T(\beta\to\gamma)}\, C_{s+t}\, v^{s+t} $$
$$ + \sum_{\alpha\in'\beta} 1_{\alpha\to\beta}\, 1_{\beta]}\, 1_{T(\alpha\to\beta)<s+t}\, C_{s+t}\, v^{s+t} \qquad (55) $$

and then

$$ (52_4) + (52_8) + (53_2) + (53_4) = -\ {}_{s+t}E_\beta(C_\tau)^\circ \qquad (52_{4,8}\ ,\ 53_{2,4}) $$

because

$$ 1_{\alpha\to\beta}\, 1_{\beta\to\gamma}\, (1_{C3} + 1_{C5}) = 1_{\alpha\to\beta}\, 1_{\beta\to\gamma}\, 1_{T(\alpha\to\beta)<s+t<T(\beta\to\gamma)} $$

and

$$ 1_{\alpha\to\beta}(1_{D1} + 1_{D2}) = 1_{\alpha\to\beta}\, 1_{T(\alpha\to\beta)<s+t}. $$

Hence,

$$ {}_{s|t}\bar{a}_\beta(c_\tau)^\circ = (52_{2,6}) + (52_{5,7}\ ,\ 53_3) + (52_{1,3}\ ,\ 53_1) + (52_{4,8}\ ,\ 53_{2,4}) $$
$$ = -\sum_{\gamma\in\beta'} {}_{s|t}\bar{A}_{\beta\to\gamma}(C_\tau)^\circ + \sum_{\alpha\in'\beta} {}_{s|t}\bar{A}_{\alpha\to\beta}(C_\tau)^\circ + {}_sE_\beta(C_\tau)^\circ - {}_{s+t}E_\beta(C_\tau)^\circ \bullet \qquad (56) $$

Proof of Theorem 3 at present value level

The Corollary of Theorem 2 holds at present value level. Then the argument of proof of Theorem 3 can be repeated at that level •

Proof of Theorem 4 at present value level

It is enough to prove relation (46) at present value level. Noticing that ${}_{s+k|1}a_\beta{}^\circ = {}_{s+k+1}E_\beta{}^\circ$, it is sufficient to verify that

$$ u\ {}_{s+1}E_\beta{}^\circ - {}_sE_\beta{}^\circ = u^{1/2}\sum_{\alpha\in'\beta} {}_{s|1}\hat{A}_{\alpha\to\beta}{}^\circ - u^{1/2}\sum_{\gamma\in\beta'} {}_{s|1}\hat{A}_{\beta\to\gamma}{}^\circ \qquad (57) $$

because then we can replace s by s+k. By (54) with $C_\tau\equiv 1$, the first member of (57) equals

$$ u\sum_{\alpha\in'\beta}\sum_{\gamma\in\beta'} 1_{\alpha\to\beta} 1_{\beta\to\gamma} 1_{T(\alpha\to\beta)<s+1<T(\beta\to\gamma)}\, v^{s+1} + u\sum_{\alpha\in'\beta} 1_{\alpha\to\beta} 1_{\beta]} 1_{T(\alpha\to\beta)<s+1}\, v^{s+1} $$
$$ -\sum_{\alpha\in'\beta}\sum_{\gamma\in\beta'} 1_{\alpha\to\beta} 1_{\beta\to\gamma} 1_{T(\alpha\to\beta)<s<T(\beta\to\gamma)}\, v^s - \sum_{\alpha\in'\beta} 1_{\alpha\to\beta} 1_{\beta]} 1_{T(\alpha\to\beta)<s}\, v^s. $$

The last member of (57) equals

$$ u^{1/2}\sum_{\alpha\in'\beta} 1_{\alpha\to\beta}\, 1_{s<T(\alpha\to\beta)<s+1}\, v^{s+1/2} - u^{1/2}\sum_{\gamma\in\beta'} 1_{\beta\to\gamma}\, 1_{s<T(\beta\to\gamma)<s+1}\, v^{s+1/2}. $$

Hence, (57) is equivalent to relation

$$ \sum_{\alpha\in'\beta}\sum_{\gamma\in\beta'} 1_{\alpha\to\beta} 1_{\beta\to\gamma} 1_{T(\alpha\to\beta)<s+1<T(\beta\to\gamma)} \qquad (58_1) $$
$$ + \sum_{\alpha\in'\beta} 1_{\alpha\to\beta} 1_{\beta]} 1_{T(\alpha\to\beta)<s+1} \qquad (58_2) $$
$$ + \sum_{\gamma\in\beta'} 1_{\beta\to\gamma}\, 1_{s<T(\beta\to\gamma)<s+1} \qquad (58_3) $$

$$= \sum_{\alpha\in'\beta}\sum_{\gamma\in\beta'} 1_{\alpha\to\beta}1_{\beta\to\gamma}1_{T(\alpha\to\beta)<s<T(\beta\to\gamma)} \tag{59$_1$}$$

$$+ \sum_{\alpha\in'\beta} 1_{\alpha\to\beta}1_{\beta]}1_{T(\alpha\to\beta)<s} \tag{59$_2$}$$

$$+ \sum_{\alpha\in'\beta} 1_{\alpha\to\beta} 1_{s<T(\alpha\to\beta)<s+1}. \tag{59$_3$}$$

(58_1) equals

$$\sum_{\alpha\in'\beta}\sum_{\gamma\in\beta'} 1_{\alpha\to\beta}1_{\beta\to\gamma}1_{T(\alpha\to\beta)<s+1} \tag{58$_{1'}$}$$

$$- \sum_{\alpha\in'\beta}\sum_{\gamma\in\beta'} 1_{\alpha\to\beta}1_{\beta\to\gamma}1_{T(\beta\to\gamma)<s+1}. \tag{60$_1$}$$

($58_{1'}$)+(58_2) equals

$$+ \sum_{\alpha\in'\beta} 1_{\alpha\to\beta} 1_{T(\alpha\to\beta)<s+1} \tag{60$_2$}$$

because

$$1_{\alpha\to\beta} [\sum_{\gamma\in\beta'} 1_{\beta\to\gamma} + 1_{\beta]}] = 1_{\alpha\to\beta}.$$

(if a transition from α to β occurs, then a transition from β to some state $\gamma\in\beta'$ occurs or state β remains active). (58_3) equals

$$+ \sum_{\gamma\in\beta'} 1_{\beta\to\gamma} 1_{T(\beta\to\gamma)<s+1} \tag{60$_3$}$$

$$- \sum_{\gamma\in\beta'} 1_{\beta\to\gamma} 1_{T(\beta\to\gamma)<s}. \tag{60$_4$}$$

Similarly, (59_1) equals

$$\sum_{\alpha\in'\beta}\sum_{\gamma\in\beta'} 1_{\alpha\to\beta}1_{\beta\to\gamma}1_{T(\alpha\to\beta)<s} \tag{59$_{1'}$}$$

$$- \sum_{\alpha\in'\beta}\sum_{\gamma\in\beta'} 1_{\alpha\to\beta}1_{\beta\to\gamma}1_{T(\beta\to\gamma)<s} \tag{61$_1$}$$

and ($59_{1'}$)+(59_2) equals

$$+ \sum_{\alpha\in'\beta} 1_{\alpha\to\beta} 1_{T(\alpha\to\beta)<s}. \tag{61$_2$}$$

(59_3) equals

$$+ \sum_{\alpha\in'\beta} 1_{\alpha\to\beta} 1_{T(\alpha\to\beta)<s+1} \tag{61$_3$}$$

$$- \sum_{\alpha\in'\beta} 1_{\alpha\to\beta} 1_{T(\alpha\to\beta)<s}. \tag{61$_4$}$$

Hence, it is enough to verify that

$$(60_1) + (60_2) + (60_3) + (60_4) = (61_1) + (61_2) + (61_3) + (61_4). \tag{62}$$

Relation (62) is correct because (60_2)≡(61_3), (61_2)+(61_4)≡0 and moreover (60_1)+(60_3)=0 and (60_4)=(61_1) because

$$1_{\beta\to\gamma} \sum_{\alpha\in'\beta} 1_{\alpha\to\beta} = 1_{\beta\to\gamma}$$

(a transition from β to γ must be preceded by a transition from some α to β)•

Chapter 15

VARIANCES (SEVERAL LIVES)

15.1. Ruin problems

The considerations of Ch.10.1–11 can obviously be adapted to life portfolios with policies on any number of lives. For instance, in the case of a contract on lives x and y, subscribed t years ago, the basic random variable S° defined by Ch.10.(2) must include the corresponding term

$$[({}_{\bullet t|}V_{xy})_{tech} - ({}_{\bullet t|}V_{xy}{}^\circ)_{true}] \qquad (1)$$

if x and y are still alive, the term

$$[({}_{\bullet t|}V_{x|y})_{tech} - ({}_{\bullet t|}V_{x|y}{}^\circ)_{true}] \qquad (2)$$

if x is dead and y alive, the term

$$[({}_{\bullet t|}V_{y|x})_{tech} - ({}_{\bullet t|}V_{y|x}{}^\circ)_{true}] \qquad (3)$$

if y is dead and x alive or the term

$$[({}_{\bullet t|}V_{x|y|})_{tech} - ({}_{\bullet t|}V_{x|y|}{}^\circ)_{true}] \qquad (4)$$

if x and y are both dead. Of course, only the non-vanishing terms must be considered. Then the problem is the calculation of variance of

$$({}_{\bullet t|}V_{xy}{}^\circ)_{true},\ ({}_{\bullet t|}V_{x|y}{}^\circ)_{true},\ ({}_{\bullet t|}V_{y|x}{}^\circ)_{true},\ ({}_{\bullet t|}V_{x|y|}{}^\circ)_{true}. \qquad (5)$$

These random variables are linear combinations of random variables

$$E_x{}^\circ, E_y{}^\circ, E_{xy}{}^\circ, \ldots\ a_x{}^\circ, a_y{}^\circ, a_{xy}{}^\circ, a_{x|y}{}^\circ, \ldots, A_x{}^\circ, A_y{}^\circ, A_{xy}{}^\circ, \ldots\ [c_\tau, {}_{s}, {}_{s|n}, {}^{(r)}, \bar{\ }, \ddot{\ }] \qquad (6)$$

(of course with x+t, y+t instead of x, y resp. and with different functions c_τ and different values of s, n and r).

In all the results of Ch.10.13–16, x and X can be replaced everywhere by σ and T_σ resp., where σ is any simple status.

This remark is useful when the variance of particular random variables of sequence (6) is considered. When linear combinations of random variables (6) are considered, then several simple statuses σ and also non simple statuses ρ may be involved. Then the remark cannot be applied.

Only time-capitals on 2 lives are discussed. The arguments can easily be adapted to time-capitals on any number of lives.

15.2. Evaluation of variances. General methodology

The same methodology as in Ch.10.12 is followed in the treatment of ruin problems in portfolios with contracts on any number of lives. In particular, $i'=i^2+2i$ and c_τ and C_τ are associated capital-functions. The connexion between c_τ and C_τ is explained in Ch.10.15 in the case of classical constant or variable, deferred and temporory annuities.

Instead of Ch.10.(23), particular instances of relation

$$\overline{a}_\beta(c_\tau)^\circ = C_0\, {}_0E_\beta + \sum_{\alpha\in'\beta} \overline{A}_{\alpha\to\beta}(C_\tau)^\circ - \sum_{\gamma\in\beta'} \overline{A}_{\beta\to\gamma}(C_\tau)^\circ \tag{7}$$

will be used. This is the present value version of Ch.14.(38) for s=0 and $t=\infty$ (see General Extension Theorem of Ch.14.8). In the last member of (7), ${}_0E_\beta=1$ if β is the initial state of the graph and ${}_0E_\beta=0$ otherwise.

The random variables of which the variance must be calculated will be displayed as

$$V^\circ := f(X,Y) + 1_{X<Y}\, g(X,Y) + 1_{Y<X}\, h(X,Y). \tag{8}$$

Then

$$\begin{aligned}(V^\circ)^2 &= f^2(X,Y) + 1_{X<Y}\, g^2(X,Y) + 1_{Y<X}\, h^2(X,Y)\\ &\qquad + 2\; 1_{X<Y}\, f(X,Y)g(X,Y) + 2\; 1_{Y<X}\, f(X,Y)h(X,Y)\\ &= f^2(X,Y) + 1_{X<Y}[g^2(X,Y) + 2f(X,Y)g(X,Y)]\\ &\qquad + 1_{Y<X}\,[h^2(X,Y) + 2\, f(X,Y)h(X,Y)]\end{aligned} \tag{9}$$

because

$$(1_{X<Y})^2 = 1_{X<Y},\ (1_{Y<X})^2 = 1_{Y<X},\ \ 1_{X<Y}\, 1_{Y<X} = 0.$$

Then

$$\mathrm{Var}(V^\circ) = E(V^\circ)^2 - E^2(V^\circ)$$

and one has to evaluate expectations such as

$$E[\varphi(X,Y)],\ \ E[1_{X<Y}\, \varphi(X,Y)],\ \ E[1_{Y<X}\, \varphi(X,Y)],$$

Due to the factor $1_{X<Y}$, the usual ^-approximations must be applied with some care in the latter expectations.

Explicitly, we proceed as follows. Of course, the number of terms is finite in any practical case. The lives x and y are supposed to be independent.

$$E[\varphi(X,Y)] = \int_{(0,\infty)} \int_{(0,\infty)} \varphi(s,t)\, d\,{}_sq_x\, d\,{}_tq_y$$
$$= \textstyle\sum_{j\geq 0} \sum_{k\geq 0} \int_{(j,j+1)} \int_{(k,k+1)} \varphi(s,t)\, d\,{}_sq_x\, d\,{}_tq_y$$
$$\approx \textstyle\sum_{j\geq 0} \sum_{k\geq 0} \int_{(j,j+1)} \int_{(k,k+1)} \varphi(j+1/2,k+1/2)\, d\,{}_sq_x\, d\,{}_tq_y$$
$$= \textstyle\sum_{j\geq 0} \sum_{k\geq 0} \varphi(j+1/2,k+1/2) \int_{(j,j+1)} \int_{(k,k+1)} d\,{}_sq_x\, d\,{}_tq_y.$$

Hence,
$$\mathbf{E[\varphi(X,Y)] \approx \textstyle\sum_{j\geq 0} \sum_{k\geq 0} \varphi(j+1/2,k+1/2)\, \Delta\,{}_jq_x\, \Delta\,{}_kq_y.} \tag{10}$$

$$E[1_{X<Y}\, \varphi(X,Y)] = \int_{(0,\infty)} \int_{(0,\infty)} 1_{s<t}\, \varphi(s,t)\, d\,{}_sq_x\, d\,{}_tq_y$$
$$= \textstyle\sum_{j\geq 0} \sum_{k\geq 0} \int_{(j,j+1)} \int_{(k,k+1)} 1_{s<t}\, \varphi(s,t)\, d\,{}_sq_x\, d\,{}_tq_y$$
$$= \textstyle\sum_{k\geq 0} (\sum_{j<k} + \sum_{j=k} + \sum_{j>k}) \int_{(j,j+1)} \int_{(k,k+1)} 1_{s<t}\, \varphi(s,t)\, d\,{}_sq_x\, d\,{}_tq_y$$
$$= \textstyle\sum_{k\geq 0} \sum_{j<k} \int_{(j,j+1)} \int_{(k,k+1)} 1_{s<t}\, \varphi(s,t)\, d\,{}_sq_x\, d\,{}_tq_y \tag{11_1}$$
$$+ \textstyle\sum_{k\geq 0} \sum_{j=k} \int_{(j,j+1)} \int_{(k,k+1)} 1_{s<t}\, \varphi(s,t)\, d\,{}_sq_x\, d\,{}_tq_y \tag{11_2}$$
$$+ \textstyle\sum_{k\geq 0} \sum_{j>k} \int_{(j,j+1)} \int_{(k,k+1)} 1_{s<t}\, \varphi(s,t)\, d\,{}_sq_x\, d\,{}_tq_y, \tag{11_3}$$

where
$$(11_1) \approx \textstyle\sum_{k\geq 0} \sum_{j<k} \int_{(j,j+1)} \int_{(k,k+1)} \varphi(j+1/2,k+1/2)\, d\,{}_sq_x\, d\,{}_tq_y$$
$$= \textstyle\sum_{k\geq 0} \sum_{j<k} \varphi(j+1/2,k+1/2) \int_{(j,j+1)} \int_{(k,k+1)} d\,{}_sq_x\, d\,{}_tq_y$$
$$= \textstyle\sum_{k\geq 0} \sum_{j<k} \varphi(j+1/2,k+1/2)\, \Delta\,{}_jq_x\, \Delta\,{}_kq_y,$$

$$(11_2) = \textstyle\sum_{k\geq 0} \int_{(k,k+1)} \int_{(k,k+1)} 1_{s<t}\, \varphi(s,t)\, d\,{}_sq_x\, d\,{}_tq_y$$
$$\approx (1/2) \textstyle\sum_{k\geq 0} \varphi(k+1/2,k+1/2) \int_{(k,k+1)} \int_{(k,k+1)} d\,{}_sq_x\, d\,{}_tq_y$$
$$= (1/2) \textstyle\sum_{k\geq 0} \varphi(k+1/2,k+1/2)\, \Delta\,{}_kq_x\, \Delta\,{}_kq_y.$$

Hence,
$$\mathbf{E[1_{X<Y}\, \varphi(X,Y)] \approx \textstyle\sum_{k\geq 0} \sum_{j<k} \varphi(j+1/2,k+1/2)\, \Delta\,{}_jq_x\, \Delta\,{}_kq_y}$$
$$\mathbf{+ (1/2) \textstyle\sum_{k\geq 0} \varphi(k+1/2,k+1/2)\, \Delta\,{}_kq_x\, \Delta\,{}_kq_y} \tag{12}$$
because $(11_3)=0$. Similarly,
$$\mathbf{E[1_{Y<X}\, \varphi(X,Y)] \approx \textstyle\sum_{j\geq 0} \sum_{k<j} \varphi(j+1/2,k+1/2)\, \Delta\,{}_jq_x\, \Delta\,{}_kq_y}$$
$$\mathbf{+ (1/2) \textstyle\sum_{k\geq 0} \varphi(k+1/2,k+1/2)\, \Delta\,{}_kq_x\, \Delta\,{}_kq_y.} \tag{13}$$

Hereafter ρ is any status and σ any simple status on the lives x and y.

15.3. Deferred life capitals

$$ {}_tE_\rho{}^\circ = 1_{\rho\uparrow t}\, v^t,\ ({}_tE_\rho{}^\circ)^2 = 1_{\rho\uparrow t}\, v^{2t} = 1_{\rho\uparrow t}\, v'^t = {}_tE_\rho(i')^\circ. $$

Hence,

$$ \mathrm{Var}({}_tE_\rho{}^\circ) = {}_tE_\rho(i') - ({}_tE_\rho{}^\circ)^2. \qquad (14) $$

When the variance of reserves of contracts is considered, the approximation

$$ {}_tE_\rho{}^{\circ\circ} = {}_{t|1}\ddot{a}_\rho{}^{\circ\circ} \approx u^{1/2}\ {}_{t|1}\bar{a}_\rho{}^{\circ\circ} \qquad (15) $$

is useful. See 15.5 for the treatment of continuous life annuity ${}_{t|1}\bar{a}_\rho{}^{\circ\circ}$ when variances are discussed.

15.4. General life insurances

By Ch.10.(25) and (26) with x replaced by σ,

$$ \mathrm{Var}[\bar{A}_\sigma(C_\tau)^\circ] = \bar{A}_\sigma(C^2{}_\tau, i') - [\bar{A}_\sigma(C_\tau)]^2. \qquad (16) $$

$$ \mathrm{Var}({}_{s|t}\bar{A}_\sigma{}^\circ) = {}_{s|t}\bar{A}_\sigma(i') - ({}_{s|t}\bar{A}_\sigma)^2. \qquad (17) $$

When the variance of reserves of contracts is considered, the following expressions are used.

$$ \bar{A}_x(C_\tau)^\circ = v^X,\quad \bar{A}_y(C_\tau)^\circ = v^Y, \qquad (18) $$

$$ \bar{A}_{xy}(C_\tau)^\circ = 1_{X<Y}\, C_X\, v^X + 1_{Y<X}\, C_Y\, v^Y, \qquad (19) $$

$$ \bar{A}_{\overline{xy}}(C_\tau)^\circ = 1_{X<Y}\, C_Y\, v^Y + 1_{Y<X}\, C_X\, v^X, \qquad (20) $$

$$ \bar{A}_{\overset{1}{x}y}(C_\tau)^\circ = 1_{X<Y}\, C_X\, v^X, \qquad (21) $$

$$ \bar{A}_{\overset{2}{x}y}(C_\tau)^\circ = 1_{Y<X}\, C_X v^X. \qquad (22) $$

$$ \bar{A}_{x\overset{1}{y}}(C_\tau)^\circ = 1_{Y<X}\, C_Y v^Y, \qquad (23) $$

$$ \bar{A}_{x\overset{2}{y}}(C_\tau)^\circ = 1_{X<Y}\, C_Y v^Y. \qquad (24) $$

15.5. Life annuities

The following expressions are useful for the evaluation of variances. They result from relation (7) applied to particular extinction graphs and from formulas of 15.4.

$$ \bar{a}_x(c_\tau)^\circ = C_0 - C_X v^X,\quad \bar{a}_y(c_\tau)^\circ = C_0 - C_Y v^Y, \qquad (25) $$

[graphs $Gr_2(x)$ and $Gr_2(y)$ at state 0]

$$\bar{a}_{x|}(c_\tau)^\circ = C_X v^X, \quad \bar{a}_{y|}(c_\tau)^\circ = C_Y v^Y, \tag{26}$$

[graphs $Gr_2(x)$ and $Gr_2(y)$ at state 1]

$$\bar{a}_{xy}(c_\tau)^\circ = C_0 - 1_{X<Y}\, C_X\, v^X - 1_{Y<X}\, C_Y\, v^Y, \tag{27}$$

[graph $Gr_5(x,y)$ at state 0]

$$\bar{a}_{x|y}(c_\tau)^\circ = 1_{X<Y}\, C_X\, v^X - 1_{X<Y}\, C_Y\, v^Y, \tag{28}$$

[graph $Gr_5(x,y)$ at state 1]

$$\bar{a}_{y|x}(c_\tau)^\circ = 1_{Y<X}\, C_Y\, v^Y - 1_{Y<X}\, C_X\, v^X, \tag{29}$$

[graph $Gr_5(x,y)$ at state 2]

$$\bar{a}_{x|^\circ y|}(c_\tau)^\circ = 1_{X<Y}\, C_Y\, v^Y, \tag{30}$$

[graph $Gr_5(x,y)$ at state 3]

$$\bar{a}_{y|^\circ x|}(c_\tau)^\circ = 1_{Y<X}\, C_X\, v^X, \tag{31}$$

[graph $Gr_5(x,y)$ at state 4]

$$\bar{a}_{x|y|}(c_\tau)^\circ = 1_{X<Y}\, C_Y\, v^Y + 1_{Y<X}\, C_X\, v^X, \tag{32}$$

[graph $Gr_4(x,y)$ at state 3]

$$\bar{a}_{\overline{xy}}{}^{[1]}(c_\tau)^\circ = \bar{A}_{xy}(C_\tau)^\circ - \bar{A}_{\overline{xy}}(C_\tau)^\circ$$

$$= 1_{X<Y}\, C_X\, v^X + 1_{Y<X}\, C_Y v^Y - 1_{X<Y}\, C_Y\, v^Y - 1_{Y<X}\, C_X v^X. \tag{33}$$

[graph $Gr_3(x,y)$ at state 1]

By (25) and (27),

$$\bar{a}_{\overline{xy}}(c_\tau)^\circ = C_0 - C_X\, v^X - C_Y\, v^Y + 1_{X<Y}\, C_X\, v^X + 1_{Y<X}\, C_Y\, v^Y$$

$$= C_0 - (1 - 1_{X<Y})\, C_X\, v^X - (1 - 1_{Y<X})\, C_Y\, v^Y.$$

Hence,

$$\bar{a}_{\overline{xy}}(c_\tau)^\circ = C_0 - 1_{Y<X}\, C_X\, v^X - 1_{X<Y}\, C_Y\, v^Y. \tag{34}$$

(25)–(34) are present values such as (8). Hence, the corresponding variances can be evaluated by the method of 15.2.

By Ch.10.(32) and (33) with x replaced by a simple status σ,

$$\delta^2\, \mathrm{Var}({}_{s|t}\bar{a}_\sigma{}^\circ)$$

$$= v'^s - {}_sE_\sigma(i') + {}_{s+t}E_\sigma(i') + {}_{s|t}\bar{A}_\sigma(i') - [v^s - {}_sE_\sigma + {}_{s+t}E_\sigma + {}_{s|t}\bar{A}_\sigma]^2, \tag{35}$$

$$\delta^2\, \mathrm{Var}({}_{s|t}\bar{a}_\sigma{}^\circ) = 2\delta[v^s\, {}_{s|t}\bar{a}_\sigma - {}_{s|t}\bar{a}_\sigma(i')] - \delta^2\, ({}_{s|t}\bar{a}_\sigma)^2. \tag{36}$$

15.6. Variance of reserves

As an illustration, we indicate how the variance of the reserve at subscription of contract

$$({}_{n|}\bar{A}^{\,1}_{xy}{}^{\circ\circ},\ p\ {}_{m}\ddot{a}_{xy}{}^{\circ\circ})\ \ (m \le n) \tag{37}$$

can be evaluated numerically. This contract is replaced by contract

$$({}_{n|}\bar{A}^{\,1}_{xy}{}^{\circ\circ},\ pu^{1/2}\ {}_{m}\bar{a}_{xy}{}^{\circ\circ})\ \ (m \le n). \tag{38}$$

Capital-functions $C_{1,\tau}$ and $C_{2,\tau}$ are fixed such that

$$ {}_{n|}\bar{A}^{\,1}_{xy}{}^{\circ} = 1_{X<Y}\, C_{1,X}\, v^X,$$

$$ {}_{m}\bar{a}_{xy}{}^{\circ} = C_{2,0} - 1_{X<Y}\, C_{2,X}\, v^X - 1_{Y<X}\, C_{2,Y}\, v^Y.$$

See (21), (27) and Ch.10.(30) with s=m and n=∞. Then the present value of the reserve at 0 of contract (38) equals

$$\begin{aligned} {}_{\bullet 0|}V_{xy}{}^{\circ} &= {}_{n|}\bar{A}^{\,1}_{xy}{}^{\circ} - pu^{1/2}\ {}_{m}\bar{a}_{xy}{}^{\circ} \\ &= -\,pu^{1/2}\, C_{2,0} + 1_{X<Y}(C_{1,X} + pu^{1/2}\, C_{2,X})v^X + 1_{Y<X}\, pu^{1/2}\, C_{2,Y}\, v^Y \\ &= -\,c + 1_{X<Y}\, C_{3,X}\, v^X + 1_{Y<X}\, C_{4,Y}\, v^Y, \end{aligned}$$

where

$$c := pu^{1/2}\, C_{2,0},\quad C_{3,\tau} := C_{1,\tau} + pu^{1/2}\, C_{2,\tau},\quad C_{4,\tau} := pu^{1/2}\, C_{2,\tau}.$$

Then $\mathrm{Var}({}_{\bullet 0|}V_{xy}{}^{\circ})$ can be calculated by the general method of 15.2. In fact, double sums can be avoided in this particular case. Indeed, c can be dropped and

$$(1_{X<Y}\, C_{3,X}\, v^X + 1_{Y<X}\, C_{4,Y}\, v^Y)^2 = 1_{X<Y}\,(C_{3,X})^2\, v^{2X} + 1_{Y<X}\,(C_{4,Y})^2\, v^{2Y}.$$

Hence,

$$\mathrm{Var}({}_{\bullet 0|}V_{xy}{}^{\circ}) = [\bar{A}^{\,1}_{xy}((C_{3,\tau})^2, i') + \bar{A}_{xy}^{\ \ 1}((C_{4,\tau})^2, i')] - [\bar{A}^{\,1}_{xy}(C_{3,\tau}) + \bar{A}_{xy}^{\ \ 1}(C_{4,\tau})]^2\,.$$

The prices in the last member can be approximated by single sums. See Ch.11.(49).

Chapter 16

POPULATION GROUPS ON A GRAPH

16.1. Closed graph model

We assume that the states of a graph are occupied by n individuals. We denote by ${}_{t}N_{\alpha}{}^{\circ}$ the number of individuals in state α at time t. The evolution of the population groups results from the following rules defining the **closed graph model**. At origin t=0, all n individuals are in state α=0 and all other states are void:

$$ {}_{0}N_{0}{}^{\circ} = n,\ \ {}_{0}N_{\alpha}{}^{\circ} = 0\ (\alpha \neq 0). \tag{1}$$

At any moment τ, any individual in state α can jump to a state $\beta \in \alpha'$. The probability that this jump occurs during time interval $d\tau$ equals ${}_{\tau}\mu_{\alpha\to\beta}\, d\tau$. Jumps akin to different individuals are independent. No individuals from outside join the graph and no individuals from the graph leave it.

We denote by ${}_{s|t}J_{\alpha\to\beta}{}^{\circ}$ the number of jumps from state α to state β during time interval (s,s+t). Obviously,

$$ {}_{s+t}N_{\beta}{}^{\circ} - {}_{s}N_{\beta}{}^{\circ} = \textstyle\sum_{\alpha\in'\beta}\, {}_{s|t}J_{\alpha\to\beta}{}^{\circ} - \sum_{\gamma\in\beta'}\, {}_{s|t}J_{\beta\to\gamma}{}^{\circ}. \tag{2}$$

This formula results also from Ch.14.(42) at present value level with δ=0. Indeed, let i=0 and let ${}_{s|t}\overline{A}_{k,\alpha\to\beta}{}^{\circ\circ}$ be the insurance of amount 1 payable to individual k at the moment of jump, if he jumps from state α to state β during time interval (s,s+t). Let us consider the population group with one person k. Then ${}_{s|t}\overline{A}_{k,\alpha\to\beta}{}^{\circ}$ is in fact the number of jumps (0 or 1) during moments s and s+t. Let ${}_{s}E_{k,\beta}{}^{\circ\circ}$ be the insurance of amount 1 payable to individual k at s if he is in state β at that moment. Then ${}_{s}E_{k,\beta}{}^{\circ}$ is the number of individuals (0 or 1) in state β at moment s. By Ch.14.(42),

$$ {}_{s+t}E_{k,\beta}{}^{\circ} - {}_{s}E_{k,\beta}{}^{\circ} = \textstyle\sum_{\alpha\in'\beta}\, {}_{s|t}\overline{A}_{k,\alpha\to\beta}{}^{\circ} - \sum_{\gamma\in\beta'}\, {}_{s|t}\overline{A}_{k,\beta\to\gamma}{}^{\circ}. \tag{3}$$

Then

$$ \textstyle\sum_{1\le k\le n}\, {}_{s+t}E_{k,\beta}{}^{\circ} - \sum_{1\le k\le n}\, {}_{s}E_{k,\beta}{}^{\circ}$$

$$ = \textstyle\sum_{\alpha\in'\beta}\sum_{1\le k\le n}\, {}_{s|t}\overline{A}_{k,\alpha\to\beta}{}^{\circ} - \sum_{\gamma\in\beta'}\sum_{1\le k\le n}\, {}_{s|t}\overline{A}_{k,\beta\to\gamma}{}^{\circ}, \tag{4}$$

where

$$ \textstyle\sum_{1\le k\le n}\, {}_{s+t}E_{k,\beta}{}^{\circ} = {}_{s+t}N_{\beta}{}^{\circ},\ \ \sum_{1\le k\le n}\, {}_{s+t}E_{k,\beta}{}^{\circ} = {}_{s+t}N_{\beta}{}^{\circ}, \tag{5}$$

$$\sum_{1\le k\le n} {}_{s|t}\overline{A}_{k,\alpha\to\beta}{}^{\circ} = {}_{s|t}J_{\alpha\to\beta}{}^{\circ},\ \sum_{1\le k\le n} {}_{s|t}\overline{A}_{k,\beta\to\gamma}{}^{\circ} = {}_{s|t}J_{\beta\to\gamma}{}^{\circ}. \tag{6}$$

Hence, relations (2) and (4) are identical. Taking expectations, we obtain

$$_{s+t}N_\beta - {}_sN_\beta = \sum_{\alpha\in'\beta} {}_{s|t}J_{\alpha\to\beta} - \sum_{\gamma\in\beta'} {}_{s|t}J_{\beta\to\gamma}, \tag{7}$$

where

$$_sN_\beta = E\ {}_sN_\beta{}^{\circ} = \sum_{1\le k\le n} {}_sE_{k,\beta} = \sum_{1\le k\le n} {}_sp_{k,\beta},$$

$$_{s|t}J_{\alpha\to\beta} = E\ {}_{s|t}J_{\alpha\to\beta}{}^{\circ} = \sum_{1\le k\le n} {}_{s|t}\overline{A}_{k,\alpha\to\beta} = \sum_{1\le k\le n} \int_{(s,s+t)} {}_\tau p_{k,\alpha}\ {}_\tau\mu_{\alpha\to\beta}\ d\tau$$

$$= \int_{(s,s+t)} \left(\sum_{1\le k\le n} {}_\tau p_{k,\alpha}\right) {}_\tau\mu_{\alpha\to\beta}\ d\tau = \int_{(s,s+t)} {}_\tau N_\alpha\ {}_\tau\mu_{\alpha\to\beta}\ d\tau$$

and where ${}_\tau p_{k,\alpha} = {}_\tau p_\alpha$ is the probability that individual k is in state α at time τ. Hence,

$$_{s+t}N_\beta - {}_sN_\beta = \sum_{\alpha\in'\beta} \int_{(s,s+t)} {}_\tau N_\alpha\ {}_\tau\mu_{\alpha\to\beta}\ d\tau - \sum_{\gamma\in\beta'} \int_{(s,s+t)} {}_\tau N_\beta\ {}_\tau\mu_{\beta\to\gamma}\ d\tau. \tag{8}$$

Theorem 1

In the closed graph model, the expected number of individuals ${}_\tau N_\beta$ in state β at moment τ satisfies the differential equation

$$\mathbf{d\ {}_\tau N_\beta = \sum_{\alpha\in'\beta} {}_\tau N_\alpha\ {}_\tau\mu_{\alpha\to\beta}\ d\tau - {}_\tau N_\beta \sum_{\gamma\in\beta'} {}_\tau\mu_{\beta\to\gamma}\ d\tau.} \tag{9}$$

Proof

Divide (8) by t>0 and let $t\downarrow 0$. Then

$$({}_sN_\beta)' = \sum_{\alpha\in'\beta} {}_sN_\alpha\ {}_s\mu_{\alpha\to\beta} - {}_sN_\beta \sum_{\gamma\in\beta'} {}_s\mu_{\beta\to\gamma},$$

where the accent represents a differentiation with respect to s. Then (9) results from the replacement of s by τ and from multiplication by $d\tau$ •

Of course Theorem 1 is based on regularity assumptions (implicitly assumed). For instance, it is enough to suppose that all functions ${}_\tau\mu_{\alpha\to\beta}$ are piecewise continuous functions of τ with left and right sided limits.

16.2. Open graph model

In the **open graph model**, we assume that ${}_{s|t}K_{out,\beta}{}^{\circ}$ individuals leave state β and the graph during time interval (s,s+t) and that ${}_{s|t}K_{in,\beta}{}^{\circ}$ new individuals join state β during that interval. Let ${}_\tau\xi_{out,\beta}d\tau$ be the expected number of individuals leaving state β and the graph in $d\tau$ and ${}_\tau\xi_{in,\beta}d\tau$ the expected number of new individuals joining β during that time interval. Then

$$_{s|t}K_{out,\beta} = E\ {}_{s|t}K_{out,\beta}{}^{\circ} = \int_{(s,s+t)} {}_\tau\xi_{out,\beta}\ d\tau \tag{10}$$

and

$$_{s|t}K_{in,\beta} = E\ {}_{s|t}K_{in,\beta}{}^{\circ} = \int_{(s,s+t)} {}_\tau\xi_{in,\beta}\ d\tau. \tag{11}$$

Theorem 2

In the open graph model, the expected number of individuals $_{\tau}N_{\beta}$ in state β at moment τ satisfies the differential equation

$$d\,_{\tau}N_{\beta} = {_{\tau}\xi_{\beta}}\, d\tau + \sum_{\alpha\in'\beta}\, {_{\tau}N_{\alpha}}\, {_{\tau}\mu_{\alpha\to\beta}}\, d\tau - {_{\tau}N_{\beta}} \sum_{\gamma\in\beta'}\, {_{\tau}\mu_{\beta\to\gamma}}\, d\tau, \tag{12}$$

where $_{\tau}\xi_{\beta} := {_{\tau}\xi_{in,\beta}} - {_{\tau}\xi_{out,\beta}}$.

Proof

Here (2) must be completed as

$$_{s+t}N_{\beta}^{\circ} - {_{s}N_{\beta}^{\circ}} = {_{s|t}K_{in,\beta}^{\circ}} - {_{s|t}K_{out,\beta}^{\circ}} + \sum_{\alpha\in'\beta}\, {_{s|t}J_{\alpha\to\beta}^{\circ}} - \sum_{\gamma\in\beta'}\, {_{s|t}J_{\beta\to\gamma}^{\circ}}. \tag{13}$$

Taking expectations,

$$_{s+t}N_{\beta} - {_{s}N_{\beta}} = {_{s|t}K_{in,\beta}} - {_{s|t}K_{out,\beta}} + \sum_{\alpha\in'\beta}\, {_{s|t}J_{\alpha\to\beta}} - \sum_{\gamma\in\beta'}\, {_{s|t}J_{\beta\to\gamma}}. \tag{14}$$

We divide by t and we notice that

$$_{s|t}K_{in,\beta}/t - {_{s|t}K_{out,\beta}}/t = [\int_{(s,s+t)} {_{\tau}\xi_{in,\beta}}\, d\tau]/t - [\int_{(s,s+t)} {_{\tau}\xi_{out,\beta}}\, d\tau]/t$$

$$\to {_{s}\xi_{in,\beta}} - {_{s}\xi_{out,\beta}} = {_{s}\xi_{\beta}} \text{ as } t\to 0.$$

The other terms of (14) are treated in the same way as in the closed graph case •

By App.D and (9) or (12), the functions $_{\tau}N_0$, $_{\tau}N_1$, $_{\tau}N_2$, ... ($t\geq 0$) can be found successively from initial conditions (1), i.e. $_0N_0=n$ and $_0N_{\alpha}=0$ ($\alpha\neq 0$). The functions $_{\tau}N_0$, $_{\tau}N_1$, $_{\tau}N_2$, ... ($\tau\geq s$) where $s>0$ is fixed, can be found from any initial values $_sN_0$, $_sN_1$, $_sN_2$, ... All involved integrals can be evaluated numerically.

16.3. Estimation of instantaneous transition rates

We now consider the estimation problem of instantaneous transition rates in graphs such as those of Ch.14.2. (In complete extinction graphs of a group of lives, these rates are $\mu_{x+\tau}$, $\mu_{y+\tau}$, ...). The functions $_{\tau}N_0$, $_{\tau}N_1$, $_{\tau}N_2$, ... ($s\leq\tau\leq t$) can be found explicitly, given the initial values $_sN_0$, $_sN_1$, $_sN_2$, ..., if all functions $_{\tau}\mu_{\alpha\to\beta}$ and $_{\tau}\nu_{\beta}$ are constant on interval (s,t). The latter assumption is not unrealistic if $t-s$ is small (e.g. $t-s=1$ in the graphs of Ch.14.2).

In order to estimate the transition rates $\mu_{\alpha\to\beta}$ on interval (s,t), treated as constant on that interval, we consider the open graph model with constant functions $\mu_{\alpha\to\beta}$ and ξ_{β} on [s,t]. Solving the differential equations (12) on [s,t], we find analytic relations connecting

$$_sN_{\alpha}\,,\ {_tN_{\alpha}}\,,\ \mu_{\alpha\to\beta}\,,\ (t-s)\xi_{\beta}\ \ (\alpha,\beta = 0,1,2,...). \tag{15}$$

These relations allow to find $\mu_{\alpha\to\beta}$ as functions of

$$ {}_sN_\alpha\,,\ {}_tN_\alpha\,,\ (t-s)\nu_\beta\ \ (\alpha,\beta=0,1,2,\ldots). $$

In the latter functions, we **replace the expected numbers by observed numbers** (see following *Remark*). In this way, estimators for $\mu_{\alpha\to\beta}$ are obtained. Hence, we replace ${}_sN_\alpha$, ${}_tN_\alpha$ (α= 0,1,2,...) by corresponding observed numbers ${}_sN_\alpha{}^\circ$, ${}_tN_\alpha{}^\circ$. Explicitly, at instant s (say now) state α=0,1,2,... is supposed to be occupied by a large fixed number ${}_sN_\alpha{}^\circ$ of individuals and then ${}_tN_\alpha{}^\circ$ is the observed number of individuals in state α, t−s years later.

We notice that

$$ {}_{s|t-s}K_\alpha := {}_{s|t-s}K_{in,\alpha} - {}_{s|t-s}K_{out,\alpha} = \int_{(s,t)} \xi_\alpha\, d\tau = (t-s)\,\xi_\alpha. $$

Hence, $(t-s)\xi_\alpha$ is the expectation of

$$ {}_{s|t-s}K_\alpha{}^\circ := {}_{s|t-s}K_{in,\alpha}{}^\circ - {}_{s|t-s}K_{out,\alpha}{}^\circ $$

and we replace $(t-s)\xi_\alpha$ by the observed difference ${}_{s|t-s}K_\alpha{}^\circ$ accordingly.

This method is worked out in the case of particular graphs in the following sections. Then simplified notations are used. Instead of

$$ {}_\tau N_\alpha\,,\ {}_{s|t}K_\alpha\,,\ \mu_{\alpha\to\beta}\,,\ \xi_\alpha\ (\alpha,\beta=0,1,2,\ldots), $$

we write $\quad M_\tau\,, N_\tau\,, \ldots, K_{s,t}\,, L_{s,t}\,, \ldots, \lambda\,, \mu\,, \ldots, \xi\,, \eta\,, \ldots$

We use the notations λ°, μ°, ..., for estimators of λ, μ, ...

Remark

Equality between expected and observed values is a very general statistical estimation method leading to classical estimators in classical situations. For instance, let N° be an integer random variable with binomial distribution with parameters n (fixed) and p (unknown). Then $EN^\circ=np$. Hence, $p=EN^\circ/n$ and the estimator for p, resulting from the indicated principle, is $p^\circ = N^\circ/n$.

16.4. Estimations in a graph with two states

We consider the graph with two states 0 and 1 of following figure. The expected number of individuals in state 0 and 1 at moment $\tau\in[s,t]$ is M_τ and N_τ resp. The instantaneous transition rate from state 0 to state 1 is μ.

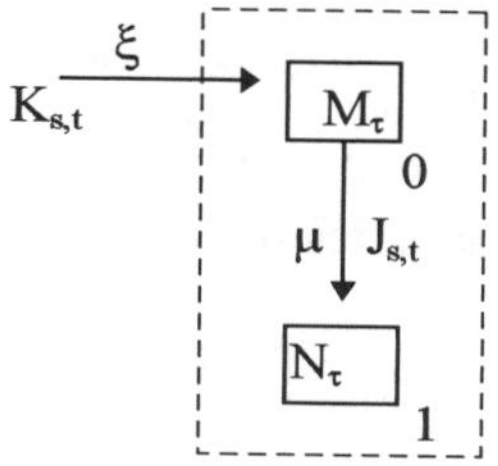

Figure 16.1. Open population graph with two states.

The expected number of jumps from state 0 to state 1 during times s and t is $J_{s,t}$. The rate of expected new entries (in fact a difference between entries and exits) in state 0 is ξ and the expected number of new entries during times s and t is $K_{s,t}$. No entries from ouside in state 1 are considered.

Solution of the differential system

By Theorem 2, the functions M_τ and N_τ satisfy the differential equations

$$dM_\tau = \xi\, d\tau - \mu\, M_\tau\, d\tau \tag{16}$$

and

$$dN_\tau = \mu\, M_\tau\, d\tau \tag{17}$$

on the small interval [s,t]. By (16) and App.D,

$$M_t = (M_s + \int_{(s,t)} \xi\, e^{(\tau-s)\mu}\, d\tau)\, e^{-(t-s)\mu} = (M_s + \xi \int_{(0,t-s)} e^{\tau\mu}\, d\tau)\, e^{-(t-s)\mu}$$

$$= [M_s + (\xi/\mu)(e^{(t-s)\mu} - 1)]\, e^{-(t-s)\mu}.$$

Hence,

$$\mathbf{M_t = \xi/\mu + (M_s - \xi/\mu)\, e^{-(t-s)\mu} = (\xi/\mu)[1 - e^{-(t-s)\mu}] + M_s\, e^{-(t-s)\mu}}. \tag{18}$$

Of course, this relation is valid for any $\tau \in [s,t]$ instead of t. Then by (17),

$$N_t - N_s = \int_{(s,t)} dN_\tau = \mu \int_{(s,t)} M_\tau\, d\tau = \xi(t-s) + (\mu\, M_s - \xi)\int_{(s,t)} e^{-(\tau-s)\mu}\, d\tau$$

$$= \xi(t-s) + (\mu\, M_s - \xi)\int_{(0,t-s)} e^{-\tau\mu}\, d\tau = \xi(t-s) + (M_s - \xi/\mu)[1 - e^{-(t-s)\mu}].$$

Hence,

$$\mathbf{N_t = N_s + \xi(t-s) + (M_s - \xi/\mu)[1 - e^{-(t-s)\mu}]}\,. \tag{19}$$

Theorem 3 (Relation for μ°)

In the model with two states of this section, the estimator μ° of μ resulting from equality between expected and observed values, satisfies the equation

$$\mathbf{M_t^\circ = K_{s,t}^\circ\, [1 - e^{-(t-s)\mu^\circ}]/[(t-s)\mu^\circ] + M_s^\circ\, e^{-(t-s)\mu^\circ}}. \tag{20}$$

Proof

By (18), $$M_t = K_{s,t}\,[1-e^{-(t-s)\mu}]/[(t-s)\mu] + M_s\,e^{-(t-s)\mu} \tag{21}$$

because $\xi(t-s)=K_{s,t}$. Then the estimator $\mu°$, resulting from equality between expected and observed values, satisfies the equation (20) •

By (19), we find the following relation for $\mu°$:

$$N_t° = N_s° + K_{s,t}° + M_s°[1-e^{-(t-s)\mu°}] - K_{s,t}°\,[1-e^{-(t-s)\mu°}]/[(t-s)\mu°]. \tag{22}$$

This relation is equivalent to (20). Indeed, by summation of (20) and (22) we obtain the correct relation

$$M_t° + N_t° = N_s° + M_s° + K_{s,t}°.$$

Approximations

Although equation (20) for $\mu°$ can easily be solved numerically when $M_s°$, $M_t°$ and $K_{s,t}°$ are fixed, explicit approximations are interesting.

By (20) and by the power series for the exponential function,

$$M_t° = K_{s,t}°\,[1-e^{-(t-s)\mu°}]/[(t-s)\mu°] + M_s°\,e^{-(t-s)\mu°}$$

$$= K_{s,t}°[1-(t-s)\mu°/2+(t-s)^2\mu^{°2}/6 - \ldots] + M_s°[1-(t-s)\mu°+(t-s)^2\mu^{°2}/2 + \ldots],$$

$$M_s° - M_t° + K_{s,t}° = (M_s° + K_{s,t}°/2)\,[(t-s)\mu°] - (M_s°/2 + K_{s,t}°/6)\,[(t-s)\mu°]^2 + \ldots \tag{23}$$

Hence,

$$J_{s,t}° = c_1°[(t-s)\mu°] - c_2°[(t-s)\mu°]^2 + c_3°[(t-s)\mu°]^3 - c_4°[(t-s)\mu°]^4 + \ldots, \tag{24}$$

where $J_{s,t}°:=M_s°-M_t°+K_{s,t}°$ is the number of jumps from state 0 to state 1 during times s and t and

$$c_k° := M_s°/k! + K_{s,t}°/(k+1)! \quad (k=1,2,\ldots). \tag{25}$$

The equation (24) for $(t-s)\mu°$ can be solved by App.E. The solution is

$$(t-s)\mu° = J_{s,t}°/c_1° + c_2°(J_{s,t}°)^2/(c_1°)^3 + [2(c_2°)^2 - c_1°c_3°](J_{s,t}°)^3/(c_1°)^5 + [5(c_2°)^3 - 5\,c_1°c_2°c_3° + (c_1°)^2c_4°](J_{s,t}°)^4/(c_1°)^7 + \ldots \tag{26}$$

In the first order approximation, terms in $(J_{s,t}°)^k (k\geq2)$ are neglected in the last member of relation (27). Hence, the **first order approximation of** $\mu°$ is the estimator

$$\boldsymbol{\mu_1° = J_{s,t}°/[(t-s)(M_s° + K_{s,t}°/2)]}. \tag{27}$$

In particular, in case of observations during one year, t=s+1 and then relation (27) becomes

$$\boldsymbol{\mu_1^\circ = J_{s,s+1}^\circ/(M_s^\circ + K_{s,s+1}^\circ/2).} \quad (28)$$

In the case of extinction graph $Gr_2(x)$ on the live x (Ch.14.1), $q_x \approx \mu_x$ and then relation (28) is compatible with relation Ch.3.(4). Estimations in $Gr_2(x)$ are discussed more extensively in 16.11.

16.5. Estimations in a graph with three states

The following graph with three states 0, 1 and 2 speaks for itself.

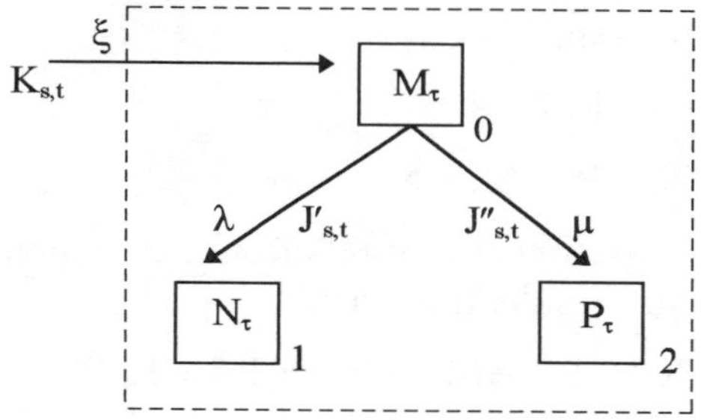

Figure 16.2. Open population graph with three states

Solution of the differential system

By Theorem 2, the functions M_τ, N_τ and P_τ satisfy the differentiel equations

$$dM_\tau = \xi\, d\tau - (\lambda+\mu)M_\tau\, d\tau, \quad (29)$$

$$dN_\tau = \lambda\, M_\tau\, d\tau \quad (30)$$

and

$$dP_\tau = \mu\, M_\tau\, d\tau \quad (31)$$

on the small interval [s,t].

Let $\sigma := \lambda+\mu$. Then equation (29) becomes

$$dM_\tau = \xi\, d\tau - \sigma\, M_\tau\, d\tau. \quad (32)$$

This is the same equation as (16) with σ instead of μ. Hence, by (18),

$$\mathbf{M_t = \xi/\sigma + (M_s - \xi/\sigma)\, e^{-(t-s)\sigma} = (\xi/\sigma)\,[1 - e^{-(t-s)\sigma}] + M_s\, e^{-(t-s)\sigma}}. \quad (33)$$

Of course, this relation is valid for any $\tau \in [s,t]$ instead of t. Then by (30),

$$N_t-N_s = \int_{(s,t)} dN_\tau = \lambda \int_{(s,t)} M_\tau\, d\tau$$
$$= \lambda\xi(t-s)/\sigma + \lambda(M_s - \xi/\sigma) \int_{(s,t)} e^{-(\tau-s)\sigma}\, d\tau$$
$$= \lambda\xi(t-s)/\sigma + \lambda(M_s - \xi/\sigma) \int_{(0,t-s)} e^{-\tau\sigma}\, d\tau$$
$$= (\lambda/\sigma)\xi(t-s) + (\lambda/\sigma)(M_s - \xi/\sigma)[1 - e^{-(t-s)\sigma}]$$

Hence,

$$\mathbf{N_t - N_s = (\lambda/\sigma)\xi(t-s) + (\lambda/\sigma)(M_s - \xi/\sigma)[1 - e^{-(t-s)\sigma}]}. \tag{34}$$

In the same way, by (31),

$$\mathbf{P_t - P_s = (\mu/\sigma)\xi(t-s) + (\mu/\sigma)(M_s - \xi/\sigma)[1 - e^{-(t-s)\sigma}]}. \tag{35}$$

By summation of (29), (30) and (31),

$$d(M_\tau+N_\tau+P_\tau) = \xi\, d\tau$$

and then

$$M_t + N_t + P_t = M_s + N_s + P_s + \xi(t-s) \tag{36}$$

by integration. The latter relation also results from summation of (33), (34) and (35). Relation (36) also results from identity

$$M_t^\circ + N_t^\circ + P_t^\circ = M_s^\circ + N_s^\circ + P_s^\circ + K_{t,s}^\circ \tag{37}$$

by taking expectations. Obviously,

$$N_s^\circ + J'^\circ_{s,t} = N_t^\circ, \quad P_s^\circ + J''^\circ_{s,t} = P_t^\circ, \tag{38}$$

where $J'^\circ_{s,t}$ is the number of jumps from state 0 to state 1 and $J''_{s,t}$ the number of jumps from state 0 to state 2 during times s and t.

The quotient of (34) and (35) furnishes the relation

$$(N_t-N_s)/(P_t-P_s) = \lambda/\mu, \quad \text{i.e. } J'_{s,t}/J''_{s,t} = \lambda/\mu. \tag{39}$$

The first relation (39) is direct from equation $\mu dN_\tau = \lambda dP_\tau$ resulting from (30) and (31). By the last relation (39),

$$J'_{s,t}/(J'_{s,t} + J''_{s,t}) = \lambda/(\lambda+\mu), \quad J''_{s,t}/(J'_{s,t} + J''_{s,t}) = \mu/(\lambda+\mu), \tag{40}$$

because $a/b=\lambda/\mu \Rightarrow a/(a+b)=\lambda/(\lambda+\mu)$, $b/(a+b)=\mu/(\lambda+\mu)$. Hence,

$$\lambda = \sigma\, J'_{s,t}/J_{s,t}\,,\ \mu = \sigma\, J''_{s,t}/J_{s,t}\,, \tag{41}$$

where $J_{s,t}=EJ_{s,t}^\circ$ and

$$J_{s,t}^\circ := J'^\circ_{s,t} + J''^\circ_{s,t} = M_s^\circ - M_t^\circ + K_{s,t}^\circ$$

is the number of jumps out of state 0.

Theorem 4 (Relations for λ° and μ°)

In the model with three states of this section, the estimators λ° and μ° for λ and μ resulting from equality between expected and observed values are

$$\lambda^\circ = \sigma^\circ J'_{s,t}{}^\circ / J_{s,t}{}^\circ \tag{42}$$

and

$$\mu^\circ = \sigma^\circ J''_{s,t}{}^\circ / J_{s,t}{}^\circ, \tag{43}$$

where σ° is the solution of equation

$$M_t{}^\circ = K_{s,t}{}^\circ \, [1 - e^{-(t-s)\sigma^\circ}]/[(t-s)\sigma^\circ] + M_s{}^\circ \, e^{-(t-s)\sigma^\circ}. \tag{44}$$

Proof

(42) and (43) result from (41). Relation (44) results from (33) in the same way as (20) has resulted from (18) •

λ° and μ° can be derived from other relations than (33) and (41), for instance from (33) and (34), or from (33) and (35). By (37), it is easily verified that the same estimators are obtained in all cases.

Approximations

Equation (44) for σ° is the same as equation (20) for μ°. Hence, approximations can be displayed for σ° by the method of 16.4. Then corresponding approximations are obtained for λ° and μ°. For instance, the **first order approximation of σ°** is the same as (27),

$$\sigma_1{}^\circ = J_{s,t}{}^\circ/[(t-s)(M_s{}^\circ + K_{s,t}{}^\circ/2)], \tag{45}$$

and the corresponding **first order approximations of λ° and μ°** are

$$\lambda_1{}^\circ = J'_{s,t}{}^\circ/[(t-s)(M_s{}^\circ + K_{s,t}{}^\circ/2)] \tag{46}$$

and

$$\mu_1{}^\circ = J''_{s,t}{}^\circ/[(t-s)(M_s{}^\circ + K_{s,t}{}^\circ/2)]. \tag{47}$$

by (42) and (43).

In the case of yearly observations, t=s+1 and then (46) and (47) become

$$\lambda_1{}^\circ = J'_{s,t}{}^\circ/(M_s{}^\circ + K_{s,s+1}{}^\circ/2) \tag{48}$$

and

$$\mu_1{}^\circ = J''_{s,t}{}^\circ/(M_s{}^\circ + K_{s,s+1}{}^\circ/2). \tag{49}$$

The latter relations can be interpreted by the argument of Ch.3.3.

16.6. Estimations in a graph with four states

We consider the following graph with four states.

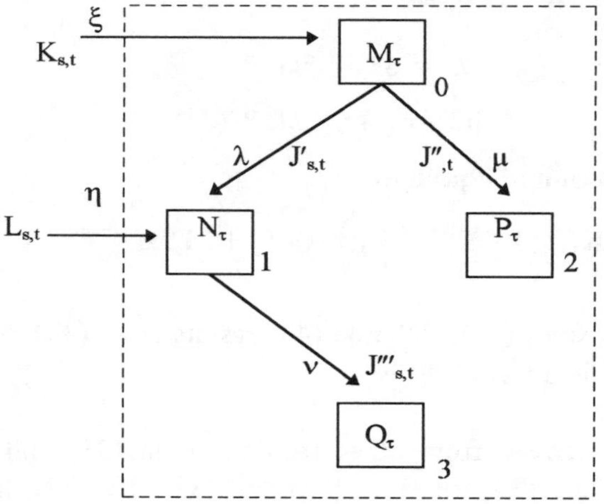

Figure 16.3. Open population graph with four states

Solution of the differential system

By Theorem 2, the functions M_τ, N_τ P_τ and Q_τ satisfy the differential equations

$$dM_\tau = \xi\, d\tau - (\lambda+\mu)M_\tau\, d\tau, \tag{50}$$

$$dN_\tau = \eta\, d\tau + \lambda\, M_\tau\, d\tau - \nu\, N_\tau\, d\tau, \tag{51}$$

$$dP_\tau = \mu\, M_\tau\, d\tau \tag{52}$$

and
$$dQ_\tau = \nu\, N_\tau\, d\tau \tag{53}$$

on the small interval [s,t]. We define $\sigma{:=}\lambda+\mu$. Then (50) becomes

$$dM_\tau = \xi\, d\tau - \sigma\, M_\tau\, d\tau, \tag{54}$$

i.e. (32). The solution is

$$\mathbf{M_t = \xi/\sigma + (M_s - \xi/\sigma)\, e^{-(t-s)\sigma} = (\xi/\sigma)\, [1 - e^{-(t-s)\sigma}] + M_s\, e^{-(t-s)\sigma}}, \tag{55}$$

i.e. (33). We introduce M_τ in (51). Then by App.D applied to that equation,

$$N_t = \big[N_s + \textstyle\int_{(s,t)} [\eta + \lambda\xi/\sigma + \lambda\, (M_s - \xi/\sigma)\, e^{-(\tau-s)\sigma}]e^{(\tau-s)\nu}d\tau\big]e^{-(t-s)\nu}$$

$$= \big[N_s + (\eta + \lambda\xi/\sigma)\textstyle\int_{(s,t)} e^{(\tau-s)\nu}d\tau + \lambda\, (M_s - \xi/\sigma)\, \int_{(s,t)} e^{(\tau-s)(\nu-\sigma)}d\tau\big]e^{-(t-s)\nu}$$

$$= [N_s + (\eta + \lambda\xi/\sigma)\int_{(0,t-s)} e^{\tau\nu}d\tau + \lambda (M_s - \xi/\sigma) \int_{(0,t-s)} e^{\tau(\nu-\sigma)}d\tau]e^{-(t-s)\nu}$$

$$= [N_s + (\eta + \lambda\xi/\sigma)[e^{(t-s)\nu}-1]/\nu + \lambda (M_s - \xi/\sigma) [e^{(t-s)(\nu-\sigma)}-1]/(\nu-\sigma)]e^{-(t-s)\nu}$$

Hence,

$$\mathbf{N_t = (\eta + \lambda\xi/\sigma)/\nu + [N_s - (\eta + \lambda\xi/\sigma)/\nu - \lambda (M_s - \xi/\sigma)/(\nu-\sigma)] e^{-(t-s)\nu}}$$
$$\mathbf{+ [\lambda (M_s - \xi/\sigma)/(\nu-\sigma)]e^{-(t-s)\sigma}}. \quad (56)$$

Relation (35) has resulted from (29) and (31). The latter relations are the same as (50) and (52). Hence, (35) is still valid here:

$$\mathbf{P_t - P_s = (\mu/\sigma)\xi(t-s) + (\mu/\sigma) (M_s - \xi/\sigma) [1 - e^{-(t-s)\sigma}]}. \quad (57)$$

By (53) and (56), $Q_t - Q_s = \nu \int_{(s,t)} N_\tau \, d\tau =$

$$(\eta + \lambda\xi/\sigma)(t-s) + [\nu N_s - (\eta + \lambda\xi/\sigma) - \lambda\nu (M_s - \xi/\sigma)/(\nu-\sigma)] \int_{(s,t)} e^{-(\tau-s)\nu} \, d\tau$$
$$+ [\lambda\nu (M_s - \xi/\sigma)/(\nu-\sigma)] \int_{(s,t)} e^{-(\tau-s)\sigma} \, d\tau$$

where $\int_{(s,t)} e^{-(\tau-s)\nu} \, d\tau = \int_{(0,t-s)} e^{-\tau\nu} \, d\tau = [1 - e^{-(t-s)\nu}]/\nu$

and $\int_{(s,t)} e^{-(\tau-s)\sigma} \, d\tau = \int_{(0,t-s)} e^{-\tau\sigma} \, d\tau = [1 - e^{-(t-s)\sigma}]/\sigma$

Hence, $\mathbf{Q_t - Q_s = (\eta + \lambda\xi/\sigma)(t-s)}$

$$\mathbf{+ [N_s - (\eta + \lambda\xi/\sigma)/\nu - \lambda (M_s - \xi/\sigma)/(\nu-\sigma)][1 - e^{-(t-s)\nu}]}$$
$$\mathbf{+ [\lambda\nu (M_s/\sigma - \xi/\sigma^2)/(\nu-\sigma)][1 - e^{-(t-s)\sigma}]}. \quad (58)$$

By summation of (50), (51), (52) and (53),

$$d(M_\tau + N_\tau + P_\tau + Q_\tau) = \xi \, d\tau + \eta \, d\tau$$

and then by integration

$$M_t - M_s + N_t - N_s + P_t - P_s + Q_t - Q_s = \xi(t-s) + \eta(t-s) = K_{s,t} + L_{s,t}. \quad (59)$$

(59) also results from the identity

$$M_t^\circ - M_s^\circ + N_t^\circ - N_s^\circ + P_t^\circ - P_s^\circ + Q_t^\circ - Q_s^\circ = K_{s,t}^\circ + L_{s,t}^\circ \quad (60)$$

by taking expectations.

By summation of (51) and (53),

$$d(N_\tau+Q_\tau) - \eta \, d\tau = \lambda \, M_\tau \, d\tau$$

and then by (52), $\mu[d(N_\tau+Q_\tau) - \eta \, d\tau] = \lambda \, dP_\tau$.

Then by integration,

$$\mu[N_t - N_s + Q_t - Q_s - \eta(t-s)] = \lambda(P_t - P_s), \quad (61)$$

where $\eta(t-s)=L_{s,t}$.

Hence, $$\lambda/\mu = [N_t - N_s + Q_t - Q_s - L_{s,t}]/(P_t - P_s)$$
and then

$$\lambda/\sigma = [N_t - N_s + Q_t - Q_s - L_{s,t}]/[N_t - N_s + P_t - P_s + Q_t - Q_s - L_{s,t}] \quad (62)$$

and $$\mu/\sigma = (P_t - P_s)/[N_t - N_s + P_t - P_s + Q_t - Q_s - L_{s,t}] \quad (63)$$

because $\lambda/\mu = a/b \Rightarrow \lambda/(\lambda+\mu) = a/(a+b),\ \mu/(\lambda+\mu) = b/(a+b)$.

Let $J_{s,t}^\circ = J'_{s,t}{}^\circ + J''_{s,t}{}^\circ$, where $J'_{s,t}{}^\circ$ is the number of jumps from state 0 to state 1 and $J''_{s,t}{}^\circ$ the number of jumps from state 0 to state 2. Then obviously,

$$K_{s,t}^\circ + M_s^\circ = M_t^\circ + J_{s,t}^\circ, \quad (64)$$

$$N_t^\circ + Q_t^\circ = N_s^\circ + Q_s^\circ + J'_{s,t}{}^\circ + L_{s,t}^\circ \quad (65)$$

and $$P_t^\circ = P_s^\circ + J''_{s,t}{}^\circ. \quad (66)$$

Hence,
$$J_{s,t}^\circ = M_s^\circ - M_t^\circ + K_{s,t}^\circ = N_t^\circ - N_s^\circ + P_t^\circ - P_s^\circ + Q_t^\circ - Q_s^\circ - L_{s,t}^\circ \quad (67)$$

by (60), $$J'_{s,t}{}^\circ = N_t^\circ - N_s^\circ + Q_t^\circ - Q_s^\circ - L_{s,t}^\circ \quad (68)$$

and $$J''_{s,t}{}^\circ = P_t^\circ - P_s^\circ. \quad (69)$$

By these relations, at expected value level, and by (62) and (63),

$$\lambda = \sigma\, J'_{s,t}/J_{s,t}\,,\quad \mu = \sigma\, J''_{s,t}/J_{s,t}. \quad (70)$$

By (56), $$N_t = N_s\, e^{-(t-s)\nu} + [\eta(t-s) + \lambda\xi(t-s)/\sigma][1-e^{-(t-s)\nu}]/[(t-s)\nu]$$
$$+ \lambda[(t-s)M_s - (t-s)\xi/\sigma][e^{-(t-s)\sigma} - e^{-(t-s)\nu}]/[(t-s)(\nu-\sigma)]$$

Hence, $$N_t = N_s\, e^{-(t-s)\nu} + [L_{s,t} + \lambda K_{s,t}/\sigma][1-e^{-(t-s)\nu}]/[(t-s)\nu]$$
$$+ \lambda[(t-s)M_s - K_{s,t}/\sigma][e^{-(t-s)\sigma} - e^{-(t-s)\nu}]/[(t-s)(\nu-\sigma)]. \quad (71)$$

By the power series of the exponential function,

$$N_t = N_s\,[1 - (t-s)\nu + (t-s)^2\nu^2/2 - \ldots]$$
$$+[L_{s,t} + \lambda K_{s,t}/\sigma][1 - (t-s)\nu/2 + (t-s)^2\nu^2/6 - \ldots]$$
$$+ \lambda[(t-s)M_s - K_{s,t}/\sigma][1 - (t-s)(\nu+\sigma)/2 + (t-s)^2(\nu^2+\nu\sigma+\sigma^2)/6 - \ldots]. \quad (72)$$

Theorem 5 (Relations for λ°, μ° and ν°)

In the model with four states of this section, let λ°, μ° and ν° be the estimators of λ, μ and ν resp. resulting from equality between expected and observed values and let $\sigma^\circ:=\lambda^\circ+\mu^\circ$. Then σ° is the solution of equation

$$M_t^\circ = K_{s,t}^\circ\,[1-e^{-(t-s)\sigma^\circ}]/[(t-s)\sigma^\circ] + M_s^\circ\, e^{-(t-s)\sigma^\circ}. \tag{73}$$

Then
$$\lambda^\circ = \sigma^\circ\, J'_{s,t}{}^\circ/J_{s,t}{}^\circ\,, \quad \mu^\circ = \sigma^\circ\, J''_{s,t}{}^\circ/J_{s,t}{}^\circ \tag{74}$$

and ν° is solution of equation

$$N_t^\circ = N_s^\circ\, e^{-(t-s)\nu^\circ} + [L_{s,t}{}^\circ + \lambda^\circ K_{s,t}{}^\circ/\sigma^\circ][1-e^{-(t-s)\nu^\circ}]/[(t-s)\nu^\circ]$$
$$+ \lambda^\circ[(t-s)M_s^\circ - K_{s,t}{}^\circ/\sigma^\circ][e^{-(t-s)\sigma^\circ} - e^{-(t-s)\nu^\circ}]/[(t-s)(\nu^\circ-\sigma^\circ)]. \tag{75}$$

Proof
By (55), (70) and (71) •

Approximations

Equation (73) for σ° is the same as equation (20) for μ°. Hence, approximations can be displayed for σ° by the method of 16.4. Then corresponding approximations are obtained for λ° and μ° by (74). In particular, the **first order approximations $\lambda_1{}^\circ$ and $\mu_1{}^\circ$ of λ° and μ°** are

$$\lambda_1{}^\circ = J'_{s,t}{}^\circ/[(t-s)(M_s^\circ + K_{s,t}{}^\circ/2)] \tag{76}$$

and
$$\mu_1{}^\circ = J''_{s,t}{}^\circ/[(t-s)(M_s^\circ + K_{s,t}{}^\circ/2)]. \tag{77}$$

In order to obtain a **first order approximation $\nu_1{}^\circ$ of ν°**, we retain two terms only in the expansions in last member of (72):

$$N_t \approx N_s\,[1-(t-s)\nu] + [L_{s,t} + \lambda K_{s,t}/\sigma][1-(t-s)\nu/2]$$
$$+ \lambda[(t-s)M_s - K_{s,t}/\sigma][1-(t-s)(\nu+\sigma)/2]$$
$$= N_s - (t-s)\nu N_s + L_{s,t} - (t-s)\nu L_{s,t}/2 + \lambda[(t-s)M_s$$
$$- \lambda(t-s)^2(\nu+\sigma)M_s/2 + \lambda(t-s)K_{s,t}/2$$

and then

$$(t-s)\nu[N_s + L_{s,t}/2 + \lambda(t-s)M_s/2] \approx N_s - N_t + L_{s,t} + \lambda(t-s)[M_s + K_{s,t}/2],$$

where the term $-\lambda(t-s)^2\sigma M_s/2$ has been neglected in the last member. But

$$\lambda(t-s)M_s \text{ and } \lambda(t-s)[M_s + K_{s,t}/2]$$

are approximations of $J'_{s,t}$, the expected number of jumps from state 0 to state 1 during times s and t. Hence,

$$(t-s)\nu[N_s + L_{s,t}/2 + J'_{s,t}/2] \approx N_s - N_t + L_{s,t} + J'_{s,t}. \quad (78)$$

Obviously,
$$N_s^\circ + L_{s,t}^\circ + J'^\circ_{s,t} = N_t^\circ + J'''^\circ_{s,t}, \quad (79)$$

where $J'''^\circ_{s,t}$ is the number of jumps from state 1 to state 3 during times s and t. Hence, the last member of (78) equals $J'''_{s,t}$. Then

$$(t-s)\nu[N_s + L_{s,t}/2 + J'_{s,t}/2] \approx J'''_{s,t}. \quad (80)$$

This relation allows to define estimator ν_1° as

$$\boldsymbol{\nu_1^\circ = J'''^\circ_{s,t}/[(s-t)(N_s^\circ + L_{s,t}^\circ/2 + J'^\circ_{s,t}/2)]}. \quad (81)$$

Remark

Let us consider the partial graph with two states 1 and 3 of the initial graph with four states. Then jumps from state 0 to state 1 in the initial graph can be regarded as jumps from outside to state 1 in the partial graph. We can apply section 16.4 with $L_{s,t}+J'_{s,t}$ instead of $K_{s,t}$, in order to estimate ν. Then approximation (81) is in complete agreement with (27).

We notice however that the partial model is not strictly a model such as that one discussed in 16.4, because the expected number of individuals coming from state 0 during time interval $d\tau$, is not a constant: it is proportional to the number of individuals in state 0 at moment τ.

16.7. Evaluation of state probabilities

In order to evaluate the price or variance of time capitals (defined in Ch.14.4. and Ch.15.4), we need the transition rates ${}_\tau\mu_{\alpha\to\beta}$ and the **state probabilities** ${}_\tau p_\alpha$ ($\alpha,\beta= 0,1,\ldots$). In the case of extinction graphs of a group of lives, these functions result from foregoing chapters. The following method can be applied to graphs such as those of Ch.14.2. For the sake of completeness, a graph with only two states is also considered.

We assume that the time axis is partitioned in intervals (s,t). For instance, the intervals (s,t) may be (k,k+1) (k=0,1,2,...). We suppose that the transition rates have already been estimated and that they are constant on each interval (s,t) of the partition. Then the state probabilities are determined by the differential equations Ch.14.(7). These equations allow to find the probabilities ${}_t p_\alpha$ when the probabilites ${}_s p_\alpha$ (α=0,1,2,...) are fixed already.

The procedure starts with the probabilities ${}_0p_0=1$, ${}_0p_\alpha=0$ $(\alpha\neq 0)$ on the first interval of the partition.

The method is developed in the case of particular graphs hereafter. Then we use notations

$$\lambda,\ \mu,\ \ldots,\ p_\tau,\ q_\tau,\ \ldots \text{ instead of } {}_\tau\mu_{\alpha\to\beta}\ ,\ {}_\tau p_\alpha\ \ (\alpha,\beta=0,1,2,\ldots).$$

16.8. State probabilities in a graph with two states.

The following graph with two states speaks for itself.

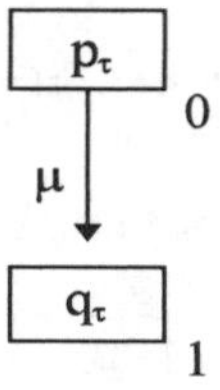

Figure 16.4. Closed probability graph with two states

The differential system of equations Ch.14.(7) becomes

$$d\,p_\tau = -\,\mu\,p_\tau\,d\tau,\quad d\,q_\tau = \mu\,p_\tau\,d\tau \tag{82}$$

on interval [s,t]. This is the same system as (16), (17) with 0, p_τ, q_τ instead of ξ, M_τ, P_τ. Then the solution of system (82) results from (18) and (19). It is

$$p_t = p_s\,e^{-(t-s)\mu},\quad q_t = q_s + p_s[1-e^{-(t-s)\mu}]. \tag{83}$$

By (82), $d(p_\tau+q_\tau)=0$ and then $p_t+q_t=p_s+q_s$ by integration. The latter relation is obvious from relations (83).

16.9. State probabilities in a graph with three states.

In case of following graph, the differential system Ch.14.(7) becomes

$$dp_\tau = -\,(\lambda+\mu)\,p_\tau\,d\tau,\quad dq_\tau = \lambda\,p_\tau\,d\tau,\quad dr_\tau = \mu\,p_\tau\,d\tau \tag{84}$$

on [s,t]. This is the same system as (29), (30), (31) with 0, p_τ, q_τ, r_τ instead of ξ, M_τ, N_τ, P_τ. Hence, the solution is furnished by (33), (34) and (35).

$$p_t = p_s\,e^{-(t-s)(\lambda+\mu)}\ , \tag{85}$$

$$q_t = q_s + \lambda\,p_s\,[1-e^{-(t-s)(\lambda+\mu)}]/(\lambda+\mu), \tag{86}$$

$$r_t = r_s + \mu\, p_s\, [1-e^{-(t-s)(\lambda+\mu)}]/(\lambda+\mu). \tag{87}$$

Now $p_t+q_t+r_t= p_s+q_s+r_s$.

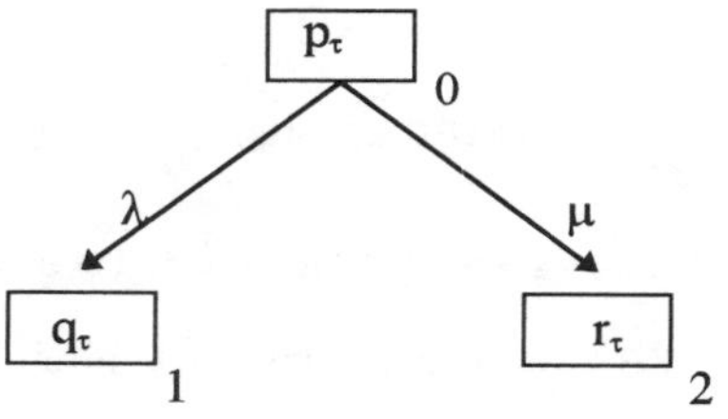

Figure 16.5. Closed probability graph with three states

16.10. State probabilities in a graph with four states.

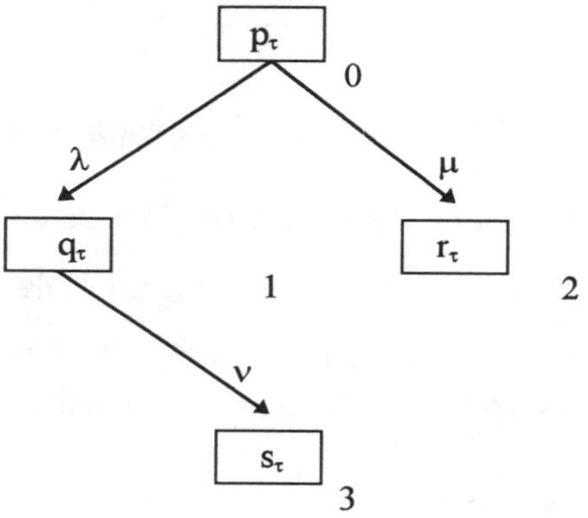

Figure 16.6. Closed probability graph with four states

The differential system of equations Ch.14.(7) becomes

$$dp_\tau = -\,(\lambda+\mu)\, p_\tau\, d\tau, \tag{88}$$

$$dq_\tau = \lambda\, p_\tau\, d\tau - \nu\, q_\tau\, d\tau, \tag{89}$$

$$dr_\tau = \mu\, p_\tau\, d\tau, \tag{90}$$

$$ds_\tau = \nu\, q_\tau\, d\tau \tag{91}$$

on [s,t]. This is the same system as (50), (51), (52), (53) with 0, 0, p_τ, q_τ, r_τ, s_τ, instead of ξ, η, M_τ, P_τ, Q_τ, R_τ. Hence, the solution of system (88), (89), (90), (91) is furnished by (55), (56), (57), (58).

$$p_t = p_s\, e^{-(t-s)(\lambda+\mu)}, \tag{92}$$

$$q_t = [q_s - \lambda\, p_s/(\nu-\lambda-\mu)]e^{-(t-s)\nu} + \lambda\, p_s\, e^{-(t-s)(\lambda+\mu)}/(\nu-\lambda-\mu), \tag{93}$$

$$r_t = r_s + \mu\, p_s\, [1-e^{-(t-s)(\lambda+\mu)}]/(\lambda+\mu), \tag{94}$$

$$s_t = s_s + [q_s\ -\lambda\, p_s\, /(\nu-\lambda-\mu)][1 - e^{-(t-s)\nu}]$$
$$+ \lambda\nu\, p_s[1 - e^{-(t-s)(\lambda+\mu)}]/[(\lambda+\mu)(\nu-\lambda-\mu)]. \tag{95}$$

Now $p_t+q_t+r_t+s_t= p_s+q_s+r_s+s_s$.

16.11. Mortality estimations

We consider following open graph with two states. Now the population of state 0 is composed of $M_{x+\tau}^{\circ}$ lifes aged $x+\tau$ ($0\leq\tau\leq1$), K_x° (positive or negative) is the number of new lives (in fact a difference between entries and exits) joining that population during observation year [0,1], J_x° is the number of deceases during that year and $\mu_{x+\tau}\equiv\mu_x$ ($0\leq\tau\leq1$) is the constant force of mortality at age $x+\tau$. The number of dead persons in state 1 is irrelevant. (In notations of Ch.3.3, M_x°, K_x° and J_x° are n_x, e_x-o_x and m_x resp.)

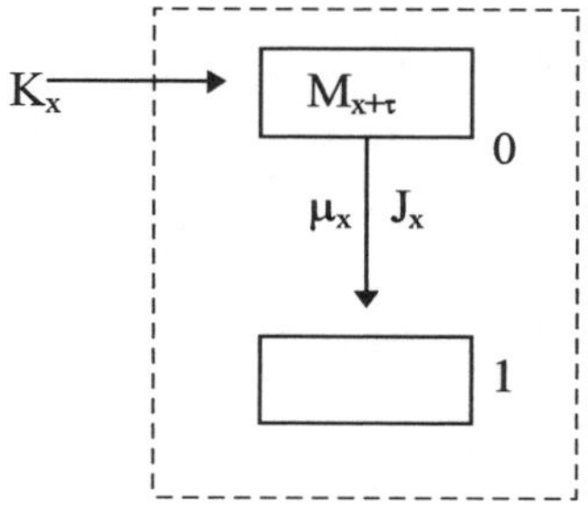

16.7. Open population graph with two states

The results of 16.4, with s=0 and t=1, can be applied here. Hence, the estimator μ_x° of μ_x based on equality of expected and observed values, satisfies equation (20):

$$M_{x+1}^{\circ} = K_x^{\circ}(1-e^{-\mu_x^{\circ}})/\mu_x^{\circ} + M_x^{\circ}\, e^{-\mu_x^{\circ}}. \tag{96}$$

The power series expansion (26) for μ_x° is

$$\mu_x^\circ = J_x^\circ/c_1^\circ + c_2^\circ(J_x^\circ)^2/(c_1^\circ)^3 + [2(c_2^\circ)^2 - c_1^\circ c_3^\circ](J_x^\circ)^3/(c_1^\circ)^5$$
$$+ [5(c_2^\circ)^3 - 5\, c_1^\circ c_2^\circ c_3^\circ + (c_1^\circ)^2 c_4^\circ](J_x^\circ)^4/(c_1^\circ)^7 + \ldots, \quad (97)$$

where $c_k^\circ := M_x^\circ/k! + K_x^\circ/(k+1)! \quad (k=1,2,\ldots).$ (98)

By Ch.2.(9), $p_x = l_{x+1}/l_x = \exp(-\int_{(0,1)} \mu_{x+\tau}\, d\tau) = e^{-\mu_x}$

and then $q_x = 1 - p_x = 1 - e^{-\mu_x} = \mu_x - \mu_x^2/2! + \mu_x^3/3! - \ldots$ (99)

The estimator of q_x resulting from this relation is

$$q_x^\circ = 1 - e^{-\mu_x^\circ} = \mu_x^\circ - (\mu_x^\circ)^2/2! + (\mu_x^\circ)^3/3! - \ldots \quad (100)$$

By (97), it has following power series expansion:

$$q_x^\circ = J_x^\circ/c_1^\circ + [c_2^\circ - c_1^\circ/2](J_x^\circ)^2/(c_1^\circ)^3 +$$
$$[2(c_2^\circ)^2 - c_1^\circ c_2^\circ - c_1^\circ c_3^\circ + (c_1^\circ)^2/6](J_x^\circ)^3/(c_1^\circ)^5$$
$$+ [5(c_2^\circ)^3 - 5c_1^\circ c_2^\circ c_3^\circ + (c_1^\circ)^2 c_4^\circ - 5c_1^\circ(c_2^\circ)^2/2$$
$$+ (c_1^\circ)^2 c_3^\circ + (c_1^\circ)^2 c_2^\circ/2 - (c_1^\circ)^3/24](J_x^\circ)^4/(c_1^\circ)^7 + \ldots \quad (101)$$

The first term in last member, J_x°/c_1°, is estimator Ch.3.(4).

Appendix A

SUMMATION BY PARTS

We consider numbers a_k and b_k, for the integer values of k occurring in the following expressions.

The **ascending difference operator** Δ is defined by the relation

$$\Delta a_k := a_{k+1} - a_k.$$

Then $$\sum_{m\leq k\leq n} \Delta a_k = a_{n+1} - a_m =: [a_k]_m^{n+1}. \quad (1)$$

Theorem

$$\sum_{m\leq k\leq n} \mathbf{a_k \Delta b_k} = [\mathbf{a_k b_k}]_m^{n+1} - \sum_{m\leq k\leq n} \mathbf{b_{k+1} \Delta a_k}. \quad (2)$$

Proof.

$$\Delta(a_k b_k) = a_{k+1} b_{k+1} - a_k b_k = a_k(b_{k+1} - b_k) + (a_{k+1} - a_k) b_{k+1}$$

Hence, $$\Delta(a_k b_k) = a_k \Delta b_k + b_{k+1} \Delta a_k,$$

$$\sum_{m\leq k\leq n} \Delta(a_k b_k) = \sum_{m\leq k\leq n} a_k \Delta b_k + \sum_{m\leq k\leq n} b_{k+1} \Delta a_k$$

and then $$[a_k b_k]_m^{n+1} = \sum_{m\leq k\leq n} a_k \Delta b_k + \sum_{m\leq k\leq n} b_{k+1} \Delta a_k$$

by (1) •

Appendix B

LINEAR INTERPOLATIONS

Single linear interpolation

Theorem 1

Let f_τ be a linear function on the interval [s,s+1]. Then

$$\mathbf{f_\tau = (s+1-\tau)f_s + (\tau-s)f_{s+1} \quad (s\leq\tau\leq s+1).} \tag{1}$$

Proof
The last member of (1) is linear in τ and it furnishes the correct value for τ=s and for τ=s+1 •

Of course, if f is linear on the open interval]s,s+1[, but not necessarily continuous on the closed interval [s,s+1], then (1) must be replaced by

$$f_\tau = (s+1-\tau)f_{s+} + (\tau-s)f_{s+1-} \quad (s<\tau<s+1). \tag{2}$$

We recall that the **right-sided limit** f_{t+} and the **left-sided limit** f_{t-} are defined as

$$f_{t+} := \lim_{\varepsilon\downarrow 0} f_{t+\varepsilon}, \quad f_{t-} := \lim_{\varepsilon\downarrow 0} f_{t-\varepsilon}\ ,$$

where the notation $\varepsilon\downarrow 0$ indicates that $\varepsilon > 0$. The functions f encountered in life insurance mathematics are very simple and then the limits f_{t+} and f_{t-} exist in any case.

In the following Lemma, r is a strictly positive integer and we use the following notations (already closely related to life insurance notations),

$${}_{s+k|1}a^{(r)}(f) := (1/r) \textstyle\sum_{1\leq v\leq r} f_{s+k+v/r-},$$

$${}_{s+k|1}\ddot{a}^{(r)}(f) := (1/r) \textstyle\sum_{0\leq v\leq r-1} f_{s+k+v/r+},$$

$${}_{s+k|1}\bar{a}(f) := \textstyle\int_{(s+k,s+k+1)} f_\tau d\tau.$$

The proof of the Lemma is easy by (2), but we provide a more instructive geometric demonstration. The next figure is akin to the case r=4.

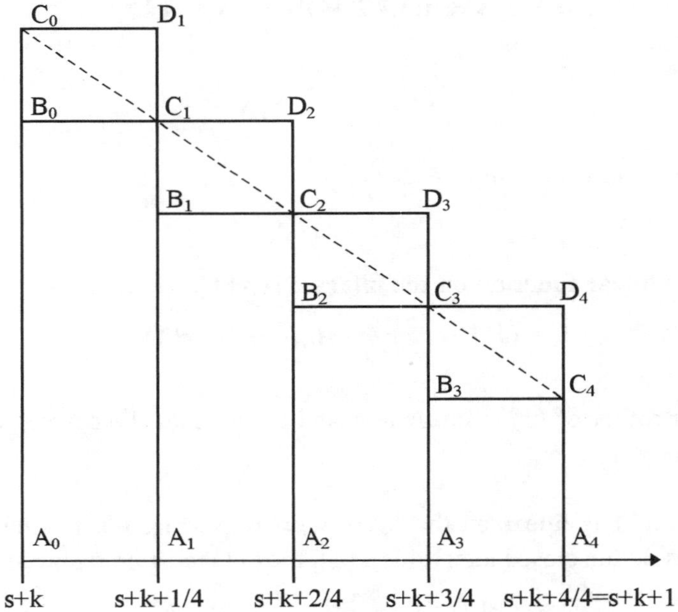

Figure A.1. Geometric proof of interpolation formulas

Lemma

If f is linear on the interval]s+k,s+k+1[,

$$\mathbf{{}_{s+k|1}a^{(r)}(f) = f_{s+k+1-} + (f_{s+k+}-f_{s+k+1-}).(r-1)/(2r),} \tag{3}$$

$$\mathbf{{}_{s+k|1}\ddot{a}^{(r)}(f) = f_{s+k+} - (f_{s+k+}-f_{s+k+1-}).(r-1)/(2r),} \tag{4}$$

$$\mathbf{{}_{s+k|1}\bar{a}(f) = (f_{s+k+} + f_{s+k+1-})/2.} \tag{5}$$

If f is decreasing on]s+k,s+k+1[(not necessarily linear),

$$\mathbf{f_{s+k+1-} \leq {}_{s+k|1}a^{(r)}(f) \leq {}_{s+k|1}\bar{a}(f) \leq {}_{s+k|1}\ddot{a}^{(r)}(f) \leq f_{s+k+}.} \tag{6}$$

Proof

Let f be linear on]s+k,s+k+1[. The graph of f is the straight line C_0C_4 and

$${}_{s+k|1}a^{(r)}(f) = \text{surface}(B_0C_1B_1C_2B_2C_3B_3C_4A_4A_0B_0),$$

$${}_{s+k|1}\ddot{a}^{(r)}(f) = \text{surface}(C_0D_1C_1D_2C_2D_3C_3D_4A_4A_0C_0),$$

$$_{s+k|1}\bar{a}(f) = \text{surface}(C_0C_4A_4A_0C_0).$$

Then

$$_{s+k|1}\bar{a}(f) = (f_{s+k+}+f_{s+k+1-})/2,$$

$$(_{s+k|1}\ddot{a}^{(r)}(f) + {}_{s+k|1}a^{(r)}(f))/2 = {}_{s+k|1}a(f).$$

Hence

$$_{s+k|1}\ddot{a}^{(r)}(f) + {}_{s+k|1}a^{(r)}(f) = f_{s+k+} + f_{s+k+1-}. \tag{7}$$

The difference $_{s+k|1}\ddot{a}^{(r)}(f) - {}_{s+k|1}a^{(r)}(f)$ equals the sum of the surface of the rectangles $C_0D_1C_1B_0$, $C_1D_2C_2B_1$, $C_2D_3C_3B_2$, $C_3D_4C_4B_3$. The surface of each rectangle equals $(1/r).(f_{s+k+}-f_{s+k+1-})/r$. Hence,

$$_{s+k|1}\ddot{a}^{(r)}(f) - {}_{s+k|1}a^{(r)}(f) = (f_{s+k+}-f_{s+k+1-})/r. \tag{8}$$

Then (3) and (4) result from (7) and (8). Relation (6) is obvious from the figure in the linear case. In the non-linear case, (6) results from a similar figure •

Multiple linear interpolation

In the following Theorem, f is defined on the interval [s,s+n] and we use the notations

$$_{s|n}a^{(r)}(f) := \sum_{0\le k\le n-1} {}_{s+k|1}a^{(r)}(f) = (1/r) \sum_{1\le \nu\le nr} f_{s+\nu/r-},$$

$$_{s|n}\ddot{a}^{(r)}(f) := \sum_{0\le k\le n-1} {}_{s+k|1}\ddot{a}^{(r)}(f) = (1/r) \sum_{0\le \nu\le nr-1} f_{s+\nu/r+},$$

$$_{s|n}\bar{a}(f) := \sum_{0\le k\le n-1} {}_{s+k|1}\bar{a}(f) = \int_{(s,s+n)} f_\tau d\tau,$$

$$_{s|n}a(f) := \sum_{0\le k\le n-1} f_{s+k+1-} = \sum_{1\le k\le n} f_{s+k-},$$

$$_{s|n}\ddot{a}(f) := \sum_{0\le k\le n-1} f_{s+k+}.$$

Theorem 2

If f is linear on each interval]s+k,s+k+1[(0≤k≤n−1),

$$_{s|n}a^{(r)}(f) = {}_{s|n}a(f) + [{}_{s|n}\ddot{a}(f) - {}_{s|n}a(f)].(r-1)/(2r), \tag{9}$$

$$_{s|n}\ddot{a}^{(r)}(f) = {}_{s|n}\ddot{a}(f) - [{}_{s|n}\ddot{a}(f) - {}_{s|n}a(f)].(r-1)/(2r), \tag{10}$$

$$_{s|n}\bar{a}(f) = [{}_{s|n}\ddot{a}(f) + {}_{s|n}a(f)]/2. \tag{11}$$

If f is decreasing on]s,s+n[,

$$_{s|n}a(f) \le {}_{s|n}a^{(r)}(f) \le {}_{s|n}\bar{a}(f) \le {}_{s|n}\ddot{a}^{(r)}(f) \le {}_{s|n}\ddot{a}(f). \tag{12}$$

Proof

The Theorem results from the application of $\sum_{0\leq k\leq n-1}$ to the relations of the Lemma •

Theorem 3

If f is continuous on [s,s+n] and linear on each interval [s+k,s+k+1] (0≤k ≤n−1),

$$ {}_{s|n}\mathbf{a}^{(r)}(\mathbf{f}) = {}_{s|n}\mathbf{a}(\mathbf{f}) + (\mathbf{f}_s-\mathbf{f}_{s+n}).(\mathbf{r}-1)/(2\mathbf{r}), \tag{13} $$

$$ {}_{s|n}\ddot{\mathbf{a}}^{(r)}(\mathbf{f}) = {}_{s|n}\ddot{\mathbf{a}}(\mathbf{f}) - (\mathbf{f}_s-\mathbf{f}_{s+n}).(\mathbf{r}-1)/(2\mathbf{r}), \tag{14} $$

$$ {}_{s|n}\bar{\mathbf{a}}(\mathbf{f}) = {}_{s|n}\mathbf{a}(\mathbf{f}) + (\mathbf{f}_s-\mathbf{f}_{s+n})/2 = {}_{s|n}\ddot{\mathbf{a}}(\mathbf{f}) - (\mathbf{f}_s-\mathbf{f}_{s+n})/2. \tag{15} $$

Proof

The Theorem results from the application of $\sum_{0\leq k\leq n-1}$ to the relations of the Lemma. In the continuous case, $f_{s+k+1-}=f_{s+k+1}$, $f_{s+k+}=f_{s+k}$ and then

$$ \sum_{0\leq k\leq n-1} (f_{s+k+}-f_{s+k+1-}) $$

$$ = (f_s-f_{s+1}) + (f_{s+1}-f_{s+2}) + \ldots + (f_{s+n-1}-f_{s+n}) = f_s-f_{s+n} \quad \bullet $$

The functions f of life insurance are not linear on intervals]s+k,s+k+1[. Then f is replaced, separately on each interval]s+k,s+k+1[, by a linear function and then the foregoing equalities of Theorem 1, 2 and 3 become approximations. In most cases the approximations are excellent, because the life insurance functions are quasi-linear on unit intervals]s+k,s+k+1[.

Appendix C

PROBABILITY THEORY

Expectations

Let X be a **random variable** with **distribution function** F. This means that

$$F(t) = P(X \leq t) \quad (t \in \mathbf{R}). \tag{1}$$

The **expectation** of the function $\varphi(X)$ of X is the number

$$E\varphi(X) := \int_{(-\infty,+\infty)} \varphi(t)dF(t) \tag{2}$$

(where the integral is supposed to exist). If F has the **density** f, then $F'=f$ and then $dF(t)$ may be replaced by $f(t)dt$ in (2). The infinitesimal interpretation of the density f is

$$f(t)dt = P(X \in dt), \tag{3}$$

where dt represents an infinitesimal number in the left member of (3) and an infinitesimal set of length dt, containing t, in the right member.

Of course, if the values of X belong to the interval I, then the integration domain $(-\infty,+\infty)$ can be replaced by I in (2).

Variances

The **variance** of $\varphi(X)$ is the number

$$\mathrm{Var}\ \varphi(X) := E\varphi^2(X) - E^2\varphi(X), \tag{4}$$

where the last term is $[E\varphi(X)]^2$.

Jensen's formula

In the following Theorem, X is any random variable such that the involved expectations exist. The function φ is **convex** on interval I if $\varphi'' \geq 0$ on I. A more general definition, applicable when φ has not necessarily a second order derivative, is the following.

The function $\varphi(\tau)$ is **convex** on the interval I, if a linear function $\lambda_t(\tau)$ exists for each point $t \in I$, such that $\lambda_t \leq \varphi$ on I and $\lambda_t(t) = \varphi(t)$. With this definition it is direct that the function $\varphi(\tau) := |\tau|$ is convex on **R**. It is well known that

$$|EX| \leq E|X|. \tag{5}$$

Jensen's formula (6) is a generalization of (5).

Theorem

Let φ be convex on the interval I and let X be a random variable with values in I. Then

$$\varphi(EX) \leq E\varphi(X). \tag{6}$$

Proof

$$\lambda_{EX}(X) \leq \varphi(X) \tag{7}$$

because $\lambda_{EX}(\tau) \leq \varphi(\tau)$. We now apply E to (7) and we observe that

$$E\lambda_{EX}(X) = \lambda_{EX}(EX) = \varphi(EX),$$

where the first equality results from the linearity of λ_{EX}. The conclusion is relation (6) •

Multiple events

A **multiple event** is a function of events A, B, ...,C. We here indicate a general method, allowing to express the probability of a multiple event as a linear combination of probabilities

1, P(A), P(B), ..., P(C), P(A and B), P(A and C), ..., P(A and B and C), ...

We first recall the **de Morgan's formulas**

$$\text{not}(A \text{ and } B \text{ and } \ldots \text{ and } C) = [(\text{not } A) \text{ or } (\text{not } B) \text{ or } \ldots \text{ or } (\text{not } C)], \tag{8}$$

$$\text{not}(A \text{ or } B \text{ or } \ldots \text{ or } C) = [(\text{not } A) \text{ and } (\text{not } B) \text{ and } \ldots \text{ and } (\text{not } C)]. \tag{9}$$

We use the following notations (related to life insurance notations) for particular multiple events.

$$A| := \text{not } A,$$

$$AB\ldots C := (A \text{ and } B \text{ and } \ldots \text{ and } C),$$

$$\overline{AB\ldots C} := (A \text{ or } B \text{ or } \ldots \text{ or } C),$$

$$\overline{AB\ldots C}^{\,r} \text{ occurs} :\Leftrightarrow \text{at least } r \text{ of the events } A, B, \ldots, C \text{ occur},$$

$\overline{AB...C}^{[r]}$ occurs :⇔ exactly r of the events A, B, ...,C occur.

In these definitions, A, B, ...,C may already be multiple events. For instance

$$A|B = (\text{not } A) \text{ and } B,$$

$$A|B| = (\text{not } A) \text{ and } (\text{not } B) = \text{not}(A \text{ or } B)$$

The indicator 1_A or $1(A)$ is a random variable taking the value 1 if A occurs and the value 0 if A does not occur. **The expectation of an indicator function of an event equals the probability of that event**. Indeed,

$$E1_A = 1.P(A) + 0.P(A|) = P(A).$$

Hence, in order to prove a relation such as

$$aP(A) + bP(B) + ... + cP(C) = 0,$$

it is enough to verify that

$$a1_A + b1_B + ... + c1_C = 0,$$

because then we can apply E to the latter relation.

The following relations hold between indicator functions.

$$1_{A|} = 1 - 1_A, \tag{10}$$

$$1_{A|B} = 1_B - 1_{AB}, \tag{11}$$

$$1_{\overline{AB}} = 1_A + 1_B - 1_{AB}, \tag{12}$$

$$1(\overline{AB}^{[1]}) = 1_A + 1_B - 2.1_{AB}, \tag{13}$$

For instance, in order to find (13) we proceed as follows. We consider the array with 4 rows of all possible occurrences or not of A and B. The number 1 corresponds to an occurrence, the number 0 to a non occurrence of the event. We complete by a column for $\overline{AB}^{[1]}$. We display $1(\overline{AB}^{[1]})$ as a linear combination of 1, 1_A, 1_B, 1_{AB} with unknown coefficients a, a_A, a_B, a_{AB}. To each row of the array corresponds one equation for the unknown coefficients. Hence, a=0, a_B=1, a_A=1, a_{AB}= −2.

Table C.1. Verification of a double event relation

A	B	$\overline{AB}^{[1]}$	$1(\overline{AB}^{[1]})$	$= a + a_A 1_A + a_B 1_B + a_{AB} 1_{AB}$
1	1	0	0	$= a + a_A.1 + a_B.1 + a_{AB}.1$
1	0	1	1	$= a + a_A.1 + a_B.0 + a_{AB}.0$
0	1	1	1	$= a + a_A.0 + a_B.1 + a_{AB}.0$
0	0	0	0	$= a + a_A.0 + a_B.0 + a_{AB}.0$

We proceed similarly in case of 3 events A, B, C. Let the event D be a function of A, B and C. We consider an array with 2^3 columns, a supplementary column for D and the relation for 1_D as a linear combination of 1_A, 1_B, 1_C, 1_{AB}, 1_{BC}, 1_{CA} and 1_{ABC}. To each column of the array corresponds an equation for the unknown coefficients.

Table C.2. Verification of a triple event relation

A	B	C	D	$1_D = a + a_A 1_A + a_B 1_B + a_C 1_C + a_{AB} 1_{AB} + a_{BC} 1_{BC} + a_{CA} 1_{CA} + a_{ABC} 1_{ABC}$
1	1	1	s_1	$s_1 = a + a_A.1 + a_B.1 + a_C.1 + a_{AB}.1 + a_{BC}.1 + a_{CA}.1 + a_{ABC}.1$
1	1	0	s_2	$s_2 = a + a_A.1 + a_B.1 + a_C.0 + a_{AB}.1 + a_{BC}.0 + a_{CA}.0 + a_{ABC}.0$
1	0	1	s_3	$s_3 = a + a_A.1 + a_B.0 + a_C.1 + a_{AB}.0 + a_{BC}.0 + a_{CA}.1 + a_{ABC}.0$
1	0	0	s_4	$s_4 = a + a_A.1 + a_B.0 + a_C.0 + a_{AB}.0 + a_{BC}.0 + a_{CA}.0 + a_{ABC}.0$
0	1	1	s_5	$s_5 = a + a_A.0 + a_B.1 + a_C.1 + a_{AB}.0 + a_{BC}.1 + a_{CA}.0 + a_{ABC}.0$
0	1	0	s_6	$s_6 = a + a_A.0 + a_B.1 + a_C.0 + a_{AB}.0 + a_{BC}.0 + a_{CA}.0 + a_{ABC}.0$
0	0	1	s_7	$s_7 = a + a_A.0 + a_B.0 + a_C.1 + a_{AB}.0 + a_{BC}.0 + a_{CA}.0 + a_{ABC}.0$
0	0	0	s_8	$s_8 = a + a_A.0 + a_B.0 + a_C.0 + a_{AB}.0 + a_{BC}.0 + a_{CA}.0 + a_{ABC}.0$

Each s_k equals 1 or 0. Let us assume that $s_8 = 0$. Then the solution of the foregoing linear system is

$$a = 0,\quad a_A = s_4,\quad a_B = s_6,\quad a_C = s_7,$$

$$a_{AB} = s_2 - (s_4 + s_6),\quad a_{BC} = s_5 - (s_6 + s_7),\quad a_{CA} = s_3 - (s_4 + s_7),$$

$$a_{ABC} = (s_1 + s_4 + s_6 + s_7) - (s_2 + s_3 + s_5).$$

The columns corresponding to the events $\overline{ABC}^{\,r}$ and $\overline{ABC}^{[r]}$ are indicated in following Table C.3.

Table C.3. Symmetrical triple events

A	B	C	$\overline{ABC}^{\,1}$	$\overline{ABC}^{\,2}$	$\overline{ABC}^{\,3}$	$\overline{ABC}^{[1]}$	$\overline{ABC}^{[2]}$	$\overline{ABC}^{[3]}$	
1	1	1	1	1	1	0	0	1	s_1
1	1	0	1	1	0	0	1	0	s_2
1	0	1	1	1	0	0	1	0	s_3
1	0	0	1	0	0	1	0	0	s_4
0	1	1	1	1	0	0	1	0	s_5
0	1	0	1	0	0	1	0	0	s_6
0	0	1	1	0	0	1	0	0	s_7
0	0	0	0	0	0	0	0	0	s_8

Then

$$1(\overline{ABC^{1}}) = 1_{ABC} = (1_A+1_B+1_C) - (1_{AB}+1_{BC}+1_{CA}) + 1_{ABC}, \qquad (14)$$

$$1(\overline{ABC^{2}}) = (1_{AB}+1_{BC}+1_{CA}) - 2.1_{ABC}, \qquad (15)$$

$$1(\overline{ABC^{3}}) = 1_{ABC}, \qquad (16)$$

$$1(\overline{ABC^{[1]}}) = (1_A+1_B+1_C) - 2.(1_{AB}+1_{BC}+1_{CA}) + 3.1_{ABC}, \qquad (17)$$

$$1(\overline{ABC^{[2]}}) = (1_{AB}+1_{BC}+1_{CA}) - 3.1_{ABC}, \qquad (18)$$

$$1(\overline{ABC^{[3]}}) = 1_{ABC}. \qquad (19)$$

Non-symmetrical formulas can be obtained by the same method. Some of them result from successive applications of (10), (11), (12) and of the general formula

$$1_{AB...C} = 1_A\, 1_B\, \dots\, 1_C.$$

For instance,

$$1_{(AB)|C} = 1_C - 1_{(AB)C} = 1_C - 1_{ABC}, \qquad (20)$$

$$1_{\overline{AB}|C} = 1_C - 1_{\overline{AB}\,C} = 1_C - 1_{\overline{AB}}1_C = 1_C - (1_A+1_B-1_{AB})1_C$$

$$= 1_C - 1_{AC} - 1_{BC} + 1_{ABC}. \qquad (21)$$

$$1_{A|BC} = 1_{BC} - 1_{ABC}. \qquad (22)$$

Events can be regarded as subsets of the basic probability space Ω. When only two events A and B are involved, the corresponding sets (denoted by the same symbols A and B) can be represented in a plane figure and then the linear relations between probabilities of multiple events are easily visualized.

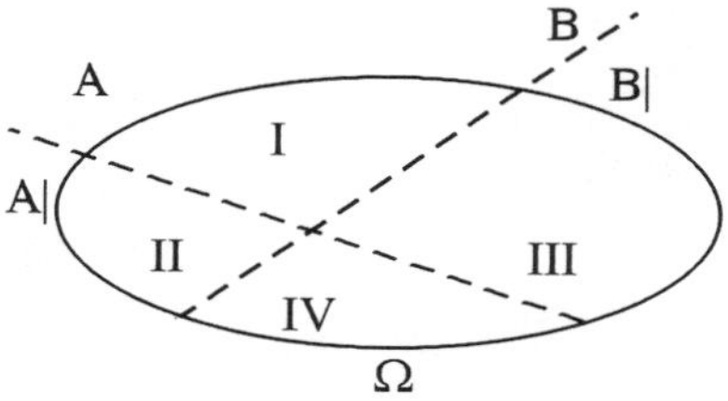

Figure C.1. Representation of double events

$$A = I+III, \;\; B = I+II,$$

$$A| = \mathbf{C}A = \Omega \backslash A = II+IV, \;\; B| = \mathbf{C}B = \Omega \backslash B = III+IV,$$

$$AB = A \cap B = I, \;\; \overline{AB} = A \cup B = I+II+III,$$

$$A|B = (\mathbf{C}A)\cap B = \mathrm{II},\quad B|A = (\mathbf{C}B)\cap A = \mathrm{III},\quad A|B| = (\mathbf{C}A)\cap(\mathbf{C}B) = \mathrm{IV},$$

$$\overline{AB}^{[1]} = \mathrm{II}+\mathrm{III}.$$

Then

$$P(A|B) = P(\mathrm{II}) = P(\mathrm{I}+\mathrm{II})-P(\mathrm{I}) = P(B) - P(AB),$$

$$P(\overline{AB}) = P(\mathrm{I}+\mathrm{II}+\mathrm{III}) = P(\mathrm{I}+\mathrm{III}) + P(\mathrm{I}+\mathrm{II}) - P(\mathrm{I}) = P(A) + P(B) - P(AB),$$

$$P(\overline{AB}^{[1]}) = P(\mathrm{II}+\mathrm{III}) = P(\mathrm{I}+\mathrm{III}) + P(\mathrm{I}+\mathrm{II}) - 2P(\mathrm{I}) = P(A) + P(B) - 2P(AB).$$

Hence,

$$P(A|B) = P(B) - P(AB), \tag{11'}$$

$$P(\overline{AB}) = P(A) + P(B) - P(AB), \tag{12'}$$

$$P(\overline{AB}^{[1]}) = P(A) + P(B) - 2P(AB). \tag{13'}$$

The linear relations between multiple events are not based on any independence assumptions.

Appendix D

A DIFFERENTIAL EQUATION

We consider the differential equation

$$d\xi(t) = f(t)dt - g(t)\xi(t)dt \quad (t \geq s), \tag{1}$$

where ξ is the unknown function and where s is fixed. The corresponding homogeneous equation is

$$d\xi(t) = \; - g(t)\xi(t)dt \quad (t \geq s). \tag{2}$$

Then

$$\xi_0(t) := \exp[-\int_{(s,t)} g(\tau)d\tau] \tag{3}$$

is a particular solution of (2). Hence, we replace ξ by η in (2), where η results from the relation

$$\xi(t) = \eta(t)\xi_0(t) = \eta(t) \exp[-\int_{(s,t)} g(\tau)d\tau]. \tag{4}$$

Then (1) becomes the differential equation

$$d\eta(\tau) = f(\tau) \exp[\int_{(s,\tau)} g(\sigma)d\sigma] \, d\tau,$$

with solution

$$\eta(t) = \eta(s) + \int_{(s,t)} f(\tau) \exp[\int_{(s,\tau)} g(\sigma)d\sigma] \, d\tau.$$

By (4), $\eta(s)=\xi(s)$. Hence,

$$\xi(t) = \{\xi(s) + \int_{(s,t)} f(\tau) \exp[\int_{(s,\tau)} g(\sigma)d\sigma] \, d\tau\} \exp[-\int_{(s,t)} g(\tau)d\tau]. \tag{5}$$

Appendix E

INVERSION OF A POWER SERIES

Theorem

If one of the power series

$$y = a_1x + a_2x^2 + a_3x^3 + \ldots \quad (1)$$

$$x = y/a_1 - a_2 y^2/a_1^3 + (2a_2^2 - a_1a_3)y^3/a_1^5 + (5a_1a_2a_3 - 5a_2^3 - a_1^2a_4)y^4/a_1^7 + \ldots \quad (2)$$

where $a_1 \neq 0$, has a strictly positive radius of convergence, then the other has a strictly positive radius of convergence and then relations (1) and (2) are equivalent when $|x|$ and $|y|$ are small enough. The coefficients in power series (2) result from the following proof.

Corollary

If one of the power series

$$y = x + a_2x^2 + a_3x^3 + \ldots \quad (3)$$

$$x = y - a_2 y^2 + (2a_2^2 - a_3)y^3 + (5a_2a_3 - 5a_2^3 - a_4)y^4 + \ldots \quad (4)$$

has a strictly positive radius of convergence, then the other has a strictly positive radius of convergence and then relations (3) and (4) are equivalent when $|x|$ and $|y|$ are small enough.

Proof

The convergences and the validity of the following proof result from general properties of power series. The Corollary results from the Theorem with $a_1=1$. Conversely, relation (1) can be displayed as

$$y/a_1 = x + (a_2/a_1)x^2 + (a_3/a_1)x^3 + \ldots$$

and then the Theorem results from its Corollary with y/a_1, a_2/a_1, a_3/a_1, ... instead of y, a_2, a_3, ... resp. Hence, Theorem and Corollary are equivalent and it is sufficient to derive the latter.

Let the radius of power series (3) be strictly positive. The solution x of equation (3) can be displayed as a power series

$$x = y + b_2y^2 + b_3y^3 + \dots$$

if |y| is small enough. Then, by substitution in (3),

$$y = (y+b_2y^2+b_3y^3+b_4y^4+\dots) + a_2(y+b_2y^2+b_3y^3+b_4y^4+\dots)^2$$
$$+ a_3(y+b_2y^2+b_3y^3+b_4y^4+\dots)^3 + a_4(y+b_2y^2+b_3y^3+b_4y^4+\dots)^4 + \dots$$
$$= (y+b_2y^2+b_3y^3+b_4y^4+\dots) + a_2[y^2+2b_2y^3+(2b_3+b_2^2)y^4+\dots] +$$
$$a_3(y^3+3b_2y^4+\dots) + a_4(y^4+\dots).$$
$$= y + (a_2+b_2)y^2 + (a_3+2a_2b_2+b_3)y^3 + (a_4+ 3a_3b_2+a_2b_2^2+ 2a_2b_3+b_4)y^4 + \dots$$

By a coefficient identification

$$a_2+b_2 = 0,$$
$$a_3+2a_2b_2+b_3 = 0,$$
$$a_4+ 3a_3b_2+a_2b_2^2+ 2a_2b_3+b_4 = 0,$$
$$\dots \quad \dots \quad \dots \quad \dots \quad \dots \quad \dots \quad \dots \quad \dots \quad \dots$$

These relations furnish successively

$$b_2 = -a_2,$$
$$b_3 = 2a_2^2 - a_3,$$
$$b_4 = 5a_2a_3 - 5a_2^3 - a_4,$$
$$\dots \quad \dots \quad \dots \quad \dots \quad \dots \quad \dots \quad \bullet$$

Appendix F

SUMMARY OF FORMULAS

ρ is any status, σ is a simple status, c_τ is any capital-function, C_τ and c_τ are associated capital-functions when occurring simultaneously in a formula.

Partitioned annuities (Ch.5, Ch.11)

$a_\rho^{(r)} \approx a_\rho + (\ddot{a}_\rho - a_\rho).(r-1)/(2r)$ $[{}_{s|n}, c_\tau]$

$\ddot{a}_\rho^{(r)} \approx \ddot{a}_\rho - (\ddot{a}_\rho - a_\rho).(r-1)/(2r)$ $[{}_{s|n}, c_\tau]$

$\bar{a}_\rho \approx (\ddot{a}_\rho + a_\rho)/2$ $[{}_{s|n}, c_\tau]$

${}_{s|n}\ddot{a}_\rho - {}_{s|n}a_\rho = {}_{s}E_\rho - {}_{s+n}E_\rho$

${}_{s|n}(I\ddot{a})_\rho - {}_{s|n}(Ia)_\rho = {}_{s|n}\ddot{a}_\rho - n\ {}_{s+n}E_\rho$

$(I_{\overline{n|}}\ddot{a})_\rho - (I_{\overline{n|}}a)_\rho = {}_{n}\ddot{a}_\rho$

${}_{n}(D\ddot{a})_\rho - {}_{n}(Da)_\rho = n - {}_{n}a_\rho$

Relations between life annuities and insurances (Ch.7, Ch.11)

$$\bar{A}_\sigma = (\ddot{a}_\sigma - a_\sigma) - \delta\ \bar{a}_\sigma \ [\ ^\circ, {}_{s|n}, \text{staircase } c_\tau]$$

$$u^{1/2}\ \hat{A}_\sigma = (\ddot{a}_\sigma - a_\sigma) - i\ a_\sigma \ [\ ^\circ, {}_{s|n}, \text{staircase } c_\tau]$$

$$v^{1/2}\ \hat{A}_\sigma = (\ddot{a}_\sigma - a_\sigma) - iv\ \ddot{a}_\sigma \ [\ ^\circ, {}_{s|n}, \text{staircase } c_\tau]$$

$${}_{s|t}\bar{A}_\sigma(C_\tau) = {}_{s}E_\sigma(C_\tau) - {}_{s+t}E_\sigma(C_\tau) - {}_{s|t}\bar{a}_\sigma(c_\tau)\ [\ ^\circ\ ]$$

Decomposition formulas (Ch.8, Ch.12)

One life. $Q = {}_{0|t}Q_x + {}_{t}E_x\ {}_{\bullet t|}Q_x + {}_{t}E_{x|}\ {}_{\bullet t|}Q_{x|}$

$Q = {}_{0|t}Q_x + {}_{t}E_x\ {}_{\bullet t|}Q_x$ if $Q^{\circ\circ}$ vanishes with x

Two lifes. $Q = {}_{0|t}Q_{xy} + {}_{t}E_{xy}\ {}_{\bullet t|}Q_{xy} + {}_{t}E_{x|y}\ {}_{\bullet t|}Q_{x|y} + {}_{t}E_{y|x}\ {}_{\bullet t|}Q_{y|x} + {}_{t}E_{x|y|}\ {}_{\bullet t|}Q_{x|y|}$

$Q = {}_{0|t}Q_{xy} + {}_{t}E_{xy}\ {}_{\bullet t|}Q_{xy}$ if $Q^{\circ\circ}$ vanishes at first decease

Reserve of time-capital at fractional instant (Ch.8, Ch.12)

${}_{\bullet k+\theta|}Q_\rho \approx (1-\theta)\ {}_{\bullet k|}Q_\rho + \theta\ {}_{\bullet k+1|}Q_\rho - [(1-\theta)\ {}_{\bullet k|1}Q_\rho - {}_{\bullet k+\theta|1-\theta}Q_\rho]$ k k+θ k+1

Particular statuses (Ch.11)

${}_{t}E_{x|y} = {}_{t}E_y - {}_{t}E_{xy}\ [\ ^\circ, ^{\circ\circ}, c_\tau]$

${}_{t}E_{\overline{xy}} = {}_{t}E_x + {}_{t}E_y - {}_{t}E_{xy}\ [\ ^\circ, ^{\circ\circ}, c_\tau]$

${}_{t}E_{\overline{xy}[1]} = {}_{t}E_x + {}_{t}E_y - 2\ {}_{t}E_{xy}\ [\ ^\circ, ^{\circ\circ}, c_\tau]$

$a_{x|y} = a_y - a_{xy}\ [\ ^\circ, ^{\circ\circ}, c_\tau, {}_{s|n}, \bar{}, \ddot{}\ ]$

$a_{\overline{xy}} = a_x + a_y - a_{xy}\ [\ ^\circ, ^{\circ\circ}, c_\tau, {}_{s|n}, \bar{}, \ddot{}\ ]$

$a_{\overline{xy}[1]} = a_x + a_y - 2\ a_{xy}\ [\ ^\circ, ^{\circ\circ}, c_\tau, {}_{s|n}, \bar{}, \ddot{}\ ]$

$A_{\overline{xy}} = A_x + A_y - A_{xy}\ [\ ^\circ, ^{\circ\circ}, c_\tau, {}_{s|n}, \bar{}, \wedge\ ]$

Reserve of contract $(C^{\circ\circ}, P^{\circ\circ})$ (Ch.9, Ch.13)

General expression. ${}_{\bullet t|}V_\rho = {}_{\bullet t|}C_\rho - {}_{\bullet t|}P_\rho$

Contract vanishing at first decease:

$${}_{\bullet t|}V_\sigma = ({}_{\bullet 0|t}P_\sigma - {}_{\bullet 0|t}C_\sigma)/{}_tE_\sigma \text{ (retrospective expression)}$$

$${}_{\bullet k+1|}V_\sigma = ({}_{\bullet k|}V_\sigma + {}_{\bullet k|1}P_\sigma - {}_{\bullet k|1}C_\sigma)/{}_1E_{\sigma+k} \text{ (recurrent expression),}$$

where σ+k is status σ with all ages augmented by k.

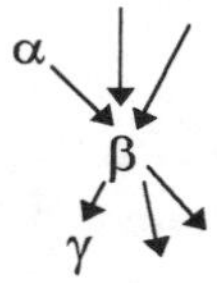

Graphs (Ch.14)

$$\delta\, \bar{a}_\beta = \Sigma_{\alpha\in'\beta}\, \bar{A}_{\alpha\to\beta} - \Sigma_{\gamma\in\beta'} \bar{A}_{\beta\to\gamma} + (\ddot{a}_\beta - a_\beta) \;\; [\,{}^\circ,\ {}_{s|n},\ \text{staircase } c_\tau\,]$$

$$i\ a_\beta = u^{1/2}\, \Sigma_{\alpha\in'\beta}\, \hat{A}_{\alpha\to\beta} - u^{1/2}\, \Sigma_{\gamma\in\beta'} \hat{A}_{\beta\to\gamma} + (\ddot{a}_\beta - a_\beta) \;\; [\,{}^\circ,\ {}_{s|n},\ \text{staircase } c_\tau\,]$$

$$iv\ \ddot{a}_\beta = v^{1/2}\, \Sigma_{\alpha\in'\beta}\, \hat{A}_{\alpha\to\beta} - v^{1/2}\, \Sigma_{\gamma\in\beta'} \hat{A}_{\beta\to\gamma} + (\ddot{a}_\beta - a_\beta) \;\; [\,{}^\circ,\ {}_{s|n},\ \text{staircase } c_\tau\,]$$

$${}_{s|t}\bar{a}_\beta(c_\tau) = \Sigma_{\alpha\in'\beta}\, \bar{A}_{\alpha\to\beta}(C_\tau) - \Sigma_{\gamma\in\beta'} \bar{A}_{\beta\to\gamma}(C_\tau) + {}_sE_\beta(C_\tau) - {}_{s+t}E_\beta(C_\tau) \;\; [\,{}^\circ\,]$$

Commutations (Ch.5, Ch.6)

$\ddot{a}_x = N_x/D_x$

${}_{m|}\ddot{a}_x = N_{x+m}/D_x$

${}_n\ddot{a}_x = (N_x - N_{x+n})/D_x$

${}_{m|n}\ddot{a}_x = (N_{x+m} - N_{x+m+n})/D_x$

$(I\ddot{a})_x = S_x/D_x$

${}_m(I\ddot{a})_x = S_{x+m}/D_x$

${}_n(I\ddot{a})_x = (S_x - S_{x+n} - nN_{x+n})/D_x$

${}_{m|n}(I\ddot{a})_x = (S_{x+m} - S_{x+m+n} - nN_{x+m+n})/D_x$

$(I_{\overline{n|}}\ddot{a})_x = (S_x - S_{x+n})/D_x$

${}_n(D\ddot{a})_x = (nN_x - S_{x+1} + S_{x+n+1})/D_x$

$\hat{A}_x = \hat{M}_x/D_x$

${}_{m|}\hat{A}_x = \hat{M}_{x+m}/D_x$

${}_n\hat{A}_x = (\hat{M}_x - \hat{M}_{x+n})/D_x$

${}_{m|n}\hat{A}_x = (\hat{M}_{x+m} - \hat{M}_{x+m+n})/D_x$

$(I\hat{A})_x = \hat{R}_x/D_x$

${}_m(I\hat{A})_x = \hat{R}_{x+m}/D_x$

${}_n(I\hat{A})_x = (\hat{R}_x - \hat{R}_{x+n} - n\hat{M}_{x+n})/D_x$

${}_{m|n}(I\hat{A})_x = (\hat{R}_{x+m} - \hat{R}_{x+m+n} - n\hat{M}_{x+m+n})/D_x$

$(I_{\overline{n|}}\hat{A})_x = (\hat{R}_x - \hat{R}_{x+n})/D_x$

${}_n(D\hat{A})_x = (n\hat{M}_x - \hat{R}_{x+1} + \hat{R}_{x+n+1})/D_x$

$a_x = N_{x+1}/D_x$

${}_{m|}a_x = N_{x+m+1}/D_x$

${}_na_x = (N_{x+1} - N_{x+n+1})/D_x$

${}_{m|n}a_x = (N_{x+m+1} - N_{x+m+n+1})/D_x$

$(Ia)_x = S_{x+1}/D_x$

${}_m(Ia)_x = S_{x+m+1}/D_x$

${}_n(Ia)_x = (S_{x+1} - S_{x+n+1} - nN_{x+n+1})/D_x$

${}_{m|n}(Ia)_x = (S_{x+m+1} - S_{x+m+n+1} - nN_{x+m+n+1})/D_x$

$(I_{\overline{n|}}a)_x = (S_{x+1} - S_{x+n+1})/D_x$

${}_n(Da)_x = (nN_{x+1} - S_{x+2} + S_{x+n+2})/D_x$

REFERENCES

[1] Bowers N.L., Gerber H.U., Hickmann J.C., Jones D.A., Nesbitt C.J. (1986). *Actuarial Mathematics.* Society of Actuaries, Itasca, Illinois

[2] De Vylder F. (1973). *Théorie Générale des Assurances Individuelles de Capitalisation.* Office des Assureurs de Belgique. Bruxelles (no longer available)

[3] De Vylder F. (1975). Maximum de vraisemblance et moindres carrés pondérés dans l'ajustement des tables de mortalité. *Bulletin de l'Association Royale des Actuaires Belges, Bruxelles*

[4] De Vylder F., Jaumain C. (1976). *Exposé Moderne de la Théorie Mathématique des Opérations Viagères.* Office des Assureurs de Belgique. Bruxelles (no longer available)

[5] Gerber H. (1986). *Life Insurance Mathematics.* Springer-Verlag & Swiss Association of Actuaries

[6] Thyrion P. (1952). Les écarts quadratiques dans les opérations viagères. *Bulletin 3 & 4, Ecole Royale Militaire, Bruxelles*

Graphs and general capital-functions are introduced in [2]. Variances of life insurances are already considered in [6]. The obsolete deterministic model for life insurance theory does not reflect the true mechanisms. It should be abandoned nowadays. The first book in which the stochastic approach is adopted systematically, including the evaluation of variances and the graph considerations, is [4].

NOTATION INDEX

SUBJECT INDEX